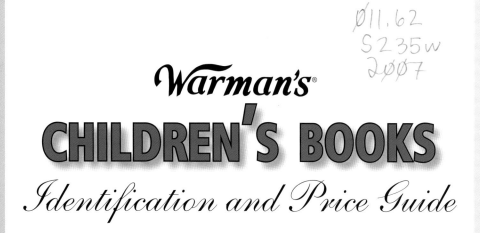

# Warman's
# CHILDREN'S BOOKS
## Identification and Price Guide

## Steve Santi

©2007 Steve Santi
Published by

**krause publications**
*An Imprint of F+W Publications*

**700 East State Street • Iola, WI 54990-0001**
**715-445-2214 • 888-457-2873**
**www.krausebooks.com**

Our toll-free number to place an order or obtain
a free catalog is (800) 258-0929.

Library of Congress Catalog Number: 2006935441

ISBN: 978-0-89689-467-9

Designed by Donna Mummery
Edited by Mary Sieber

Printed in China

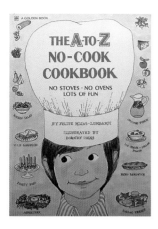

# *Contents*

**How to Use This Book** — 5

**Section 1: Golden Books** — 6

Big Golden Books, Giant Golden Books,
  Deluxe Golden Books and Golden Books — 10

Big Disney Golden Books — 50

Tiny Golden Libraries — 60

Golden Story Books & Sandpiper Books — 64

See Saw Books — 67

**Section 2: Whitman Books** — 68

Tell-A-Tale Books — 68

Top Top Tales — 122

A Cozy Corner Book — 131

Tiny Tales — 138

Tiny-Tot Tales — 140

Fuzzy Wuzzy Story Books — 143

Story Hour Series — 145

**Section 3: Rand McNally** — 150

Elf Books — 150

Jr. Elf Books — 181

**Section 4: Wonder Books** — 202

**Section 5: Treasure Books** — 245

**Section 6: Jolly Books** — 251

**Section 7: Little Owl Books** — 253

**Section 8: Pied Piper Books** — 254

**Section 9: Star-Bright Books** — 256

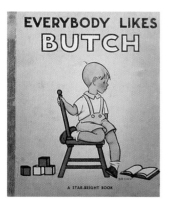

# Dedication

# Acknowledgments

John Wharton, Judy and Elmer Waldmann, Holly Everson, Mary Janaky, Don Wirf

# Author's Note

Any questions can be directed to the author either by e-mailing Steve@theSantis.com, visiting his web page at http://www.thesantis.com, or by sending a self-addressed, stamped envelope to:

Steve Santi
19626 Ricardo Ave.
Hayward, CA 94541

# Foreword

I met Steve Santi in late 1987. Since then, I've come to know him as a man who cares. What I mean by that is Golden Books®. What? Golden Books®? Yes. I'm not sure how long he has been collecting them ... since who knows when. I don't consider him a collector, though, but a historian. Think back on how we have been raised on the Little Golden Book—as much as we have been raised on the Disney animated film. He has taken of his time, energy, money, and knowledge to accumulate the history of a treasure—the Little Golden Book. Without him, not even the Golden Book publishers would know all about Golden Book's recorded history.

It has been a pleasure to know Steve, a man with a golden vision. Thanks, Steve.

*Ron Dias*

## Note

Ron Dias has illustrated or collaborated on many Walt Disney children's books since getting his first job as an animator/illustrator for the Walt Disney Studios in the late 1950s. He is credited with illustrating 12 Little Golden Books®, but he worked on many before Disney Studios started allowing illustrators to be given name credit. Dias received national attention in 1956 when he was invited to visit President Dwight D. Eisenhower in Washington, D.C., as a result of winning a national contest on designing a "Children's Friendship" postal stamp. He is still very active in the animation industry. http://www.RonDias.com

This guide lists book titles alphabetically by series category. The values shown are for first edition books in very fine or better condition. You will need to deduct from the values for reprints and books in lesser condition.

**How much to deduct from the listed value for reprints:**

Many of you would love to hear that there's a magic formula for reprints to be deducted from the shown price. Because some titles had many reprints and others maybe only one, there is no magic formula for pricing reprints.

A second edition of a title with only two printings would have a lesser value deduction than a second edition of a title with 10 reprints. If you know the book had many reprints, then the percentage off the book value would be more than for a title with one or two printings. If the book had only one reprint, it could sell for close to original value. Reprints of books that have fewer pages than the original will be worth less than a full-page edition.

You may also want to know how many reprints a book had. I wish I could tell you, but I can't. Much of this information has been lost or misplaced during company moves over the years.

**Condition Value Percentages**

I find the following definitions of condition terms to be the best.

**100% Mint:** *No marks of any kind on book. Should look like it just came off the store shelf.*

**80%-90% Very Fine:** *This is a book that would be mint condition except for very few scuff marks.*

**75% Fine:** *Clean, tight book. May have some light erasable pencil marks. Name may be written on inside cover in space provided. A little of the cover luster may be gone. Overall condition of the book should be one that was read but well cared for.*

**60%-70% Very Good:** *Above average condition. Well taken care of book with no major flaws.*

**50% Good:** *May have some light soiling or chipping on front cover. No tears or scrapes on the cover. The inside pages may have small creases or folded corners, could have small tears no more than a quarter-inch long. No tape. Some of the spine cover may be missing or chipping. The book is well read but still in complete condition.*

**25% Fair:** *The spine is getting loose. The cover is soiled. There is no crayon scribbling or ink that distracts from any part of the book. There may be some tape on pages. The book is well-read and not taken care of.*

**0%-10% Poor:** *A damaged book. Crayon, ink on pages, missing pages, chewed pages, missing activities. The book probably looks like it just came out of the trash.*

# Section 1: *Golden Books*®

## The History of Western Printing & Lithographing Co., Whitman Publishing Company, Golden Books®, and Western Publishing Company

**The History of Little Golden Books**®

Western Publishing Company, Inc., one of the largest printers of children's books in the world, had its beginning in the basement of 618 State Street in Racine, Wisconsin.

Edward Henry Wadewitz, the 30-year-old son of German immigrants, had been working two jobs—one at a paint store and the other for West Side Printing Company—while taking bookkeeping classes at night. When the owner of the printing company was unable to pay Wadewitz his wages, he offered to sell Wadewitz the business. With dreams of owning his own business, Wadewitz, with $2,504 (some of it borrowed from his brother, Al), purchased the West Side Printing Company in 1907.

Wadewitz knew that if the printing company were to make it, he would need someone with more knowledge than he had. Roy A. Spencer, a printer with the Racine Journal Company, was one of the first people Wadewitz hired.

West Side Printing Company, with four employees, showed sales of $5,000 at the end of its first year. In 1908, with commercial job sales increasing, the company hired more employees. That year it also left a $10-a-month rental building and moved into a larger one and purchased a new automatic cutting machine and three new presses.

In 1910, after the purchase of the company's first lithographic press, the name was changed to Western Printing and Lithographing Company.

Less than four years later, the company moved into an even larger space—the basement of the Dr. Clarendon I. Shoop Building located at State and Wisconsin Avenue in Racine. Dr. Shoop was famous for bottled medications and tonics. Western Printing and Lithographing Company had become so successful that when Dr. Shoop retired in 1914, the company took over all six floors of the Shoop Building.

By its seventh year, sales had topped $127,000 and two new departments were formed: electrotyping and engraving. The company also purchased a new 28-inch by 42-inch offset press.

Wadewitz was approached by the Hamming-Whitman Publishing Company of Chicago to print its line of children's books. What Wadewitz did not foresee was that Hamming-Whitman would soon be going out of business. Unable to pay its bills, Hamming-Whitman left Western with thousands of books in its warehouse and in production.

Trying to cut its losses, Wadewitz entered Western into the retail book market for the first time. It proved so successful that the remaining Hamming-Whitman books were liquidated.

After acquiring Hamming-Whitman on Feb. 9, 1916, Western formed a subsidiary corporation called Whitman Publishing Company. Whitman employed two salesmen the first year and grossed more than $43,500 in children's book sales.

Sam Lowe, who later owned Bonnie Books, joined the Western team in 1916. Lowe sold Western and Whitman on the idea of bringing out a 10-cent children's book in 1918. Disaster almost followed when an employee misread a book order from S.S. Kresge Company, confusing dozens for gross, resulting in too many books being printed. Lowe was able to sell F.W. Woolworth Company and other chains the idea of having children's books on sale all year round. Until that time, stores usually treated children's books as Christmas items.

Toward the end of 1918, Western was outgrowing the Shoop Building, so another one was purchased—named Plant 2—to house the bookbinding and storage departments. In order to print a 6-inch by 9-inch book, Western purchased a 38-inch by 52-inch Potter offset press in 1923. This same year, Western started producing games and puzzles.

With sales of more than $1 million in 1925, Western decided to add another product, playing cards, to its growing line of merchandise. To be able to handle this, Western obtained the Sheffer Playing Card Company and formed another subsidiary corporation, the Western Playing Card Company.

By 1928, Western had built a new, modern, air-conditioned plant on Mound Avenue in Racine, and by 1929, sales were more than $2.4 million. The print run for children's books exceeded $10 million, playing cards $5 million, and games and puzzles $1 million. As a result, the company had to make plans to expand its new building.

In 1929, Western

*Western Publishing Company started in 1907 in this basement print shop. "Pioneer employees" were (from left) Roy A. Spencer, Catherine Bongarts Rutledge, E. H. Wadewitz, W. R. Wadewitz, and William Bell. The shop consisted of not much more than two battered presses, a few fonts of worn type, and a hand-powered cutting machine.*

*A major sign of Western Publishing Company's growth was the 1929 move to the new main plant in Racine, Wisconsin.*

*In 1910 West Side Printing Company changed its name to Western Printing and Lithographing Company and moved to the imposing building seen here, which was owned by Dr. Shoop's Laboratories.*

purchased Stationer's Engraving Company of Chicago, a manufacturer of stationery and greeting cards. This was the second operation the company had outside of Racine.

Western was able to keep its plant operational during the Depression years (1929-1933) by introducing a couple of new products: The Whitman jigsaw puzzle became very popular during this time of uncertainty, and a new series of books called Big Little Books was marketed. Brought out in 1932, the 10-cent Big Little Books became very popular during the years when people were looking for inexpensive entertainment. The first Big Little Book title was *The Adventures of Dick Tracy*. With this line of books, Western was setting the stage for future inexpensive reading material like comic books and Little Golden Books®. People love to copy success, and many publishers started bringing out their own books styled after the Big Little Book.

By the end of 1933, the Depression was coming to a close, Disney's Big Bad Wolf had been beaten by the Three Little Pigs, and Western and Walt Disney signed their first contract, giving Western exclusive rights to Disney's major characters.

Western, seeing a problem in having its plants and offices so far from the rest of the publishing industry, purchased a plant in Poughkeepsie,

New York, in 1934. This event marked the beginning of a close relationship with Dell Publishing Company and Simon & Schuster, Inc. Dell Publishing and Western produced Color Comics, which contained many of Western's licensed characters, from 1939 to 1962. *A Children's History* was the first joint effort between Western and Simon & Schuster in 1938.

Western formed the Artists and Writers Guild Inc. in the 1930s to handle the development of new children's books. This company, located on Fifth Avenue in New York City, would later have an immense hand in the conception of Little Golden Books®.

Western expanded its operations to the West Coast when it opened an office in Beverly Hills, California, sometime in the early 1940s. Being closer to the movie capital of the world made it a lot easier to do business with the studios that owned the characters the company licensed.

During World War II, Western did its part to help with the war effort. The company had a contract with the U.S. Army Map Service to produce maps for American soldiers in the fields. Along with the maps and other projects it did for the military, Western also manufactured many of its own products that were sent to the soldiers and the Red Cross overseas, such as playing cards and books.

In 1940, Sam Lowe left the company and George Duplaix replaced

him as head of the Artists and Writers Guild. While the guild and Simon & Schuster were collaborating on a book about Walt Disney's Bambi, Duplaix came up with the concept of a colorful children's book that would be durable and affordable to more American families than those being printed at that time. In 1941, children's books sold for between $2 and $3—a luxury for a lot of families. With the help of Lucile Olge, also of the guild, Duplaix contacted Albert Leventhal—a vice president and sales manager at Simon & Schuster— and Leon Shimkin, also of Simon & Schuster, with his idea.

The group decided on 12 titles to be released at the same time. Each title would have 42 pages, 28 printed in two-color and 14 printed in four-color. The book's binding was designed after a side-staple binding being done in Sweden.

These books were to be called Little Golden Books®.

The group originally discussed a 50-cent price for Little Golden Books, but Western did not want to compete with the other 50-cent books already on the market. The group did some more figuring and found that if it printed 50,000 copies of each book instead of 25,000, the books could be sold for 25 cents each. In September 1942, the first 12 titles were printed and released to stores in October.

Little Golden Books®, with their colorful, bright pages, were designed to be handled by children and were inexpensive enough that children could read or handle their books whenever they wanted. With these qualities and many more, the books became very popular with parents, but not with librarians in these early years, who felt these books did not contain the quality of literature a child should be reading. They did not consider that a book a child could handle was better than one stored out of reach on a shelf, or that an affordable book was better than not owning one at all, but this attitude has mellowed quite a bit since the 1940s.

Golden® Books were published by Simon & Schuster, Inc. They were produced by Artists and Writers Guild and printed at Western Printing and Lithographing.

During World War II, there was a paper shortage in the United States. To help ease this shortage, in 1943 the War Production Board put restrictions on paper use. As a result, retailers were receiving only one of every 10 books they ordered. Once the paper shortage was over, backorders that had piled up during the shortage began to be filled, and the company now had thousands of new customers.

Sales of Little Golden Books® were doing so well that in 1944, Simon & Schuster decided to create a new division headed by George Duplaix, called Sandpiper Press. Duplaix hired Dorothy Bennett—who was formerly employed as the assistant curator at the Museum of Natural History—as the general editor. She was responsible for many of the subjects used in Little Golden Books®

through the mid-1950s, and she authored numerous books, including The Giant Golden Book Encyclopedia. Bennett fought very hard to keep television and movies out of Little Golden Books®; she felt the quality and context of the books would be weakened. She hated to see the book *J. Fred Muggs* printed and thought it poetic justice when the monkey bit the host and the television show was taken off the air. Bennett wanted the books to teach children something of the world they lived in, whether it was history, geography, science, or the experiences a child has while growing up.

In 1958, Western Publishing and Lithographing Co., Inc. and Pocket Books Inc. became joint publishers, and the company name then became Golden Press, Inc. But in 1960, Western Printing and Lithographing became Western Publishing Company, Inc. and Pocket Books' interest in Golden Press was acquired in 1964.

Golden Books® became part of Random House on March 1, 2002.

## The Golden Book Numbering System

Prior to 1979, Golden Books® had a three- to six-digit book number printed on the front or back covers.

In 1979, Western changed its numbering to a code-based numbering system using three digits, a dash, and two digits. For example, with 101-42, 1 indicates assortment, 01 indicates category, and -42 indicates position in category. These dash numbered books were not printed numerically, and this number on the book may or may not have changed with a title's reprinting. I recommend that if you are a new collector trying to collect a title that was printed with a dash number, that you try to collect the first edition.

## How to Determine Golden Book Editions

1. **1942-1946** Edition number will be found on the first or second page of book.

2. **1947-1970** Depending on the book series, there is a letter of the alphabet on the inside front cover, bottom left, or at the bottom lower right-hand corner of the last page of the book

by the spine. A few larger Golden Books® had the letter at the bottom of the back inside cover. This letter will correspond with the book's edition. For example: A=1st, Z=26th, AA=27.

3. **1971-1991** On the bottom of one of the first two pages, you will see something like ABCDEFGHIJKLM. The first letter to the far left is the edition. A= first edition.

4. **1991–2001** Books printed during these years will have a copyright date as well as a printing date in Roman numerals. If a book from this period does not have a Roman numeral date, it is a first printing and the number was left off by mistake. If the letter "A" precedes the Roman numerals, the book is a first edition. If an "R" precedes the Roman numerals, the book is a revised edition. If no letter precedes the Roman numerals, the numerals themselves state when the book was printed, and there is no way to determine the edition.

For those of you not familiar with Roman numerals, "MCMXCI" is 1991. When reading Roman numerals, you subtract the number on the left from the one on the right when the one on the left is smaller. M =1,000, C=100, X=10, IX=9 (or 10 minus 1), VIII=8, VII=7, VI=6, V=5, IV=4 (or 5 minus 1), III=3, II=2, I=1. With the number "MCMXCI," you have "M"=1000, "CM"=900 (or 1000 minus 100), "XC"=90 (or 100 minus 10), "I"=1 for 1000 + 900 + 90 + 1 = 1991.

5. **2001–Present** In 2001 the Roman numerals were dropped for the industry standard way of determining book editions. Using this method, the last number to the right of a row of numbers is the edition/printing.

10 9 8 7 6 5 4 3 2 1 is a first edition. Most first editions will also state "First Edition."

10 9 8 7 6 5 4 3 is a third edition/ printing.

## How to Determine Whitman Book Editions

Whitman books never had edition information printed in the books. In the different Whitman series chapters, I mention ways to assist you in making an educated guess to a book's year of printing.

# The First 12 Little Golden Books

**#1 Three Little Kittens**
Illustrator: Masha
#1    1942   42 Pages
1st Edition  **$50**
Four-color and black & white
Blue spine with dust jacket **$50-$200**

**#2 Bedtime Stories**
Illustrator: Tenggren, Gustaf
Author: Misc. Authors
#2    1942   42 Pages
1st Edition  **$50**
Four-color and black & white
Blue spine with dust jacket **$50-$150**
Five Stories: Chicken Little, The Three
Bears, The Three Little Pigs, Little Red
Riding Hood, The Gingerbread Man

**#3 Alphabet A-Z, The**
Illustrator: Blake, Vivienne
#3    1942   42 Pages
1st Edition  **$50**
Four-color and black & white
Blue spine with dust jacket **$50-$200**

**#4 Mother Goose**
Illustrator: Elliott, Gertrude
Author: Fraser, Phyllis
#4    1942   42 Pages
1st Edition  **$50**
Four-color and black & white
Blue spine with dust jacket **$50-$200**

**#5 Prayers for Children**
Illustrator: Dixon, Rachel Taft
#5    1942   42 Pages
1st Edition  **$40**
Four-color and black & white
Blue spine with dust jacket **$50-$200**

**#6 Little Red Hen, The**
Illustrator: Freund, Rudolf
Author: Potter, Marion
#6    1942   42 Pages
1st Edition  **$50**
Four-color and black & white
Blue spine with dust jacket **$50-$200**

**#7 Nursery Songs**
Illustrator: Malvern, Corinne
Author: Gale, Leah
#7    1942   42 Pages
1st Edition  **$40**
Four-color and black & white
Blue spine with dust jacket **$50-$200**

**#8 Poky Little Puppy, The**
Illustrator: Tenggren, Gustaf
Author: Lowrey, Janet Sebring
#8    1942   42 Pages
1st Edition  **$50**
Four-color and black & white
Blue spine with dust jacket **$50-$200**

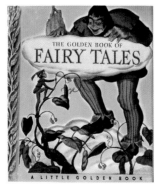

**#9 Golden Book of Fairy Tales, The**
Illustrator: Hoskins, Winfield
#9       1942       42 Pages
1st Edition  **$50**
Four-color and black & white
Blue spine with dust jacket $50-$200
Four stories: Jack and the Beanstalk,
Cinderella, Puss in Boots, Sleeping Beauty

**#10 Baby's Book**
Illustrator: Smith, Bob
Author: Smith, Bob
#10  1942   42 Pages
1st Edition  **$50**
Four-color and black & white
Blue spine with dust jacket **$75-$300**

**#11 Animals of Farmer Jones, The**
Illustrator: Freund, Rudolf
Author: Gale, Leah
#11  1942   42 Pages
1st Edition  **$50**
Four-color and black & white
Blue spine with dust jacket **$50-$200**

**#12 This Little Piggy**
Illustrator: Paflin, Roberta
#12  1942   42 Pages
1st Edition  **$60**
Four-color and black & white
Blue spine with dust jacket **$60-$250**

For more Little Golden Books, please see *Warman's Little Golden Books Identification and Price Guide* by Steve Santi (Krause Publications, 2006).

# Section 1: Golden Books
## *Big Golden Books®,*
## *Giant Golden Books®, Deluxe Golden Books®,*
## *and Golden Books®*

In this section you'll find Golden Books®, Big Golden Books®, Giant Golden Books®, and Deluxe Golden Books®. They are listed together to avoid causing confusion to the collector because some of these books were published under different types over the years.

Big Golden Books® and Giant Golden Book were first published around 1944. Deluxe Giant Golden Books® followed them in 1946.

The titles are listed in alphabetical order and different numbers are given, if applicable. It is possible that you could own a book with a different number than listed.

### How to determine editions:
1) Look for a letter of the alphabet corresponding with the edition number, which can be found on the inside front cover, bottom left. It will look like A100100 or B100100. An "A" means a first edition, and the 100100 means that its suggested retail price was $1.
2) Look on the last page of the book at the bottom right corner for a letter of the alphabet. An "A" means first edition, "B" means second, "C" means third, etc.
3) Look for a row of letters, either on the copyright page or back inside cover. ABCDEFGHIJ = first edition, BCDEFGHIJK = second, etc.
4) Look on the copyright page for something like: Fifth printing, 1972.
5) If there are Roman numerals at the bottom of the copyright page and no "A" directly in front of it, it's a reprint.
6) If none of the above applies, there's a good chance that the book is a first edition. Sorry, but there are no guarantees.

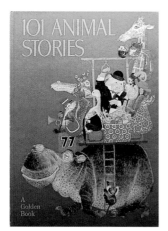

**101 Animal Stories**
Illustrator: Benvenuti
Author: Dalmais, Anne-Marie
15565   1972   8 x 11         144 pp.   **$15**

**12 Folk and Fairy Tales**
Illustrator: Durand, Paul
13578   1970   10 x 11-3/4        64 pp.      **$7**

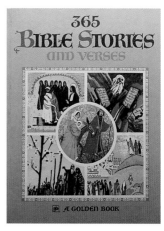

**365 Bible Stories and Verses**
Author: Grainger, Muriel
16819   1973   8-1/2 x 11         240 pp.   **$8**

**366 Goodnight Stories**
Illustrator: Various
15568   1969   8-3/8 x 10 7/8   240 pp.   **$5**

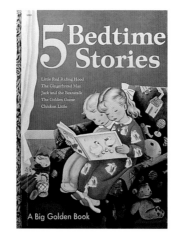

**5 Bedtime Stories**
Illustrator: Tenggren, Gustaf
8002   1957   7-3/4 x 10 7/8   48 pp.      **$8**

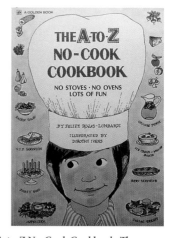

**A-to-Z No-Cook Cookbook, The**
Illustrator: Ivens, Dorothy
Author: Rojas-Lombardi, Felipe
15784   1974   9-1/4 x 12 5/8   62 pp.      **$6**

**About the Big Sky…Hills…Earth and the Deep Sea**
Illustrator: Kaufman, Joe
Author: Kaufman, Joe
16805   1978   10-1/4 x 12      72 pp.   **$10**

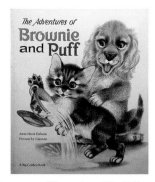

**Adventures of Brownie and Puff, The**
Illustrator: Giannini
Author: Dalmais, Anne-Marie
13544   1971   10-1/4 x 11 7/8  62 pp.   **$16**

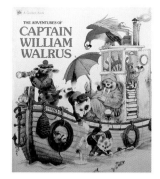

**Adventures of Captain William Walrus, The**
Illustrator: Giannini
Author: Duplaix, Michel
13545   1972   10-1/4 x 11 7/8  28 pp.   **$15**

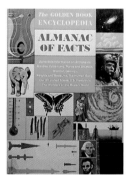

**Adventures of Little Rabbit, The**
Illustrator: Durand, Paul
Author: Dalmais, Anne-Marie
13633   1972   10-3/4 x 11 7/8  64 pp.   **$6**

*Dust jacket*

*Book cover*

**Aesop's Fables**
Illustrator: Provensen, Alice & Martin
Author: Untermeyer, Louis
15509   1965   10-1/2 x 12-1/8 92 pp.   **$25**

**Almanac of Facts**
Illustrator: Hess, Lowell
Author: Parker Morris, Bertha
No #   1962   7-1/2 x 10-1/2  94 pp.   **$8**

**Alphabet of Many Things**
Illustrator: Rojankovsky, Feodor
Author: Rojankovsky, Feodor
13529   1970   9-1/2 x 12-3/4  64 pp.   **$12**

**Amazing Travels of Ingrid Our Turtle, The**
Illustrator: Lippman, Peter
Author: Lippman, Peter
12500   1973   9-1/4 x 12-1/2  28 pp.   **$7**

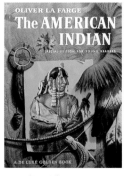

**American Indian, The**
Illustrator: Various
Author: Le Farge, Oliver
17846   1960   8 x 11      214 pp.   **$15**

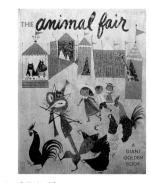

**Animal Fair, The**
Illustrator: Provensen, Alice & Martin
Author: Provensen, Alice & Martin
751   1952   9 5/8 x 12-3/4  80 pp.   **$16**

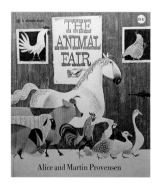

**Animal Fair, The**
Illustrator: Provensen, Alice & Martin
Author: Provensen, Alice & Martin
15709   1952   10-1/2 x 12-1/8 64 pp.   **$7**

**Animal Stories**
Illustrator: Rojankovsky, Feodor
Author: Duplaix, Georges
8008   1944   7-3/4 x 10 7/8   48 pp.   **$12**

**Animal Stories**
With dust jacket
Illustrator: Rojankovsky, Feodor
Author: Duplaix, Georges
No #    1944   10-1/4 x 13     92 pp.   **$40**

**Animal Stories**
With dust jacket
Illustrator: Rojankovsky, Feodor
Author: Duplaix, George
710   1944   10 x 12 7/8     96 pp.   **$35**

**Animal Talk "A Pop-Up Book"**
Illustrator: Gergely, Tibor
Author: Leydenfrost, Robert
13542   1960   6-3/4 x 9-1/2   32 pp.   **$25**

**Animals' Merry Christmas, The**
Illustrator: Scarry, Richard
Author: Jackson, Kathryn
556   1950   9-3/4 x 13     98 pp.   **$65**

**Animals' Merry Christmas, The**
Illustrator: Scarry, Richard
Author: Jackson, Kathryn
10315   1950   8-1/2 x 11-1/4   48 pp.   **$8**

**Animals' Merry Christmas, The**
Illustrator: Scarry, Richard
Author: Jackson, Kathryn
15612   1950   9-1/2 x 12-3/4   80 pp.   **$10**

**Animals Around the Year**
Illustrator: Simon, Romain
Author: Verite, Marcelle
17858   1972   7-3/4 x 10-3/8   160 pp.   **$8**

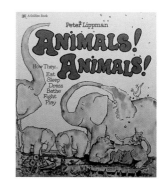

**Animals! Animals!**
Illustrator: Lippman, Peter
Author: Lippman, Peter
16808   1976   10-1/2 x 12-1/8 72 pp.   **$10**

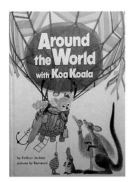

**Around the World With Koa Koala**
Illustrator: Benvenuti
Author: Jackson, Kathryn
16817   1974   8 x 11-1/4         144 pp.   **$6**

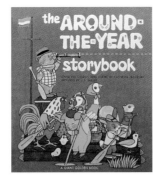

**Around-the-Year Story Book, The**
Illustrator: Miller, J.P.
Author: Jackson, Kathryn
15769   1971   10-1/4 x 11 7/8  96 pp.   **$10**

**Astronauts, The**
Illustrator: Photos
Author: the 7 Astronauts of Project Mercury
11125   1961   7 x 10-1/8   96 pp.   **$18**

**Baby Animals**
Illustrator: Williams, Garth
477   1952   6-3/4 x 8         22 pp.   **$10**

**Baby Brown Bear's Big Bellyache**
Illustrator: Nez, John
Author: Coco, Eugene Bradley
12088   1989   8-1/4 x 11         24 pp.   **$5**

**Baby Farm Animals**
Illustrator: Williams, Garth
481   1953   6-3/4 x 8         22 pp.   **$10**

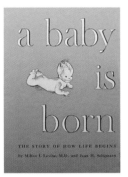

**Baby is Born, A**
Illustrator: Wilkin, Eloise
Author: Levine, Milton & Seligmann, Jean
576   1949   9-1/4 x 6-1/2   60 pp.   **$18**

**Baby's First Book**
Illustrator: Williams, Garth
489   1955   6-3/4 x 8         22 pp.   **$10**

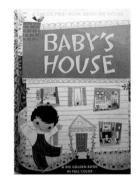

**Baby's House**
Illustrator: Blair, Mary
Author: McHugh, Gelolo
10412   1950   9-1/4 x 12-1/2   24 pp.   **$16**

**Baby's Mother Goose**
Illustrator: Wilkin, Eloise
10411   1958   9-1/4 x 12-1/2   24 pp.   **$5**

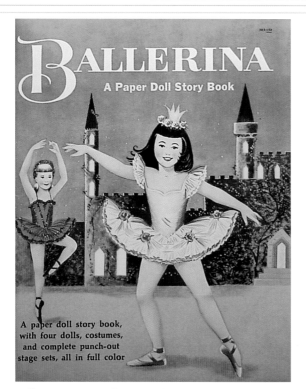

**Bamm-Bamm With Pebbles Flintstone**
Illustrator: Pratt, Hawley & McGary, Norm
Author: Lewis, Jean
10845   1963   9-1/4 x 12-1/2   24 pp.   **$25**

**Bedtime Stories**
Illustrator: Scarry, Richard
Author: Jackson, Kathryn
10727   1957   7-1/2 x 10-1/2   96 pp.   **$25**

**Ballerina, A Paper Doll Story Book**
Illustrator: Lockwood, Judy
Author: Lockwood, Judy
383   1960   8-3/4 x 11-1/4   40 pp.   **$75**

**Bedtime Tales**
Illustrator: Malvern, Corinne
Author: Packard, Hazel
558   1951   8-1/4 x 10-3/4   130 pp.   **$16**

**Betsy McCall's Paper Doll Story Book**
Illustrator: Miloche, Hilda & Kane, Wilma
Author: Fletcher, Steffi
483   1954   8-3/4 x 11-1/4   52 pp.   **$175**

**Betsy's Adventure**
Illustrator: Mamlok, Gwyneth
Author: Mamlok, Gwyneth
10852   1964   9 5/8 x 12-3/4   28 pp.   **$7**

**Bible Songs and Stories**
Illustrator: Rojankovsky, Feodor
Author: Nast, Elsa Ruth
GRC10 1957   12-1/4 x 12-1/4 23 pp.   **$15**

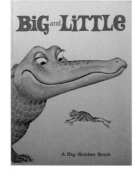

**Big and Little**
Illustrator: Kaufman, Joe
Author: Kaufman, Joe
10475   1966   9 5/16 x 12      28 pp.   **$6**

**Big Brown Bear, The**
Illustrator: Tenggren, Gustaf
Author: Duplaix, George
10413   1947   9-1/4 x 12-1/2   24 pp.   **$10**

**Big Brown Bear, The**
Illustrator: Tenggren, Gustaf
Author: Duplaix, George
No #    1947    8-1/8 x 11    56 pp.    **$25**

**Big Elephant, The**
Illustrator: Rojankovsky, Feodor
Author: Jackson, Kathryn & Byron
No #    1949    8-1/8 x 13-1/4    28 pp.    **$25**

**Big Farmer Big & Little Farmer Little**
Illustrator: Rojankovsky, Feodor
Author: Jackson, Kathryn & Byron
No #    1948        5-1/2 x 12-1/2
64 pp.                    **$60**

**Big Golden Animal A B C, The**
Illustrator: Williams, Garth
Author: Williams, Garth
457    1957    9-1/2 x 12-3/4    28 pp.    **$10**

**Big Golden Animal A B C, The**
Illustrator: Williams, Garth
Author: Williams, Garth
10457    1957    9-1/4 x 12-1/2    28 pp.    **$5**

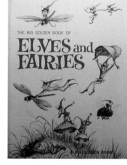

**Big Golden Book of Elves and Fairies, The**
Illustrator: Williams, Garth
Author: Werner, Jane
12067    1951    10 x 13        78 pp.    **$100**

**Big Golden Book of Bible Stories, The**
Illustrator: Von Carolsfeld, Schnorr
Author: Sporri, Samuel
584    1958    8-3/16 x 10-3/4 72 pp.    **$15**

**Big Golden Book of Fairy Tales, The**
Illustrator: Manson, Beverlie
Author: Lette-Hodge, Lornie
15545    1981    8 5/8 x 11 7/8    158 pp.    **$8**

**Bill Dugan's Busy Town**
Illustrator: Dugan, William
Author: Dugan, William
12298    1969    9-1/4 x 11-3/8    64 pp.    **$6**

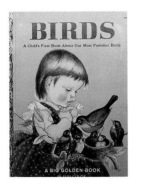

**Birds**
Illustrator: Wilkin, Eloise
Author: Watson, Jane Werner
10544   1958   9-1/4 x 12-1/2   28 pp.   **$12**

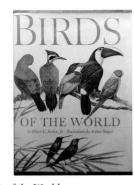

**Birds of the World**
Illustrator: Singer, Arthur
Author: Austin, Oliver L.
69502   1961   10 x 13-1/4       300 pp.   **$25**

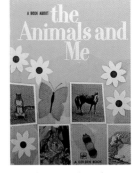

**Book About the Animals and Me, A**
Illustrator: Various Photos
Author: Dwyer, Jane
10888   1971   9-3/8 x 12-1/2   28 pp.       **$5**

*Dust jacket*                *Book cover*

**Boswell's Life of Boswell**
Illustrator: Leavens, Evelyn
Author: Leavens, Evelyn
416       1958   7-3/4 x 11       28 pp.   **$15**

**Boy Engineer, The**
Author: Throm, Edward
841       1960   6 5/8 x 9 5/8     242 pp.   **$25**

**Boy Mechanic, The**
Author: Popular Mechanics Editors
824       1952   6 5/8 x 9 5/8     314 pp.   **$35**

**Boy Scientist, The**
Illustrator: Barker, Robert
Author: Leweilen, John
827       1955   6 5/8 x 9 5/8     272 pp.   **$25**

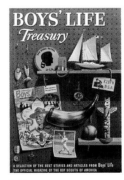

**Boy's Life Treasury**
Illustrator: Various
Author: Editors of Boys' Life
835       1958   7-1/4 10-1/4     480 pp.   **$15**

**Bugs Bunny in Escape From Noddington Castle**
Illustrator: Baker, Darrell
Author: Graham, Kennon
10827-2   1980   9-3/8 x 12-1/2   24 pp.     **$4**

**Bugs Bunny Stories**
Illustrator: Various
Author: Various
15827   1990   8-1/2 x 11         68 pp.     **$6**

**Bugs Bunny's Book**
Illustrator: Bradbury, Jack & Grant, Campbell
Author: Bedford, Annie North
472       1951   8-1/2 x 11-1/4   56 pp.   **$16**

**Bugs Bunny's Book**
Illustrator: Bradbury, Jack & Grant, Campbell
Author: Bedford, Annie North
10316   1951   8-1/2 x 11-1/4   48 pp.   **$12**

**Butterflies**
Illustrator: Durenceau, André
Author: Claarke, J. F. Gates
13765   1963   8 x 11            68 pp.     **$8**

**Canterbury Tales of Geoffrey Chaucer**
Illustrator: Tenggren, Gustaf
Author: Hieatt, Kent & Hieatt, Constance
16744   1961   8 x 11            140 pp.    **$8**

**Captain Kangaroo and His Animal Friends**
Illustrator: Nonast, Marie
Author: Memling, Carl
399     1959   8-3/8 x 10 7/8   28 pp.     **$8**

**Caroline at the Ranch**
Illustrator: Probst, Pierre
Author: Probst, Pierre
11126   1961   9 x 12-1/4       26 pp.     **$75**

**Caroline In Europe**
Illustrator: Probst, Pierre
Author: Witty, Susan
12008   1960   9 x 12-1/4       28 pp.     **$75**

**Cat Book, The**
Illustrator: Goodenow, Gig
Author: Daly, Kathleen
10837   1964   9 5/16 x 12-1/2  28 pp.     **$18**

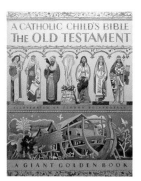

**Catholic Child's Bible, A—The Old Testament**
Illustrator: Rojankovsky, Feodor
Author: Werner,Elsa Jane & Hartman, Charles
30665   1958   10 x 13          132 pp.    **$18**

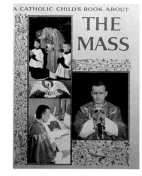

**Catholic Child's Book About the Mass**
Illustrator: Rutherfoord, William De J.
Author: Gales, Father
686     1958   8-3/4 x 11       50 pp.     **$16**

**Child's Garden of Verses, A**
Illustrator: Provensen, Alice & Martin
Author: Stevenson, Robert Louis
13583   1951   8 5/8 x 11-1/4   68 pp.     **$10**

**Child's Garden of Verses, A**
Illustrator: Tiffany, Virginia
Author: Stevenson, Robert Louis
10873   1969   9-3/8 x 12-1/2   28 pp.     **$6**

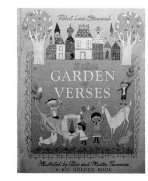

**Child's Garden of Verses, A**
Illustrator: Provensen, Alice & Martin
Author: Stevenson, Robert Louis
557     1951   8 7/8 x 11-1/4   78 pp.     **$25**

**Children Come Running, The**
UNICEF
Illustrator: Various
Author: Coatsworth, Elizabeth
523     1960   6-1/4 x 8-3/4    94 pp.     **$16**

*Book cover*

*Box cover art*

**Children's Bible, The**
19100   1965   7 X 10          520 pp.   **$10**

**Children's Bible, The**
16520   1965   7-1/4 10-1/4     520 pp.   **$12**

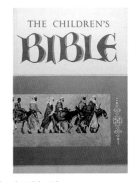

**Children's Bible, The**
No #   1965   8-1/4 x 11-1/2   80 pp.   **$8**

**Chinese Fairy Tales**
Illustrator: Rizzato, Serge
Author: Ponsot, Marie
16780   1960   10-1/8 x 13-3/4 156 pp.   **$45**

**Christmas Carols**
Author: Van Loon, Hendrik Willem
818     1937   9-3/4 x 12        64 pp.   **$35**

**Christmas Treasure Book, The**
Illustrator: Various
Author: Marx, Hilda
No #    1950   8-1/4 x 10-3/8   38 pp.   **$40**

**Christopher for President**
Illustrator: Crawford, Mel
Author: Addie
13751   1973   10-1/2 x 12-1/8 48 pp.   **$12**

**Chuckle Book, The**
Illustrator: Crawford, Mel
13538   1971   8 5/8 x 12 5/16  72 pp.   **$6**

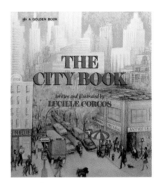

**City Book, The**
Illustrator: Corcos, Lucille
Author: Corcos, Lucille
15772   1972   10-1/2 x 12-1/8 94 pp.   **$12**

**Color Kittens**
Illustrator: Provensen, Alice & Martin
Author: Brown, Margaret Wise
546     1958   9-3/8 x 12-1/2   28 pp.   **$10**

**Color Kittens**
Illustrator: Provensen, Alice & Martn
Author: Brown, Margaret Wise
10546   1958   9-1/4 x 12-1/2   28 pp.   **$8**

**Cookie Monster and the Cookie Tree**
Illustrator: Mathieu, Joe
Author: Korr, David
10821-21977   9-3/8 x 12-1/2   24 pp.   **$4**

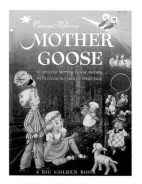

**Corinne Malvern's Mother Goose**
Illustrator: Malvern, Corinne
480    1953   8-3/8 x 11        64 pp.    **$16**

**Curly the Pig**
Illustrator: Livraghi, Virginio
Author: Pezzi, Maria Pia
10844   1964   9 5/16 x 12-1/2  28 pp.   **$15**

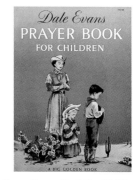

**Dale Evans Prayer Book For Children**
Illustrator: Dart, Eleanor
Author: Evans, Dale
448    1956   9 5/16 x 12-1/2  28 pp.   **$15**

**Dennis the Menace**
Illustrator: Pratt, Hawley & Holley, Lee
Author: Memling, Carl
10832   1959   9 5/16 x 12-1/2  28 pp.   **$15**

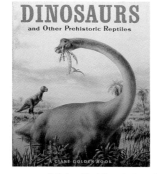

**Dinosaurs and Other Prehistoric Reptiles**
Illustrator: Zallinger, Rudolph
Author: Watson, Jane Werner
764    1960   10-3/8 x 11 7/8  64 pp.   **$7**

**Dog Stories**
Illustrator: Rojankovsky, Feodor
Author: Coatsworth, Elizabeth
578    1953   9 7/8 x 13        68 pp.   **$16**

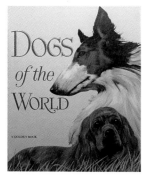

**Dogs of the World**
Illustrator: Stirnweis, Shannon
Author: Lawson, Patrick
15518   1965   10-1/8 x 12-1/2 96 pp.   **$16**

**Easy How-To Book, The**
Illustrator: Dugan, William
Author: Reit, Seymour
13573   1973   10-1/4 x 11 7/8  48 pp.   **$7**

**Enchanted Princess and Other Fairy Tales**
Illustrator: Benvenuti
Author: King, Léon
15621   1959   9 7/8 x 12-3/4  155 pp.  **$35**

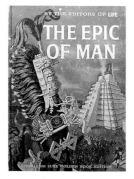

**Epic of Man, The**
Illustrator: Various
Author: Rachlis, Eugene
16502   1962   8-1/8 x 11-1/4  176 pp.  **$6**

**Fairy Tale Book, The**
Illustrator: Segur, Adrienne
Author: Ponest, Marie
760    1958   9-3/4 x 12-3/4  156 pp.  **$150**

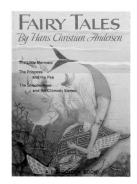

**Fairy Tales By Hans Christian Andersen**
Illustrator: Vanni, Gian Berto
Author: Daly, Kathleen
10839   1964   9 5/16 x 12-1/2  28 pp.   **$10**

**Fantasy Voyage Through Outer Space**
Illustrator: Brewer, Linda & John
Author: Hassell, Jon
15791   1974   9-1/2 x 12-3/4   28 pp.   **$12**

**Fantasy Voyage Through Prehistoric Time**
Illustrator: Brewer, Linda & John
Author: Hassell, Jon
15792   1974   9-1/2 x 12-3/4   32 pp.   **$12**

**Farm Stories**
Illustrator: Tenggren, Gustaf
Author: Jackson, Kathryn & Byron
No #   1946   10-1/4 x 13   92 pp.   **$20**

**Farm Stories**
Illustrator: Tenggren, Gustaf
Author: Jackson, Kathryn & Byron
No #   1946   10-1/4 x 13   92 pp.   **$20**

**Favorite Christmas Carols**
Illustrator: Spier, Peter
Author: Boni, Margaret Bradford
519   1957   8 x 11   128 pp.   **$25**

**Favorite Fairy Tales**
Illustrator: Rojankovsky, Feodor
No #   1949   8-1/8 x 13-1/4   28 pp.   **$40**

**Fireside Book of Favorite American Songs**
Illustrator: Battaglia, Aurelius
Author: Boni, Margaret Bradford
822   1952   8 x 11   360 pp.   **$15**

**Fireside Book of Love Songs**
Illustrator: Provensen, Alice & Martin
Author: Boni, Margaaret Bradford
826   1954   8 x 11   324 pp.   **$15**

**First Noel, The**
Illustrator: Provensen, Alice & Martin
610   1959   5 x 9   24 pp.   **$12**

**Five Fairy Tales**
Illustrator: Laite, Gordon
8010   1962   7-3/4 x 10 7/8   48 pp.   **$7**

**Flintstones, The**
Illustrator: Pratt, Hawley & White, Al
Author: Memling, Carl
8012   1962   7-3/4 x 10 7/8   36 pp.   **$18**

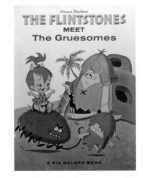

**Flintstones Meet the Gruesomes, The**
Illustrator: De Santis, George
Author: Lewis, Jean
10586   1965   9-1/2 x 12-3/4   28 pp.   **$30**

**Four Seasons, The**
Illustrator: Gottlieb, William P.
Author: Gottlieb, William P.
413     1957   9 x 12            28 pp.     **$7**

**Fourteen Bears Summer and Winter, The**
Illustrator: Parsons, Virginia
Author: Scott, Evelyn
13579   1973   10-1/4 x 11 7/8 64 pp.   **$150**

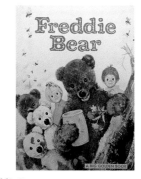

**Freddie Bear**
Illustrator: Durand, Paul
Author: Laydu, Claude
10476   1965   9-1/2 x 12-3/4  28 pp.     **$6**

**Frosty the Snow Man**
Illustrator: Malvern, Corinne
Author: Bedford, Annie North
10321   1951   9 5/16 x 12-1/2 28 pp.    **$12**

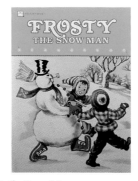

**Frosty the Snow Man**
Illustrator: Malvern, Corinne
Author: Bedford, Annie North
10201   1951   8 x 10-3/4          24 pp.     **$7**

**Fun-To-Make Book, The**
Illustrator: Lamarque, Colette
Author: Lamarque, Colette
10485   1970   9-1/4 x 12-1/2  28 pp.     **$6**

**Funny Bunny**
Illustrator: Provensen, Alice & Martin
Author: Leonard, Rachel
414     1950   9-1/2 x 13          28 pp.    **$45**

**Gay Purr-Ee**
Illustrator: White, Al
Author: Memling, Carl
10408   1962   9-1/4 x 12-1/2  24 pp.    **$25**

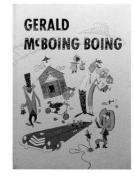

**Gerald McBoing Boing**
Illustrator: Crawford, Mel
479     1952   7-1/2 x 10          28 pp.    **$35**

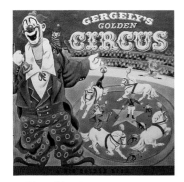

**Gergely's Golden Circus**
Illustrator: Gergely, Tibor
Author: Archer, Peter
485     1954   10-3/4 x 10-3/4 28 pp.   **$25**

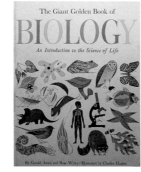

**Giant Golden Book of Biology**
Illustrator: Harper, Charles
Author: Ames, Gerald & Whler, Rose
15702   1961   10-1/4 x 13       100 pp.    **$6**

**Giant Golden Book of Birds, The**
Illustrator: Singer, Allen
Author: Allen, Robert Porter
15986   1962   10-1/8 x 13       100 pp.   **$25**

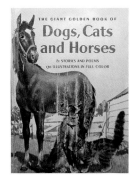

**Giant Golden Book of Cat Stories**
Illustrator: Rojankovsky, Feodor
Author: Coatsworth, Elizabeth
572    1953    9 7/8 x 13        66 pp.    **$22**

**Giant Golden Book of Dogs, Cats and Horses, The**
Illustrator: Rojankovsky, Feodor
Author: Coatsworth, Elizabeth & Barnes, Kat
699    1957    9 5/8 x 12-1/2    128 pp.    **$18**

**Giant Golden Book of Elves and Fairies**
Illustrator: Williams, Garth
Author: Werner, Jane
561    1951    10-1/8 x 13        76 pp.    **$150**

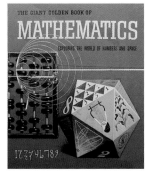

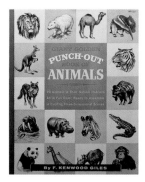

**Giant Golden Book of Mathematics**
Illustrator: Hess, Lowel
Author: Adler, Irving
762    1960    10-3/8 x 11 7/8   96 pp.    **$7**

**Giant Golden Book of Nature Stamps, The**
Illustrator: Various
Author: Various
360    1958    8-1/2 x 10 7/8    208 pp.    **$75**

**Giant Golden Punch-Out Book of Animals**
11385    1961    **$50**
385    1961    **$50**
10 x 12-3/4 on heavy card stock

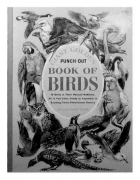

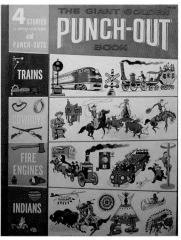

**Giant Golden Punch-Out Book of Birds**
19 Birds in their natural habitats.
11386    1961    **$50**
386    1961    **$50**
10 x 12-3/4 on heavy card stock

**Giant Panda Book, The**
Illustrator: Hildebrandt, Greg & Tim
Author: Hiss, Anthony
13753    1973    10-1/2 x 12-1/8   46 pp.    **$6**

**Giant Punch-Out Book**
18 pages of punch-outs.
Trains, cowboys, fire engines and Indians.
Originally published individually as Funtime Books.
Illustrator: Buettner, Carl & McGary, Norman
11388    1961    **$50**
388    1959    **$50**
10 x 12-3/4 on heavy card stock

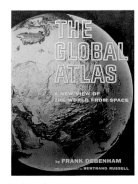

**Gingerbread Man, The**
Illustrator: Rutherford, Bonnie & Bill
Author: Rutherford, Bonnie & Bill
10460    1972    9-3/8 x 12-1/2    28 pp.    **$8**

**Global Atlas, The**
Illustrator: Various
Author: Debenham, Frank
850    1958    10-3/8 x 13 7/8   100 pp.    **$7**

*Dust jacket art*

*Book cover art*

**Golden Almanac, The**
Illustrator: Masha
Author: Bennett, Dorothy
No #   1954   9 x 11-1/496 pp.        **$35**

**Golden Animal A B C, The**
Illustrator: Williams, Garth
484   1954   6-3/4 x 8        22 pp.   **$10**

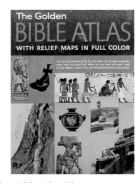

**Golden Anniversary Book of Scouting, The**
Illustrator: Rockwell, Norman & Various
Author: Bezucha, R. D.
843   1959   8 x 11        168 pp.   **$25**

**Golden Bedtime Book, The**
Illustrator: Scarry, Richard
Author: Jackson, Kathryn
752   1955   8 5/16 x 10-3/4 240 pp.   **$75**

**Golden Bible**
Illustrator: Rojankovsky, Feodor
Author: Watson, Jane Werner
No #   1946   10 x 13        124 pp.   **$15**

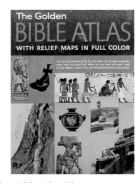

**Golden Bible Atlas, The**
Illustrator: Bolin, William
Author: Terrien, Samuel
749   1957   10-1/4 x 13        100 pp.   **$15**

**Golden Bible, The: The New Testament**
Illustrator: Provensen, Alice & Martin
Author: Werner, Elsa Jane
705   1953   10-1/4 x 13        95 pp.   **$35**

**Golden Bible, The: The Old Testament**
Illustrator: Rojankovsky, Feodor
Author: Werner, Elsa Jane
704   1946   10-1/4 x 13        124 pp.   **$35**

**Golden Birthday Book, The**
Illustrator: Weisgard, Leonard
Author: Brown, Margaret Wise
12096   1989   9-1/2 x 12-3/4   28 pp.   **$7**

**Golden Book of 365 Stories, The**
Illustrator: Scarry, Richard
Author: Jackson, Kathryn
13752   1955   8-3/8 x 11        236 pp.   **$25**

**Golden Book of America, The**
Illustrator: Various
Author: Shapiro, Irwin
833   1957   8 x 11        216 pp.   **$7**

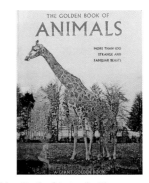

**Golden Book of Animals, The**
Illustrator: Suschitzky, W.
Author: White, Anne Terry
521   1958   10-1/4 x 13        96 pp.   **$12**

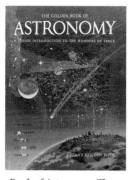

**Golden Book of Astronomy, The**
Illustrator: Polgreen, John
Author: Wyler, Rose & Ames, Gerald
753    1955    10 x 12-3/4    100 pp.    **$12**

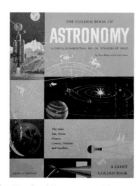

**Golden Book of Astronomy, The**
Illustrator: Polgreen, John
Author: Wyler, Rose & Ames, Gerald
15753    1955    10 x 12-3/4    100 pp.    **$6**

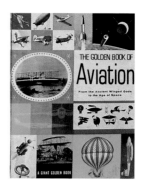

**Golden Book of Aviation**
Illustrator: McNaught, Hary
Author: Lewellen, John & Shapiro, Irwin
15761    1959    10 x 12-3/4    100 pp.    **$6**

**Golden Book of California**
Author: Shapiro, Irwin
13502    1961    7-1/4 10-1/8    96 pp.    **$8**

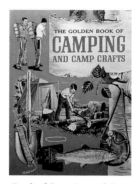

**Golden Book of Camping and Camp Crafts, The**
Illustrator: Barth, Ernest Kurt
Author: Lynn, Gordon
587    1959    8-3/8 x 11    112 pp.    **$12**

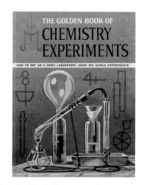

**Golden Book of Chemistry Experiments, The**
Illustrator: Lazarus, Harry
Author: Brent, Robert
612    1960    8-3/8 x 11    112 pp.    **$120**

**Golden Book of Christmas Tales, The**
Illustrator: Lewicki, Lillian
Author: Lewicki, James
454    1956    10 5/8 x 13-1/2    28 pp.    **$12**

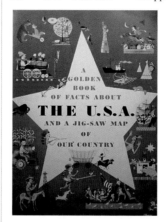

**Golden Book of Facts About the U.S.A., A**
Illustrator: McNaught.
Author: Conger, Marion
478    1952    11 x 15    24 pp.    **$65**

**Golden Book of Crafts and Hobbies**
Illustrator: Hunt, W. Ben
Author: Hunt, W. Ben
585    1957    8-3/8 x 11    112 pp.    **$30**

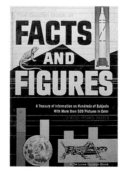

**Golden Book of Facts and Figures, The**
Illustrator: Hess, Lowell
Author: Parker, Barbara Morris
16506    1962    7-1/4 x 10-1/4    144 pp.    **$6**

**Golden Book of Fairy Tales**
Illustrator: Ségur, Adrienne
Author: Ponsot, Marie
17025    1999    9 7/8 x 13    156 pp.    **$15**

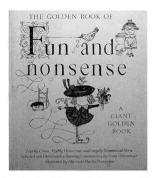

**Golden Book of Fun and Nonsense, The**
Illustrator: Provensen, Alice & Martin
Author: Untermeyer, Louis
16507   1970   10-1/2 x 12-1/8 96 pp.   **$6**

**Golden Book of Gardening, The**
Illustrator: Sayles, William & Tierney, Tom
Author: Giannoni, Frances
12586   1962   8-3/8 x 11   69 pp.   **$12**

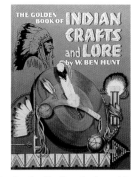

**Golden Book of Indian Crafts and Lore, The**
Illustrator: Hunt, W. Ben
Author: Hunt, W. Ben
581   1954   8-3/8 x 11   112 pp.   **$40**

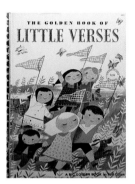

**Golden Book of Little Verses, The**
Illustrator: Blair, Mary
Author: Potter, Miriam Clark
574   1953   9-1/2 x 12-1/2   28 pp.   **$22**

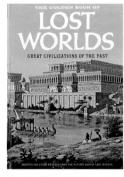

**Golden Book of Lost Worlds, The**
Author: Chenery, Janet
16519   1963   8-1/8 x 11-1/4   180 pp.   **$7**

**Golden Book of Magic, The**
Illustrator: Dugan, William
Author: Rawson, Clayton
12057   1964   8-3/8 x 11   104 pp.   **$22**

**Golden Book of Nature Crafts, The**
Illustrator: Pinney, Roy & Martin, Rene
Author: Saunders, John R.
608   1958   8-3/8 x 11   68 pp.   **$12**

**Golden Book of Nursery Tales, The**
Illustrator: Gergely, Tibor
Author: Werner, Elsa Jane
505   1948   8-3/16 10-3/4   128 pp.   **$25**

**Golden Book of Nursery Tales, The**
Illustrator: Gergely, Tibor
Author: Werner, Elsa Jane
No #   1948   8-3/4 x 11-1/8   128 pp.   **$35**

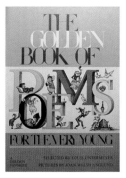

**Golden Book of Poems For the Very Young, The**
Illustrator: Anglund, Joan Walsh
Author: Untermeyer, Louis
12037   1971   8 7/8 x 12 5/8   34 pp.   **$6**

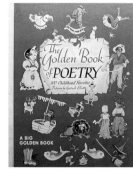

**Golden Book of Poetry, The**
**100 Childhood Favorites**
Illustrator: Elliott, Gertrude
Author: Werner, Jane
No #   1947   9 x 11-1/4   96 pp.   **$50**

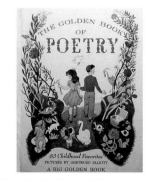

**Golden Book of Poetry, The**
**83 Childhood Favorites**
Illustrator: Elliott, Gertrude
Author: Werner, Jane
No #   1949   8 7/8 x 11-1/4   68 pp.   **$25**

**Golden Book of Poetry, The**
85 Childhood Favorites
Illustrator: Elliott, Gertrude
Author: Werner, Jane
13584   1949   8 5/8 x 11-1/4   68 pp.   **$25**

**Golden Book of Science, The**
Illustrator: NcNaught, Harry
Author: Parker, Bertha Morris
754   1956   10-1/4 x 13   98 pp.   **$12**

**Golden Book of Science, The (Revised)**
Illustrator: McNaught, Harry
Author: Parker, Bertha Morris
15563   1956   8 x 11   108 pp.   **$6**

**Golden Book of Story Time Tales, The**
Illustrator: Kane, Sharon
Author: Editors of Golden Press
13524   1962   8-1/2 x 11   164 pp.   **$18**

**Golden Book of the American Revolution, The**
Illustrator: Various
Author: Cook, Fred
844   1959   8 x 11   194 pp.   **$6**

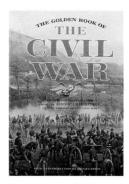

**Golden Book of the Civil War, The**
Illustrator: Various
16841   1961   8 x 11   216 pp.   **$6**

**Golden Book of the Mysterious, The**
Illustrator: Lee, Alan
Author: Watson, Jane Werner
17862   1976   8 x 11   144 pp.   **$6**

**Golden Book of the Renaissance, The**
Author: Shapiro, Irwin
16501   1962   8 x 11   168 pp.   **$8**

**Golden Book of Wild Animal Pets, The**
Illustrator: Pinney, Ron
Author: Pinney, Ron
611   1959   8-3/8 x 11   68 pp.   **$12**

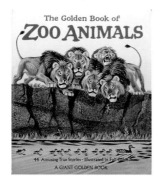

**Golden Book of Zoo Animals, The**
Illustrator: Johnston, Scott
Author: Bridges, William
13525   1962   10 5/8 x 12-1/8 62 pp.   **$8**

**Golden Bunny, The**
Illustrator: Weisgard, Leonard
Author: Brown, Margaret Wise
573   1953   9-1/2 x 12-3/4   28 pp.   **$15**

Golden Christmas Book, The
Illustrator: Malvern, Corinne
Author: Crampton, Gertrude
No #    1947    8 7/8 x 11-1/4    96 pp.    **$75**

Golden Christmas Book, The
Illustrator: Malvern, Corinne
Author: Crampton, Gertrude
433    1955    11-1/4 x 8-3/4    56 pp.    **$25**

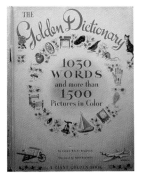

Golden Christmas Book, The
Illustrator: Malvern, Corinne
Author: Crampton, Gertrude
10433    1955    9 5/8 x 12-3/4    28 pp.    **$12**

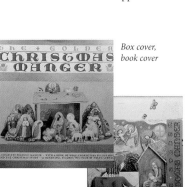

*Box cover,
book cover*

Golden Christmas Manger, The
Illustrator: Sewell, Helen
Author: Sewell, Helen
579    1948    9-1/2 x 10    28 pp.    **$60**

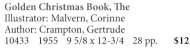

Golden Dictionary, The
Illustrator: Elliott, Gertrude
Author: Walpole, Ellen Wales
No #    1944    10-1/4 x 13    94 pp.    **$15**

Golden Dictionary, The
Illustrator: Elliott, Gertrude
Author: Walpole, Ellen Wales
551    1944    10-1/4 x 13    94 pp.    **$12**

Golden Digest, The
Illustrator: Various Golden Book Artists
Author: Editors of Golden Books*
1    1954    5-1/2 x 7-1/2    98 pp.    **$25**

Golden Egg Book, The
Illustrator: Weisgard, Leonard
Author: Brown, Margaret, Wise
462    1947    9 5/8 x 13-1/4    28 pp.    **$27**

Golden Egg Book, The
Illustrator: Weisgard, Leonard
Author: Brown, Margaret Wise
10853    1947    9 5/8 x 12-3/4    28 pp.    **$8**
10419    1975    9 5/8 x 12-3/4    28 pp.    **$5**

Golden Encyclopedia, The
Illustrator: De Witt, Cornelius
Author: Bennett, Dorothy A.
No #    1946    10-1/4 x 13    125 pp.    **$15**
703    1946    10-1/4 x 13    126 pp.    **$12**

Golden English-French Dictionary, The
Illustrator: Elliott, Gertrude
Author: Walpole, Ellen Wales
15002    1961    10-1/8 x 13    98 pp.    **$17**

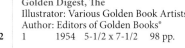

**Golden Funny Book, The**
Illustrator: Miller, J. P.
Author: Crampton, Gertrude
469    1950    8 7/8 x 11-1/4    76 pp.    **$25**

**Golden Geographic Encyclopedia, The**
Illustrator: Eigener, Wilhelm & August
Author: Shabad, Theodore & Stern, Peter
713    1958    10 x 13-1/4    232 pp.    **$8**

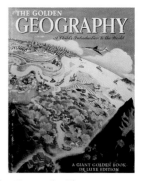

**Golden Geography, The**
Illustrator: De Witt, Cornelius
Author: Werner, Elsa Jane
750    1952    10-1/8 x 13    96 pp.    **$15**

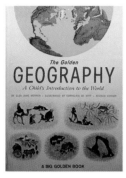

**Golden Geography, The**
Illustrator: De Witt, Cornelius
Author: Werner, Elsa Jane
12123    1964    9-1/2 x 12-3/4    62 pp.    **$6**

**Golden Grab Bag, The**
Illustrator: Gergely, Tibor
Author: Wyckoff, Jerome
559    1951    8 7/8 x 11-1/4    76 pp.    **$12**

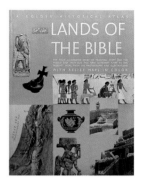

**Golden Historical Atlas Lands of the Bible**
Illustrator: Bolin, William
Author: Terrien, Samuel
749    1957    10-1/4 x 13    98 pp.    **$15**

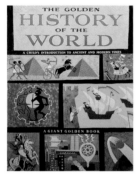

**Golden History of the World, The**
Illustrator: De Witt, Cornelius
Author: Watson, Jane Werner
829    1955    10 x 12-1/2    160 pp.    **$12**

**Golden Mother Goose, The**
Illustrator: Provensen, Alice & Martin
Author: Werner, Jane
555    1948    9-3/4 x 13    100 pp.    **$25**

**Golden Mother Goose, The**
Illustrator: Provensen, Alice & Martin
Author: Werner, Jane
555    1948    9-3/4 x 13    100 pp.    **$20**

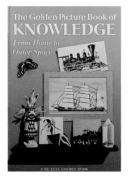

**Golden Picture Book of Knowledge, The**
Illustrator: Pothorn, Herbert
Author: Pothorn, Herbert
16503    1961    8-1/8 x 11-1/4    165 pp.    **$6**

**Golden Picture Dictionary, The**
Illustrator: Krush, Beth & Joe
Author: Moore, Lillian
11004    1954    8-1/2 x 11-1/8    80 pp.    **$8**

**Golden Song Book, The**
Illustrator: Elliott, Gertrude
Author: Wessells, Katharine Tyler
No #    1945    9 x 11-1/4    76 pp.    **$40**

**Golden Song Book, The**
56 Stories
Illustrator: Elliott, Gertrude
Author: Wessells, Katharine Tyler
13582   1945   8-1/2 x 11-1/4   70 pp.   **$15**

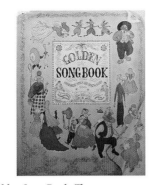

**Golden Song Book, The**
60 Stories
Illustrator: Elliott, Gertrude
Author: Wessells, Katharine Tyler
461   1945   8-7/8 x 11-1/4   76 pp.   **$22**

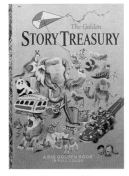

**Golden Story Treasury, The**
Illustrator: Gergely, Tibor
8003   1951   7-3/4 x 10-7/8   48 pp.   **$10**

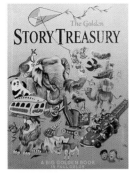

**Golden Story Treasury, The**
Illustrator: Gergely, Tibor
10319   1951   8-1/2 x 11-1/4   48 pp.   **$8**

**Golden Storybook of River Bend, The**
Illustrator: Gergely, Tibor
Author: Scarry, Patricia
15576   1969   8-1/2 x 11   96 pp.   **$12**

**Golden Treasure Book, The**
Illustrator: Various
Author: Various
560   1951   8-1/4 x 10-3/4   128 pp.   **$18**

**Golden Treasury of Animal Stories and Poems**
Author: Untermeyer
17844   1971   7-1/2 x 10-1/8   324 pp.   **$25**

**Golden Treasury of Caroline and Her Friends, The**
Illustrator: Probst, Pierre
Author: Probst, Pierre
15501   1961   12 x 9-1/16   160 pp.   **$300**

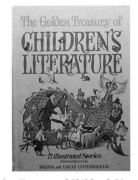

**Golden Treasury of Children's Literature, The**
Illustrator: Untermeyer, Bryan & Louis
Author: Untermeyer, Bryna & Louis
16522   1966   7-1/2 x 10-3/8   544 pp.   **$25**

**Golden Treasury of Myths and Legends**
Illustrator: Provensen, Alice & Martin
Author: White, Anne Terry
747   1959   8 x 11   168 pp.   **$16**

**Golden Treasury of Natural History, The**
Author: Parker, Bertha Morris
823   1952   8 x 11   224 pp.   **$8**

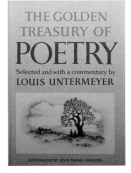

**Golden Treasury of Poetry, The**
Illustrator: Anglund, Joan Walsh
Author: Untermeyer, Louis
852   1959   7-3/8 x 10   324 pp.   **$40**

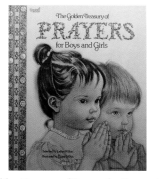

**Golden Treasury of Prayers for Boys and Girls, The**
Illustrator: Wilkin, Eloise
Author: Wilkin, Esther
13744   1975   10-1/2 x 12-1/8 46 pp.   **$10**

**Golden Treasury of Wonderful Fairy Tales, The**
Illustrator: Cremonini
15620   1961   9-3/4 x 12-3/4   160 pp.   **$18**

**Good Morning Farm**
Illustrator: Weinman, Fred
Author: Wright, Betty Ren
10885   1964   9-3/8 x 12-1/2   28 pp.   **$5**

**Good Night, Sleep Tight Book, The**
Illustrator: Vasiliu, Mircea
Author: Vasiliu, Mircea
12504   1973   9-1/4 x 12-1/2   28 pp.   **$6**

**Great Alphabet Race, The**
Illustrator: O'Sullivan, Tom
Author: Campbell, Janet & Roger
13755   1972   10-1/2 x 12-1/8 50 pp.   **$15**

**Great Big Animal Book, The**
Illustrator: Rojankovsky, Feodor
468   1950   9-3/4 x 12   24 pp.   **$8**

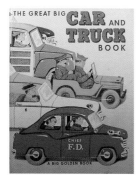

**Great Big Car and Truck Book, The**
Illustrator: Scarry, Richard
473   1951   10-1/2 x 13-1/2 20 pp.   **$15**

**Great Big Fire Engine Book, The**
Illustrator: Gergely, Tibor
470   1950   10-1/2 x 13-1/2 20 pp.   **$16**

**Great Big Fire Engine Book, The**
Illustrator: Gergely, Tibor
10470   1950   9-1/4 x 12-1/2   24 pp.   **$7**

**Great Big Wild Animal Book, The**
Illustrator: Rojankovsky, Feodor
452   1951   10-1/2 x 13-1/2 28 pp.   **$15**

**Great Big Wild Animal Book, The**
Illustrator: Rojankovsky, Feodor
563   1951   10-1/2 x 13-1/2 28 pp.   **$7**

**Grin and Giggle Book, The**
Illustrator: Pierce, Robert
Author: Pierce, Robert
13760   1972   10-1/2 x 12-1/8 48 pp.   **$10**

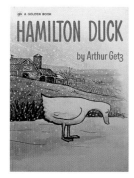

**Hamilton Duck**
Illustrator: Getx, Arthur
Author: Getz, Arthur
12055   1972   9 5/8 x 12-3/4   28 pp.   **$25**

**Hans Christian Andersen Fairy Tale Book, The**
Illustrator: Benvenuti
Author: Scott, Ann
15979   1959   9-3/4 x 12-3/4   156 pp.   **$35**

**Hans Christian Andersen Favorite Fairy Tales**
Illustrator: Durand, Paul
Author: Andersen, Hans Christian
16814   1972   8 X 11-1/4   144 pp.   **$7**

**Happy Rabbit, The**
Illustrator: Barton, Patricia
Author: Barton, Patricia
10854   1963   9-1/2 x 12-3/4   28 pp.   **$8**

**Hey There—It's Yogi Bear!**
Illustrator: Pratt, Hawley; White, Al
Author: Memling, Carl
10842   1964   9 5/16 x 12-1/2   28 pp.   **$12**

**Hilary Knight's A B C**
Illustrator: Knight, Hilary
13556   1961   9-3/8 x 12-1/2   62 pp.   **$40**

**Hilary Knight's Mother Goose**
Illustrator: Knight, Hilary
13557   1962   9-3/8 x 12-1/2   62 pp.   **$40**

**Hippopotamus Book, The**
Illustrator: Hildebrandt, Greg & Tim
Author: Carey, Winifred Rosen
15779   1975   10-1/2 x 12-1/8 48 pp.   **$6**

**History of Flight, The**
Illustrator: Various
Author: Eimerl, Sarel
15503   1964   8-1/8 x 11-1/4   106 pp.   **$8**

**Hoagy Carmichael's Songs For Children**
Illustrator: Miller, J. P.
Author: Carmichael, Hoagy
562   1957   8 x 11   64 pp.   **$25**

**Home For a Bunny**
Illustrator: Williams, Garth
Author: Brown, Margaret Wise
446   1956   9-3/8 x 12-1/2   28 pp.   **$7**

**Horse Stories**
Illustrator: Rojankovsky, Feodor
Author: Coatsworth, Elizabeth; Barnes, Kate
486   1954   9-1/2 x 12-3/4   28 pp.   **$15**

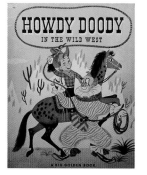

**Howdy Doody in the Wild West**
Illustrator: Seiden, Art
Author: Kean, Edward
475    1952    8 7/8 x 11-1/4    36 pp.    **$55**

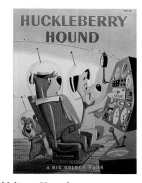

**Huckleberry Hound**
Illustrator: McGary, Norman & Pratt, Hawley
Author: Memling, Carl
10384    1960    8-3/8 x 10 7/8    28 pp.    **$15**

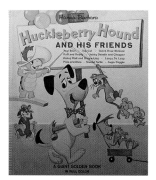

**Huckleberry Hound and His Friends**
Illustrator: Various
Author: Various
13549    1962    10-1/4 x 11 7/8    60 pp.    **$22**

**Huckleberry Hound and Yogi Bear**
Illustrator: Various
Author: Various
8006    1960    7-3/4 x 10 7/8    48 pp.    **$18**

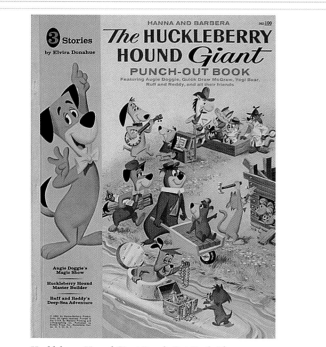

**Huckleberry Hound Giant Punch-Out Book, The**
Augie Doggie's Magic Show, Huckleberry Hound Master
Builder, and Ruff and Reddy's Deep Sea Adventure
Author: Donahue, Elvira
10362    1961            **$75-$125**
362    1961            **$75-$125**
10 x 12-3/4 on heavy card stock

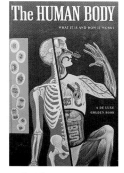

**Huckleberry Hound Treasury**
Illustrator: Various
Author: Various
516    1960    7 x 9            120 pp.    **$25**

**Human Body, The**
Illustrator: De Witt, Cornelius
Author: Wilson, Mitchell
842    1959    8 x 11            144 pp.    **$10**

**I Can Count**
Illustrator: Rojankovsky, Feodor
Author: Memling, Carl
10833    1963    9 5/16 x 12-1/2    28 pp.    **$10**

**Iliad and the Odyssey, The**
Illustrator: Provensen, Alice & Martin
Author: Watson, Jane Werner
756    1956    10 x 13            96 pp.    **$12**
13581    1964    8-3/4 x 11-1/4    104 pp.    **$8**

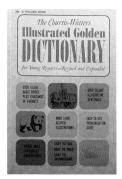

**Illustrated Golden Dictionary**
Author: Courtis, Stuart & Watter, Garnette
15544   1965   6 7/8 x 10-1/8   670 pp.   **$10**

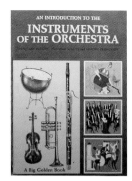

**Introduction to the Instruments of the Orchestra, An**
Illustrator: Provensen, Alice & Martin
Author: Bunche, Jane
12563   1962   8-1/8 x 11-1/8 42 pp.   **$7**

**Japanese Fairy Tales**
Illustrator: Benvenuti
Author: Marmur, Mildred
15630   1960   10-3/8 x 14-3/8 66 pp.   **$35**

**Jetsons, The**
Illustrator: White, Al & Pratt, Hawley
Author: Memling, Carl
10358   1963   9-1/2 x 12-3/4   24 pp.   **$25**

**Joe Kaufman's Book About Busy People and How They Do Their Work**
Illustrator: Kaufman, Joe
Author: Kaufman, Joe
15774   1973   10-1/2 x 12 1/4 94 pp.   **$15**

**Joe Kaufman's How We Are Born**
Illustrator: Kaufman, Joe
Author: Kaufman, Joe
15793   1975   10-1/2 x 12-1/8 94 pp.   **$16**

**Joe Kaufman's What Makes It Go?**
Illustrator: Kaufman, Joe
Author: Kaufman, Joe
15767   1971   10-1/2 x 12-1/8 94 pp.   **$15**

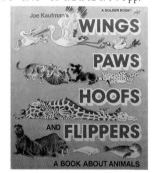

**Joe Kaufman's Wings, Paws, Hoofs, and Flippers**
Illustrator: Kaufman, Joe
Author: Kaufman, Joe
15813   1981   10-1/2 x 12-1/8 48 pp.   **$12**

**Judy and Jim, A Paper Doll Story Book**
Illustrator: Miloche, Hilda & Kane, Wilma
Author: Miloche, Hilda & Kane, Wilma
430     1947   8 7/8 x 11-1/4   48 pp.   **$125**

**King Arthur and the Knights of the Round Table**
Illustrator: Tenggren, Gustaf
Author: Sterne, Emma; Lindsay, Barbara
16748   1962   7-1/2 x 10-1/4   140 pp.   **$16**

**Kittens Three Complete Stories**
Illustrator: Masha & Tenggren & Wilkin
Author: Schurr, Cathleen & Scarry, Patsy
8009     1958   7-3/4 x 10 7/8   48 pp.   **$15**

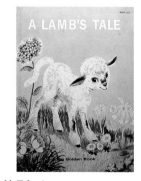

**Lamb's Tale, A**
Illustrator: Reyn, Jenny
Author: Reyn, Jenny
B0924   1963   8-1/4 x 11 \1/8   28 pp.   **$8**

**Lassie and the Secret Friend**
Illustrator: Schaar, Bob
Author: Graham, Kennon
10459   1972   9-3/8 x 12-1/2   24 pp.   **$8**

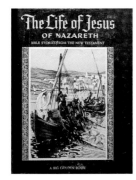

**Lassie Finds a Way**
Illustrator: Greene, Hamilton
Author: Shapiro, Irwin
456   1957   9-1/2 x 12-3/4   28 pp.   **$16**

*Book cover*

*Fish and fishing pole that came in book*

**Let's Go Fishing**
Illustrator: Scarry, Richard
Author:
Jackson, Kathryn & Byron
412   1949   **$75**
8-3/4 x 8-1/2   14 pp.

**Life of Jesus of Nazareth, The**
Illustrator: Hole, William
Author: Ferrari, Erma
837   1958   7-1/4 x 9-3/4   180 pp.   **$8**

**Little Golden Book Story Land**
Illustrator: Various
Author: Various
16561   1992   7 5/8 x 10-1/4   256 pp.   **$10**

**Litterbugs Come in Every Size**
Illustrator: Bracke, Charles
Author: Smaridge, Norah
10455   1972   9-3/8 x 12-1/2   24 pp.   **$25**

**Little Black Sambo**
Illustrator: Rutherford, Bonnie & Bill
Author: Bannerman, Helen
10503   1961   9-3/8 x 12-1/2   20 pp.   **$40**

**Little LuLu and the Magic Paints**
Illustrator: Baker, Darrell
Author: Drake, Arnold
10498   1974   9-1/4 x 12-1/2   24 pp.   **$15**

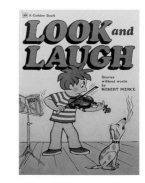

**Look and Laugh**
Illustrator: Pierce, Robert
Author: Pierce, Robert
12046   1974   9 5/8 x 12-3/4   28 pp.   **$8**

**Lt. Robin Crusoe, U.S.N.**
Illustrator: DaGradi, Don & Jonas, David
Author: Jacobs, Frank
2611    1966    8-3/8 x 11-1/4    48 pp.    $8

**Lucky Mrs. Ticklefeather and Other Funny Stories**
Illustrator: Miller, J.P. & Williams, Garth
Author: Kunhardt, Dorothy
15781    1973    10 5/8 x 12-1/8    70 pp.    $15

**Madeline**
Illustrator: Bemelmans, Ludwig
Author: Bemelmans, Ludwig
808    1939    9-1/8 x 12-1/8    50 pp.    $22

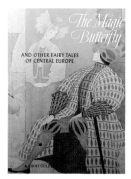

**Magic Butterfly, The**
Illustrator: Fontana, Ugo
Author: Obligado, George
15977    1963    10-1/4 x 14    64 pp.    $25

**Magilla Gorilla**
Illustrator: Crawford, Mel
Author: Memling, Carl
10847    1964    9-1/2 x 12-3/4    28 pp.    $25

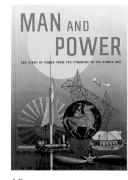

**Man and Power**
Illustrator: Various
16742    1961    8-1/8 x 11-1/4    189 pp.    $8

**Margaret Wise Brown's Wonderful Storybook**
Illustrator: Miller, J.P.
Author: Brown, Margaret Wise
504    1948    8-3/4 x 11-1/8    96 pp.    $25

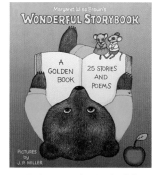

**Margaret Wise Brown's Wonderful Storybook**
Illustrator: Miller, J.P.
Author: Brown, Margaret Wise
15777    1974    10-1/2 x 12-1/8    64 pp.    $10

**McCall's Giant Golden Make-It Book**
Illustrator: Malvern, Corinne & Riley, Bob
Author: Peter, John
707    1953    8-1/2 x 11    256 pp.    $15
15570    1953    8-1/4 x 11-1/8    156 pp.    $8

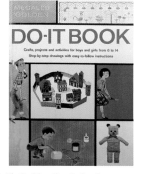

**McCall's Golden Do-It Book**
Illustrator: Dugan, William
Author: Wyckoff, Joan
13697    1960    8-1/2 x 11-1/8    156 pp.    $10

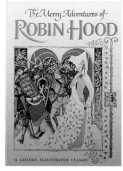

**Merry Adventures of Robin Hood, The**
Illustrator: Benvenuti
Author: Pyle, Howard
16751    1962    7-1/2 x 10-1/4    288 Pp.    $12

**Miss Frances' Ding Dong School Book**
Illustrator: Evans, Katerine
Author: Horwich, Dr. Frances R &
Werrenrath Jr., Reinald
357    1960    8-1/4 x 11-1/8    56 Pp.    $18

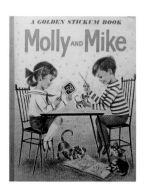

**Molly and Mike, A Golden Stickum Book**
345     1960    10 x 12-3/4     30 pp.    **$45**

**Monster at the End of This Book, The**
Illustrator: Smollin, Mike
Author: Stone, Jon
10506    1977    9-3/8 x 12-1/2    24 pp.    **$5**

**Moon, The**
Author: Brenna, Virgilio
15561    1963    8 x 11           108 pp.    **$10**

**More Please**
Illustrator: Kunhardt, Dorothy
Author: Kunhardt, Dorothy
802     1946    4-1/4 x 5-1/2    18 pp.    **$35**

**Mother Goose**
Illustrator: LaMont, Violet
8001    1957    7-3/4 x 10 7/8    48 pp.    **$8**

**Mother Goose Land With Judy and Jim**
Illustrator: Miloche, Hilda & Kane, Wilma
Author: Miloche, Hilda & Kane, Wilma
431     1949    8 7/8 x 11-1/4    52 pp.    **$125**

**Mr. Porcupine's Marvelous Flying Machine**
Illustrator: Benvenuti
Author: Dalmais, Anne-Marie
12053    1972    9-1/2 x 12-3/4    28 pp.    **$15**

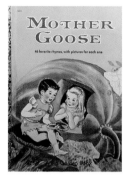

**My Big Book of Cat Stories**
Illustrator: Ségur, Adrienne
Author: Various
15611    1967    9-1/2 x 12-3/4    108 pp.    **$35**

**My Big Book of Finger Plays**
Illustrator: Aufustiny, Sally
Author: Hogstrom, Daphne
10500    1974    9-3/8 x 12-1/2    24 pp.    **$5**

**My Big Book of the Seasons**
Illustrator: Wilkin, Eloise
Author: Parker, Barbara Morris
10390    1966    9-1/4 x 12-1/2    24 pp.    **$10**

**My Christmas Treasury**
Illustrator: Hess, Lowell
10356    1957    9-1/4 x 12-1/2    31 pp.    **$10**

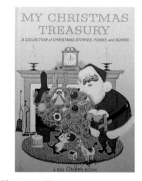

**My Christmas Treasury**
Illustrator: Hess, Lowell
10356    1968    9 5/8 x 12-3/4    31 pp.    **$8**

**My Elephant Book**
Illustrator: Battaglia, Aurelius
Author: Daly, Kathleen
10443   1966   9-1/2 x 12-3/4   28 pp.   **$6**

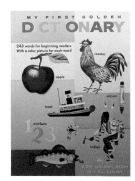

**My First Golden Dictionary**
Illustrator: Scarry, Richard
Author: Reed, Mary & Osswald, Edith
8004   1957   7-3/4 x 10 7/8   48 pp.   **$8**

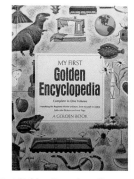

**My First Golden Encyclopedia**
Illustrator: Dugan, William
Author: Watson, Jane Werner
16549   1969   7-3/4 x 10-3/8   384 pp.   **$10**

**My Golden Book About God**
Illustrator: Wilkin, Eloise
Author: Watson, Jane Werner
676   1957   6-3/4 x 8   22 pp.   **$18**

**My Learn to Cook Book**
Illustrator: Mayhew, Martin
Author: Sedgwick, Ursula
13585   1967   9-1/4 x 12-1/2   62 pp.   **$5**

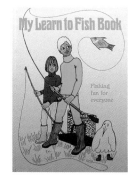

**My Learn to Fish Book**
Illustrator: White, David; Travers, Philip & Wheeler, Sandra
Author: Denham, Ken
13589   1971   9-1/4 x 12-1/2   62 pp.   **$8**

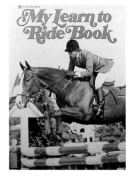

**My Learn to Ride Book**
Illustrator: Streek, Tony & Kesteven, Peter
Author: Owen, Robert
13746   1973   9-1/4 x 12-1/2   46 pp.   **$8**

**My Learn to Sew Book**
Illustrator: Lyon, Belinda
Author: Barber, Janet
13588   1970   9-1/4 x 12-1/2   62 pp.   **$5**

**My Little Golden Writing Paper**
Illustrator: Various
351   1951   6-3/4 x 8-1/2   **$150**

*Book cover*

*Stationery*

**My Nursery Tale Book**
Illustrator: Scarry, Richard
12066   1961   9-3/8 x 123/4   64 pp.   **$25**

**Nature Around the Year**
Illustrator: Probst, Pierre
Author: Leclercq, Henri
17857   1972   7-3/4 x 10-3/8   156 pp.   **$35**

**Never Talk to Strangers**
Illustrator: Buckett, George
Author: Joyce, Irma
10876   1967   9-3/8 x 12-1/2   28 pp.   **$6**

**New Golden Almanac, The**
Illustrator: Scarry, Richard
Author: Jackson, Kathryn
569   1952   8-3/16 x 10-3/4 128 pp.   **$15**

**New Golden Book of Astronomy, The**
Illustrator: Polgreen, John
Author: Wyler, Rose & Ames, Gerald
13517   1965   8 x 11   108 pp.   **$10**

**New Golden Dictionary, The**
Illustrator: Battaglia, Aurelius
Author: Parker, Barbara Morris
16837   1972   10-1/2 x 12-1/8 120 pp.   **$7**

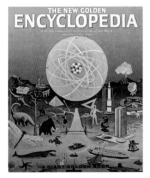

**New Golden Encyclopedia, The**
Illustrator: DeWitt, Cornelius
Author: Bennett, Dorothy & Watson, Jane
16515   1963   10-1/2 x 12-1/8 160 pp.   **$8**

**New Golden Song Book, The**
Illustrator: Blair, Mary
Author: Lloyd, Norman
708   1955   10-1/8 x 13   96 pp.   **$25**

**New Golden Song Book, The**
Illustrator: Blair, Mary
Author: Lloyd, Norman
13708   1955   10-1/8 x 13   96 pp.   **$15**

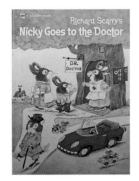

**Nicky Goes to the Doctor**
Illustrator: Scarry, Richard
Author: Scarry, Richard
12056   1972   9-1/2 x 12-3/4   28 pp.   **$16**

**Night Before Christmas, The**
Illustrator: Malvern, Corinne
Author: Moore, Clement C.
518   1950   9-1/2 x 12-3/4   28 pp.   **$15**

**Night Before Christmas, The**
Illustrator: Malvern, Corinne
Author: Moore, Clement C.
10518   1950   9-1/4 x 12-1/2   32 pp.   **$6**

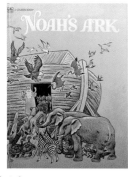

**Noah's Ark**
Illustrator: Gergely, Tibor
Author: Hazen, Barbara Shook
10482   1969   9-3/8 x 12-1/2   28 pp.   **$5**

**Nursery Tales**
Illustrator: Scarry, Richard
8005   1958   7-3/4 x 10 7/8   48 pp.   **$16**

**Nursery Tales**
Illustrator: Gergely, Tibor
Author: Watson, Jane Werner
10726   1957   7-1/2 x 10-1/2   96 pp.   **$15**

**Oklahoma!**
Illustrator: Cummings, Alison
Author: Rogers & Hammerstein
438   1956   8-3/4 x 11-1/8   48 pp.   **$95**

**Once Upon a Time Folk and Fairy Tales of the World**
Illustrator: Kubasta, Vojtech
Author: Green, Roger Lancelyn
15507   1962   8-1/4 x 11-1/4   144 pp.   **$45**

**One Monster After Another**
Illustrator: Mayer, Mercer
Author: Mayer, Mercer
15794   1974   10-1/2 x 12-1/8 48 pp.   **$12**

**One Word Storybook, The**
Illustrator: Wagner, Ken
Author: Wagner, Ken
10867   1968   9 5/8 x 12-3/4   28 pp.   **$8**

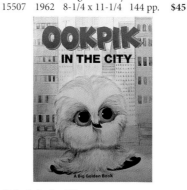

**Ookpik In the City**
Illustrator: Wilde, Irma
Author: Hazen, Barbara Shook
10868   1968   9 5/8 x 12-3/4   28 pp.   **$40**

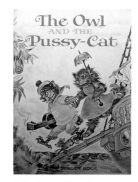

**Owl and the Pussy-Cat, The**
Illustrator: Masha
Author: Lear, Edward
10846   1964   9 5/16 x 12-1/2 28 pp.   **$8**

**Pat the Bunny**
Illustrator: Kunhardt, Dorothy
Author: Kunhardt, Dorothy
800   1940   4-1/4 x 5-1/2   16 pp.   **$50**

**Pebbles Flintstone**
Illustrator: Crawford, Mel
Author: Lewis, Jean
10834   1963   9 5/16 x 12-1/2 28 pp.   **$25**

**Pictures from Mother Goose**
Illustrator: Rojankovsky, Feodor
702   1945   14-1/2 x 19   8 pp.   **$150**

**Pink Elephant With Golden Spots, The**
Illustrator: Fix, Phillippe & Rejane
Author: Fix, Phillippe & Rejane
10889   1971   9-3/8 x 12-1/2   28 pp.   **$35**

**Pinocchio**
Illustrator: Rizzato, Sergio
Author: Collodi, Carlo
16508   1963   10 x 13-1/4   120 pp.   **$35**

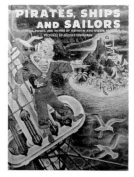

**Pirates, Ships and Sailors**
Illustrator: Tenggren, Gustaf
Author: Jackson, Kathryn & Byron
601   1950   9-3/4 x 13   100 pp.   **$26**

**Planet Earth**
Illustrator: De Witt, Cornelius
Author: Ames, Gerald; Wyler, Rose
15562   1963   8 x 11   108 pp.   **$6**

**Poky Little Puppy's First Christmas, The**
Illustrator: Winship, Florence
Author: Holl, Adelaide
10395   1973   9-3/8 x 12-1/2   24 pp.   **$5**

**Prayers For Children**
Illustrator: Wilkin, Eloise
432   1952   9-3/4 x 13-1/8   24 pp.   **$8**

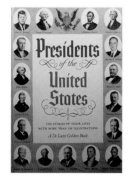

**Presidents of the United States**
Author: Lengyel, Cornel
13518   1964   8 x 11-1/4   108 pp.   **$12**

**Puss In Boots and the Sleeping Beauty**
Illustrator: Durand, Paul
Author: Daly, Kathleen
10838   1964   9 5/16 x 12-1/2   28 pp.   **$10**

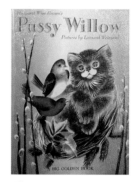

**Pussy Willow**
Illustrator: Weisgard, Leonard
Author: Brown, Margaret Wise
564   1951   9-3/4 x 13-1/8   28 pp.   **$7**

**Quick Draw McGraw**
Illustrator: White, Al & Pratt, Hawley
Author: Memling, Carl
10312   1961   8 5/8 x 11-1/8   28 pp.   **$18**

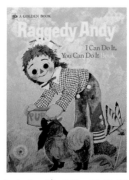

**Raggedy Andy—The I Can Do It, You Can Do It Book**
Illustrator: Goldsborough, June
Author: Smaridge, Norah
10494   1973   9-1/4 x 12-1/2   24 pp.   **$15**

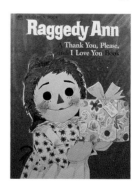

**Raggedy Ann—A Thank You, Please, and I Love You Book**
Illustrator: Goldsborough, June
Author: Smaridge, Norah
10487   1969   9-1/4 x 12-1/2   24 pp.   **$15**

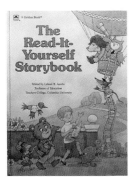

**Read-It-Yourself Storybook, The**
Author: Jacobs, Leland J.
16824　1971　9-3/4 x 12　　214 pp.　**$12**

**Richard Scarry's Animal Mother Goose**
Illustrator: Scarry, Richard
Author: Scarry, Richard
12069　1964　9-3/8 x 12-3/4　64 pp.　**$25**

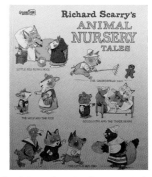

**Richard Scarry's Animal Nursery Tales**
Illustrator: Scarry, Richard
Author: Scarry, Richard
16810　1975　10-1/2 x 12-1/8 70 pp.　**$20**

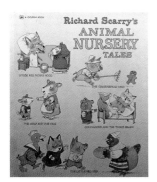

**Richard Scarry's Animal Nursery Tales**
Illustrator: Scarry, Richard
Author: Scarry, Richard
16810　1975　10-1/2 x 12-1/8 70 pp.　**$15**

**Richard Scarry's Best Mother Goose Ever**
Illustrator: Scarry, Richard
Author: Scarry, Richard
15578　1970　10-1/2 x 12-1/8 96 pp.　**$10**

**Richard Scarry's Best Story Book Ever**
Illustrator: Scarry, Richard
Author: Scarry, Richard
15510　1963　10-3/8 x 11 7/8　96 pp.　**$15**

**Richard Scarry's Best Word Book Ever**
Illustrator: Scarry, Richard
Author: Scarry, Richard
15510　1963　10-3/8 x 11 7/8　96 pp.　**$10**

**Richard Scarry's Busy, Busy World**
Illustrator: Scarry, Richard
Author: Scarry, Richard
15511　1965　10-1/2 x 12-1/8 94 pp.　**$75**

**Richard Scarry's Cars and Trucks and Thing That Go**
Illustrator: Scarry, Richard
Author: Scarry, Richard
15785　1974　10-1/2 x 12-1/8 72 pp.　**$18**

**Richard Scarry's Hop Aboard! Here We Go!**
Illustrator: Scarry, Richard
Author: Scarry, Richard
13756　1972　10-1/2 x 12-1/8 48 pp.　**$20**

**Richard Scarry's Mother Goose**
Illustrator: Scarry, Richard
10383　1972　9-3/8 x 12-1/2　24 pp.　**$15**

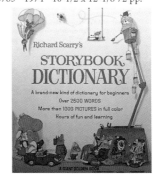

**Richard Scarry's Storybook Dictionary**
Illustrator: Scarry, Richard
Author: Scarry, Richard
15548　1966　10-1/2 x 12-1/8 126 pp.　**$25**

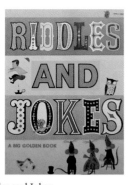

**Riddles and Jokes**
Illustrator: Miller, J. P.
Author: Crampton, Gertrude
B0911   1961   8-1/4 x 11-1/8   28 pp.   **$15**

**Rin Tin Tin and the Hidden Treasure**
Illustrator: Crawford, Mel
Author: Verral, Charles Spain
391   1958   8 5/8 x 11-1/8   28 pp.   **$16**

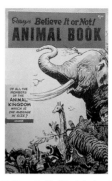

**Ripley's Believe It Or Not! Animal Book**
Illustrator: Ripley's Staff
Author: Ripley's Staff
397   1956   6-3/8 x 9-3/4   96 pp.   **$25**

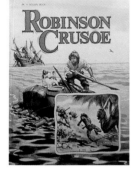

**Robinson Crusoe**
Illustrator: Rojankovsky, Feodor
Author: Defoe, Daniel
698   1960   10 x 12-3/4   100 pp.   **$10**

**Roy Rogers, King of the Cowboys**
Illustrator: Alvarado, Peter
Author: Beecher, Elizabeth
575   1953   8-1/2 x 11   112 pp.   **$25**

**Rudolph the Red-Nosed Reindeer**
Illustrator: Scarry, Richard
Author: Hazen, Barbara Shook
10849   1958   9 5/8 x 12-3/4   24 pp.   **$6**

**Russian Fairy Tales**
Illustrator: Benvenuti
Author: Ponsot, Marie
15631   1960   10-3/8 x 14-3/8 64 pp.   **$35**

**Saggy Baggy Elephant's Great Big Counting Book, The**
Illustrator: Campana, Manny
10442   1983   9-3/8 x 12-1/2   24 pp.   **$4**

**Sailor Dog, The**
Illustrator: Williams, Garth
Author: Brown, Margaret Wise
16533.   1953   8 5/8 x 11-1/4   28 pp.   **$8**

**Santa Claus Book, The**
Illustrator: Worcester, Retta
Author: Jackson, Kathryn
568   1952   8-3/16 x 10-3/4 128 pp.   **$35**

**Scandinavian Fairy Tales**
Illustrator: Santin, Federico
Author: King, Leon
16505   1962   10-1/4 x 13-1/2 160 pp.   **$35**

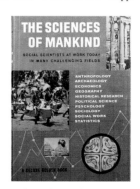

**Sciences of Mankind, The**
Illustrator: Various
Author: Watson, Jane Werner
765   1960   8-1/8 x 11-1/4   180 pp.   **$8**

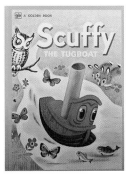

**Scuffy the Tugboat**
Illustrator: Gergely, Tibor
Author: Crampton, Certrude
10490   1955   9-1/4 x 12-1/2   24 pp.   **$5**

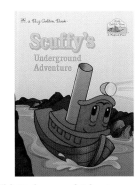

**Scuffy's Underground Adventure**
Illustrator: Baker, Darrell
Author: Carey, Mary
12058   1989   8-1/2 x 11         24 pp.   **$4**

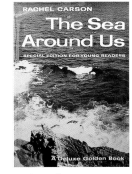

**Sea Around Us, The**
Illustrator: Various
Author: Carson, Rachel
745   1958   8 x 11         168 pp.   **$8**

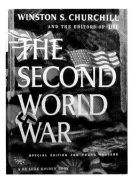

**Second World War, The**
Author: Churchill, Winston
740   1960   8-1/2 x 11-3/4   384 pp.   **$10**

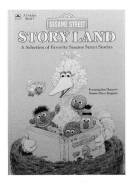

**Sesame Street Story Land**
Illustrator: Various
Author: Various
16530   1986   7-3/8 x 10-1/4   190 pp.   **$8**

**Smokey Bear's Camping Book**
Illustrator: Crawford, Mel
Author: Shapiro, Irwin
15797   1976   10-1/2 x 12-1/8 48 pp.   **$25**

**Snow Queen and Other Tales, The**
Illustrator: Ségur, Adrienne
Author: Ponsot, Marie
15763   1961   9-3/4 x 12-3/4   140 pp.   **$45**

**Snowy, the Little White Horse**
Illustrator: Studio Brambilla, Milanm Italy
Author: Reynolds, Suzanne
10858   1965   9 5/16 x 12-1/2 32 pp.   **$15**

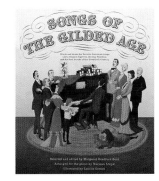

**Songs of the Gilded Age**
Illustrator: Corcos, Lucille
Author: Boni, Margaret Bradford
9408   1960   10-1/2 x 12-1/8 156 pp.   **$10**

**Songs We Sing From Rodgers and Hammerstein**
Illustrator: Dugan, William
Author: Beaty, Mary Rodgers
759   1957   10-1/4 x 13         78 pp.   **$20**

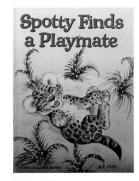

**Spotty Finds a Playmate**
Illustrator: Brroks, Mary
Author: Brooks, Mary & Carrick, Bruce R.
10835   1963   9 5/16 x 12-1/2 28 pp.   **$7**

**Stories From Mary Poppins**
Illustrator: Elliott, Gertrude
Author: Travers, P. L.
565   1952   8 7/8 x 11-1/4   36 pp.   **$24**

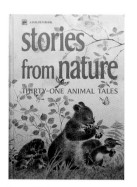

**Stories From Nature**
Illustrator: Muller, Gerda
Author: Watson, Jane Werner
16822   1973   8-1/8 x 11-1/4   140 pp.   **$8**

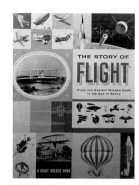

**Story of Flight, The**
Illustrator: McNaught, Harry
Author: Lewellen, John & Shapiro, Irwin
761   1959   10 x 12-3/4   100 pp.   **$12**

**Story of Fourteen Bears, The**
Illustrator: Parsons, Virginia
Author: Parsons, Virginia
10481   1970   9-1/4 x 12-1/2   28 pp.   **$150**

**Story of Franklin D. Roosevelt, The**
Illustrator: Ball, Frances M.
Author: Rosenblum, Marcus
577   1949   6-1/2 x 9-1/4   52 pp.   **$15**

**Story of Harmony Lane, The**
Illustrator: Crawford, Mel
Author: Dickson, Naida
12447   1972   9 5/16 x 12-1/2   28 pp.   **$8**

**Storytime Tales**
Illustrator: Malvern Corinne
471   1950   8-1/4 x 10-3/4   208 pp.   **$16**

**Sun Shone on the Elephant, The**
Illustrator: Mamlok, Gwyneth
Author: Mamlok, Gwyneth
10866   1967   9-1/2 x 12-3/4   28 pp.   **$15**

**Sunshine**
Illustrator: Bemelmans, Ludwig
Author: Bemelmans, Ludwig
817   1950   9-1/8 x 12-1/8   44 pp.   **$45**

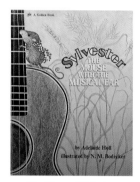

**Sylvester—The Mouse With the Musical Ear**
Illustrator: Bodecker. N.M.
Author: Holl, Adelaide
12503   1973   9-1/4 x 12-1/2   28 pp.   **$6**

**Tale of Tails, A**
Illustrator: Williams, Garth
Author: Macpherson, Elizabeth H.
10351   1962   9-1/4 x 12-1/2   24 pp.   **$8**

**Tales From the Arabian Nights**
Illustrator: Tenggren, Gustaf
Author: Soifer, Margaret; Shapiro, Erwin
13580   1957   8 x 11   96 pp.   **$18**

*Dust jacket*

*Book cover*

**Tales From the Ballet**
Illustrator: Provensen, ALice & Martin
Author: Untermeyer, Louis
17852   1968   10-1/2 x 12-1/8 92 pp.   **$12**

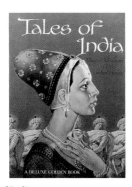

**Tales of India**
Illustrator: Rizzato
Author: Ponsot, Marie
16504    1961    10-1/8 x 13-3/4 156 pp.    **$35**

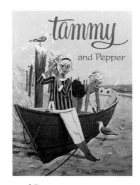

**Tammy and Pepper**
Illustrator: Crawford, Mel
Author: Hitte, Kathryn
10848    1964    9-1/2 x 12-3/4    28 pp.    **$25**

**Tarzan**
Illustrator: Crawford, Mel
Author: Weiner, Gina Ingoglia
10843    1964    9 5/16 x 12-1/2    28 pp.    **$16**

**Telephone Book, The**
Illustrator: Kunhardt, Dorothy
Author: Kunhardt, Dorothy
801    1942    4-1/4 x 5-1/2    16 pp.    **$35**

**Tell Me, Cat**
Illustrator: Tiffany, Virginia
Author: Fisher, Ellen
10813    1965    9-3/8 x 12-1/2    28 pp.    **$5**

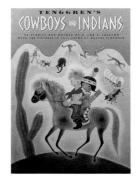

**Tenggren's Cowboys and Indians**
Illustrator: Tenggren, Gustaf
Author: Soifer, Margaret & Shapiro, Irwin
No #    1948    9 7/8 x 13    96 pp.    **$35**

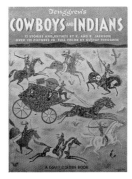

**Tenggren's Cowboys and Indians**
Illustrator: Tenggren, Gustaf
Author: Soifer, Margaret & Shapiro, Irwin
600    1948    9 7/8 x 13    96 pp.    **$16**

**Tenggren's Cowboys and Indians**
Illustrator: Tenggren, Gustaf
Author: Soifer, Margaret & Shapiro, Irwin
15558    1948    9 7/8 x 13    96 pp.    **$18**

**Tenggren's Farm Stories**
Illustrator: Tenggren, Gustaf
Author: Jackson, Kathryn & Byron
711    1946    10-1/8 x 13    76 pp.    **$35**

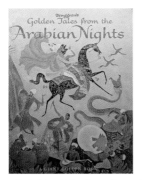

**Tenggren's Golden Tales from the Arabian Nights**
Illustrator: Tenggren, Gustaf
Author: Soifer, Margaret; Shapiro, Irwin
755    1957    10-1/8 x 13    100 pp.    **$25**

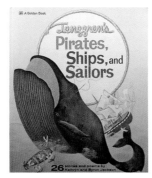

**Tenggren's Pirates, Ships, and Sailors**
Illustrator: Tenggren, Gustaf
Author: Jackson, Kathryn & Byron
601    1959    10 x 12-3/4    100 pp.    **$18**

**Tenggren's Story Book**
Illustrator: Tenggren, Gustaf
712    1944    10 x 13    90 pp.    **$35**

*Dust jacket*

*Book cover*

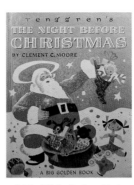

**Tenggren's Story Book**
Illustrator: Tenggren, Gustaf
No #     1948    8 7/8 x 11-1/4    68 pp.     **$25**

**Tenggren's The Night Before Christmas**
Illustrator: Tenggren, Gustaf
Author: Moore, Clement C.
474     1951    8 7/8 x 11-1/4    28 pp.     **$25**

**Three Bedtime Stories**
Illustrator: Williams, Garth
392     1958    9 5/16 x 12-1/2    28 pp.     **$8**

**Three Favorite Fairy Tales**
Illustrator: Torchio
12070    1964    9-3/8 x 12-3/4    56 pp.     **$8**

**Three Golden Book Favorites**
Illustrator: Various
Author: Various
60003-3          9-3/8 x 12-1/2    68 pp.     **$4**

**Tibor Gergely's Great Big Book of Bedtime Stories**
Illustrator: Gergely, Tibor
Author: Various
16529    1967    7-3/8 x 10-3/8    384 pp.     **$8**

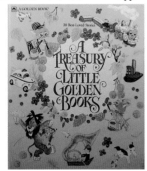

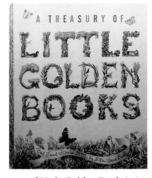

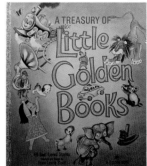

**Tootle and Katy Caboose: A Special Treasure**
Illustrator: Mones, Isidre
Author: Ingoglia, Gina
12087    1989    8-1/4 x 11            24 pp.     **$5**

**Treasury of Little Golden Books®, A**
Illustrator: Various
Author: Various
15766    1960    10 5/8 x 12-1/8    156 pp.     **$12**

**Treasury of Little Golden Books®, A**
Illustrator: Various
Author: Various
16540    1972    10 5/8 x 12-1/8    156 pp.     **$10**

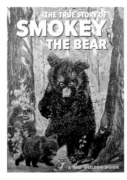

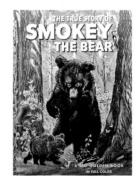

**Treasury of Little Golden Books®, A**
Illustrator: Various
Author: Various
16540-21982    10 5/8 x 12-1/8    92 pp.     **$8**

**True Story of Smokey the Bear, The**
Illustrator: Rojankovsky, Feodor
Author: Watson, Jane Werner
429     1955    9-3/8 x 12-3/4    28 pp.     **$18**

**True Story of Smokey the Bear, The**
Illustrator: Rojankovsky, Feodor
Author: Watson, Jane Werner
10429    1955    9-1/4 x 12-1/2    28 pp.     **$15**

**Uncle Sam's 200th Birthday Parade**
Illustrator: Brugos, Frank
Author: Shapiro, Irwin
13745   1974   10-1/2 x 12-1/8 48 pp.   **$6**

**Up and Down Book, The**
Illustrator: Blair, Mary
Author: Blair, Mary
10618   1964   6-1/2 x 12      28 pp.   **$35**

**Warrior and the Princess, The**
Illustrator: De Gaspari
Author: Obligado, George
15978   1961   10-3/8 x 14-3/8 58 pp.   **$35**

**Weekly Reader Parade, The**
Illustrator: Freund, Rudolf; Knight, Clayton
Author: Editors of Weekly Reader
No #   1948   8 7/8 x 11-1/48 120 pp.   **$16**

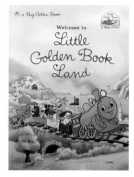

**Welcome to Little Golden Book Land**
Illustrator: Mateu
Author: West, Cindy
12084   1989   8 x 10-3/4      24 pp.   **$5**

**What Is a Color?**
Illustrator: Provensen, Alice & Martin
Author: Provensen, Alice & Martin
13620   1967   9 5/8 x 12-3/4   28 pp.   **$15**

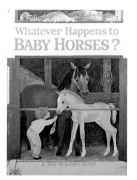

**Whatever Happens to Baby Horses?**
Illustrator: Parsons, Virginia
Author: Hall, Wm. N.
10851   1965   9-1/2 x 12-3/4   26 pp.   **$5**

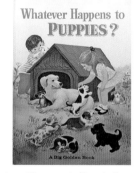

**Whatever Happens to Puppies?**
Illustrator: Parson, Virginia
Author: Hall, Bill
10855   1965   9-1/2 x 12-3/4   24 pp.   **$5**

**Whatever Happens to Bear Cubs?**
Illustrator: Parsons, Virginia
Author: Hall, Bill
10865   1968   9-1/2 x 12-3/4   28 pp.   **$5**

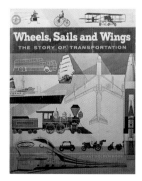

**Wheels, Sails and Wings**
Illustrator: Bukor & Peschke & Voh
Author: Deitrich, Fred & Reit Seymour
15701   1961   10-1/8 x 13      98 pp.   **$6**

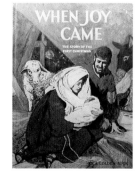

**When Joy Came, The Story of the First Christmas**
Illustrator: Stirnwies, Shannon
Author: Meek, Pauline Palmer
10887   1971   9-3/8 x 12-1/2   28 pp.   **$5**

**Who's In the Egg?**
Illustrator: Provensen, Alice & Martin
Author: Provensen, Alice & Martin
13577   1970   9 5/8 x 12-3/4   28 pp.   **$5**

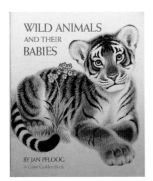

**Wild Animals and Their Babies**
Illustrator: Pfloog, Jan
Author: Pfloog, Jan
15768   1971   10-3/8 x 12-1/8 70 pp.   **$8**

**Willy's Silly Glasses**
Illustrator: Kalish, Muriel & Lionel
Author: Kalish, Muriel & Lionel
13530   1963   9 5/16 x 12-1/2 48 pp.   **$5**

**Witches, Ghosts, and Goblins**
Illustrator: Durand, Paul
Author: Long, Ruth
16818   1974   8-1/4 x 11-1/4   142 pp.   **$35**

**Wonderful Picture Book**
Illustrator: Rojankovsky, Feodor
16836   1972   10-1/2 x 12-1/8 122 pp.   **$8**

**Wonders of Life On Earth, The**
Illustrator: Various
Author: Barnett, Lincoln
16847   1960   8-1/8 x 11-1/4   216 pp.   **$8**

**Wonders of Nature**
Illustrator: Wilkin, Eloise
Author: Watson, Jane Werner
405       1958   9-1/2 x 12-3/4   28 pp.   **$15**

**Wonders of the Seasons, The**
Illustrator: Wilkin, Eloise
Author: Parker, Barbara Morris
10477   1966   9-1/2 x 12-3/4   28 pp.   **$15**

**Woody Woodpecker—The Pirate Treasure**
Illustrator: Walter Lantz Productions
10505   1977   9-3/8 x 12-1/2   24 pp.   **$5**

**Woody Woodpecker—The Pirate Treasure**
Illustrator: Walter Lantz Productions
10505-21977   9-3/8 x 12-1/2   24 pp.   **$4**

**World of Science, The**
Illustrator: Various
Author: Watson, Jane Werner
746       1958   8 x 11               216 pp.   **$8**

**World We Live In, The**
Illustrator: Various
Author: Watson, Jane Werner
832       1956   8-1/8 x 11-1/4   216 pp.   **$8**

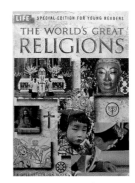

**World's Great Religions, The**
Illustrator: Various
Author: Various
839       1958   8 x 11               180 pp.   **$15**

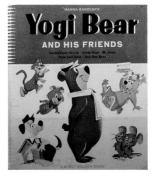

**Yogi Bear**
Illustrator: McGary, Norman
Author: Memling, Carl
10311   1961   8-1/2 x 11-1/8   28 pp.   **$16**

**Yogi Bear—A Christmas Visit**
Illustrator: Mattinson, Sylvia & Burnett
Author: Hyatt, S. Quentin
10357   1961   9-1/4 x 12-1/2   24 pp.   **$15**

**Yogi Bear and His Friends**
Illustrator: Various
Author: Various
13548   1961   10-1/2 x 12   62 pp.   **$30**

**Animals of Farmer Jones, The**
Illustrator: Scarry, Richard
10422   1953   9-1/2 x 12-3/4   28 pp.   **$7**

**Baby Farm Animals**
Illustrator: Williams, Garth
Author: Williams, Garth
545   1959   8-3/8 x 10 7/8   28 pp.   **$7**

**Bedtime Stories**
Illustrator: Gergely, Tibor
13758   1972   9 7/8 x 10   48 pp.   **$5**

**Come Play With Me**
Illustrator: Korsch, Munich
Author: Watts, Mable
10886   1971   9-3/8 x 12-1/2   24 pp.   **$10**

**Counting Rhymes**
Illustrator: Malvern, Corrine
10419   1947   9-1/4 x 12-1/2   28 pp.   **$7**

**David and Goliath**
Illustrator: Lee, Robert J.
Author: Hazen, Barbara Shook
10864   1968   9-1/4 x 12-1/2   28 pp.   **$5**

**Dennis the Menace**
Giant Punch-Out Book
10310   1963   **$50-$75**
310   1963   **$50-$75**
10 x 12-3/4 on heavy card stock

**Duffy On the Farm**
Illustrator: McCue, Lisa
Author: Elson, Marilyn
10407   1984   9-1/8 x 12-1/4   24 pp.   **$5**

**Fuzzy Duckling, The**
Illustrator: Provensen, Alice & Martin
Author: Werner, Jane
10841   1964   9 5/16 x 12-1/2   32 pp.   **$6**

**Giant Golden Book of Robinson Crusoe**
Illustrator: Rojankovsky, Feodor
Author: Defoe, Daniel
15698   1960   10 x 12-3/4   100 pp.   **$8**

**Giant Punch-Out Book No.2**
18 pages of punch-outs.
The Farm, Prehistoric Animals, Trucks and
Tractors & Airplanes.
Originally published individually as Funtime
Books.
Illustrator: Buettner, Carl & McGary,
Norman
11388   1961   **$50**
388   1960   **$50**
10 x 12-3/4 on heavy card stock

**Happy-Go-Hoppy**
Illustrator: Vasiliu, Mircea
Author: Lockwood, Myna
12446   1972   9 5/16 x 12-1/2   28 pp.   **$6**

**Know About the World**
Illustrator: Embleton, Ronald
Author: Holmes, Edward
15564   1972   9 5/16 x 12 7/8   80 pp.   **$8**

**Lion's Paw, The**
Illustrator: Tenggren, Gustaf
Author: Watson, Jane Werner
355   1960   9 5/16 x 12-1/2   28 pp.   **$15**

**Little Red Caboose**
Illustrator: Gerrely, Tibor
Author: Potter, Marian
10423   1952   9-1/2 x 12-3/4   24 pp.   **$7**

**Little Red Riding Hood**
Author: Dwyer, Jane
10874   1969   9-1/4 x 12-1/2   28 pp.   **$5**

**Miss Jaster's Garden**
Illustrator: Bodecker, N.M.
Author: Bodecker, N. M.
12445   1972   9 5/16 x 12-1/2   28 pp.   **$15**

**My Bedtime Book**
Illustrator: Williams, Garth
Author: Brown, Margaret; Werner, Jane
12065   1964   9-3/16 x 12-1/2 64 pp.   **$16**

**My Big Book of the Outdoors**
Illustrator: Wilkin, Eloise
Author: Watson, Jane Werner
10385   1958   9-1/8 x 12-1/4   24 pp.   **$10**

**My Big Golden Counting Book**
Illustrator: Williams, Garth
Author: Moore, Lilian
458   1957   8-3/8 x 10 7/8   28 pp.   **$7**

**My Golden Book of Manners**
Illustrator: Scarry, Richard
Author: Parish, Peggy
10416   1962   9-1/2 x 12-3/4   36 pp.   **$7**

**New Baby, The**
Illustrator: Wilkin, Eloise
Author: Shane, Ruth & Harold
487   1948   7-1/2 x 10   28 pp.   **$16**

**Night Before Christmas, The**
Illustrator: Wilburn, Kathy
Author: Moore, Clement C.
10202   1985   8 x 10-3/4   24 pp.   **$6**

**Planes, Trains, Cars, and Boats**
Illustrator: Kalish, Muriel & Lionel
Author: Kalish, Muriel & Lionel
13531   1963   9-1/4 x 12-1/2   28 pp.   **$10**

**Poky Little Puppy and the Patchwork
Blanket**
Illustrator: Chandler, Jean
Author: Chandler, Jean
10387   1983   9-1/8 x 12-1/4   24 pp.   **$6**

**Poky Little Puppy, The**
Illustrator: Tenggren, Gustaf
Author: Lowery, Janet Sebring
10418   1942   9-1/2 x 12-3/4   24 pp.   **$7**

**Step By Step Cook Book For Boys and
Girls**
Illustrator: Sayles, William
Author: Kiene, Julia
607   1956   6-3/8 x 9-1/4   128 pp.   **$10**

**Story of Geology, The**
Illustrator: McNaught, Harry & Sayles,
William
Author: Wyckoff, Jerome
16845   1960   8-1/4 x 11-1/4   180 pp.   **$8**

**Tale of Peter Rabbit, The**
Illustrator: Ruth, Rod
Author: Potter, Beatrix
10486   1963   9-1/4 x 12-1/2   24 pp.   **$5**

**Tall Tales of America**
Illustrator: Schmidt, Al
Author: Shapiro, Irwin
709   1959   6 x 8 5/8   128 pp.   **$10**

**Teddy Bear's Book of 1 2 3**
Author: Wright, Betty Ren
10875   1969   9-1/4 x 12-1/2   28 pp.   **$5**

**Tenggren's Pirates, Ships and Sailors**
Illustrator: Tenggren, Gustaf
Author: Jackson, Kathryn & Byron
13590   1971   10 5/8 x 12-1/8 62 pp.   **$45**

**There's an Elephant in the Bathtub**
Illustrator: Bradfield, Roger
Author: Bradfield, Roger
10812   1964   12-1/2 X 9-1/2   28 pp.   **$22**

**Three Bears, The**
Illustrator: Rojankovsky, Feodor
10421   1948   9-1/2 x 12-3/4   24 pp.   **$7**

**Three Little Kittens**
Illustrator: Masha
10410   1942   9-1/4 x 12-1/2   36 pp.   **$5**

**Top Cat**
Illustrator: Pratt, Hawley & White, Al
Author: Memling, Carl
10831   1693   9 5/16 x 12-1/2   28 pp.   **$25**

**Want to Read, I**
Illustrator: Aliki
Author: Wright, Betty Ren
10879   1970   9-3/8 x 12-1/2   28 pp.   **$5**

**What Makes It Go?**
Illustrator: Kaufman, Joe
Author: Kaufman, Joe
15767   1971   10-1/2 x 12-1/8 96 pp.   **$5**

**Whatever Happens to Kittens?**
Illustrator: Parsons, Virginia
Author: Hall, Bill
10862   1967   9-1/2 x 12-3/4   28 pp.   **$5**

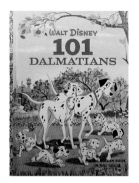

**101 Dalmatians**
Illustrator: Mc Gary, Norman &
Mattinson, Sylvia
Author: Buettner, Carl
10540   1961   9-1/2 x 12-3/4   28 pp.   **$15**

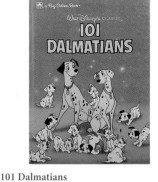

**101 Dalmatians**
Illustrator: Langley, Bill, Dias, Ron
Author: Walt Disney Studios
12346   1991   8 x 10-3/4   24 pp.   **$5**

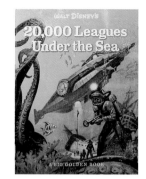

**20,000 Leagues Under the Sea**
Illustrator: Grant, Campbell
Author: Beecher, Elizabeth
488   1954   8-1/2 x 11   66 pp.   **$20**

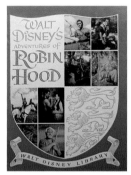

**Adventures of Robin Hood**
Illustrator: Scenes from the Movie
436   1955   8-1/2 x 11-1/8   46 pp.   **$25**

**Adventures of Mr. Toad, The**
Illustrator: Hench, John
Author: Grahame, Kenneth
No #   1949   8-1/4 x 13-1/8   28 pp.   **$25**

**Adventures of Zorro**
Illustrator: Steel, John
Author: Verral, Charles Spain
398   1958   9 5/8 x13-1/4   32 pp.   **$25**

**Alice in Wonderland**
Illustrator: Dempster, Al
Author: Carroll, Lewis
426   1951   9-3/4 x 13-1/8   28 pp.   **$10**

**Alice in Wonderland**
Illustrator: Slater, Teddy; Mateu, Franc
Author: Walt Disney Studios
12341   1991   8 x 10-3/4   24 pp.   **$5**

**Alice in Wonderland (with record)**
Illustrator: Crawford, Mel
Author: Hibler, Winston
No #   1951   10-1/2 x 13-1/4 22 pp.   **$60**

**Aladdin**
Illustrator: Baker, Darrell
Author: Kreider, Karen
12348   1992   8-1/4 x 11
24 pp.   **$5**

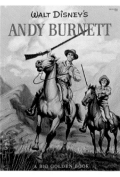

**Andy Burnett**
Illustrator: Dreany, E. Joseph
Author: Verral, Charles Spain
395   1958   8 5/8 x 11-1/8
44 pp.   **$18**

**Aristocats, The**
Illustrator: Walt Disney Prod.
Author: Walt Disney Studios
10880   1970   9-3/8 x 12-1/2   26 pp.   **$12**

**Art of Animation, The**
Illustrator: Walt Disney Studios
Author: Thomas, Bob
840   1958   8-1/4 x 11-1/4   190 pp.   **$250**

**Babes in Toyland**
Illustrator: Hess, Lowell
Author: Sherman, George & Carey, Mary
10314   1961   9-1/4 x 12-1/2   32 pp.   **$12**

**Babes in Toyland**
Giant Punch-Out Book
75 figures to punch-outs and assemble.
Story on the left side of every page.
Illustrator: Collom, Chester
Author: Sherman, George
10363   1961                   **$75-$100**
363   1961                     **$75-$100**
10 x 12-3/4      30 pages
**Bambi**
Illustrator: Shaw, Melvin
Author: Salten, Felix
Many black and white pencil sketches and
full-color preliminary drawings. Includes
four pictures to cut out and frame.
No #   1941
   9 x 11-1/8   54 pp.          **$150**
No #   1941
   Without four cut-out pictures   **$25**

**Bambi**
Illustrator: Shaw, Melvin
Author: Salten, Felix
443   1949   8-1/8 x 11-1/4   32 pp.   **$25**
10450   1949   9-1/2 x 12-3/4   28 pp.   **$7**

**Bambi**
Illustrator: Dias, Ron
Author: Walt Disney Studios
10380   1984   8-1/4 x 11   24 pp.   **$5**

**Beauty and the Beast**
Illustrator: Dias, Ron & Gonzalez, Rid
Author: Slater, Teddy
12343   1991   8-1/4 x 11   20 pp.   **$5**

**Bedknobs and Broomsticks**
Illustrator: Walt Disney Studios
Author: Walt Disney Studios
10489   1971   9-3/8 x 12-1/2   28 pp.   **$15**

**Black Cauldron Storybook, The**
Illustrator: Walt Disney Studio
Author: Walt Disney Studios
15830   1985   8-3/4 x 11-1/4   48 pp.   **$8**

**Bongo**
Illustrator: Starr, Edgar
Author: Lewis, Sinclair
No #   1947   8-1/4 x 13-1/4   28 pp.   **$35**

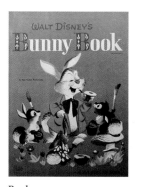

**Bunny Book**
Illustrator: Kelsey, Dick & Justice, Bill
Author: Werner, Jane
10424  1951  9-3/8 x 12-1/2  28 pp.  **$15**

**Chicken Little**
Illustrator: Walt Disney Studio
Author: Walt Disney Studios
10436  1983  9-1/8 x 12-1/4  24 pp.  **$6**

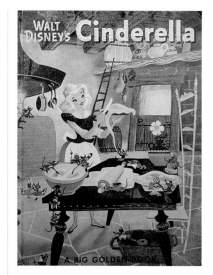

**Cinderella**
With pop-up pumpkin attached to inside front cover.
Illustrator: Worcester, Retta Scott
Author: Werner, Jane
425  1950  9 5/8 x13-1/4  28 pp.  **$50**
Without pop-up pumpkin
425  1950  9 5/8 x13-1/4  28 pp.  **$35**

**Cinderella**
Illustrator: Worcester, Retta Scott
Author: Werner, Jane
10425  1950  9-1/2 x 12-3/4  28 pp.  **$15**

**Cinderella**
Illustrator: Worcester, Retta Scott
Author: Werner, Jane
10425  1950  9-1/4 x 12-1/2  28 pp.  **$7**

**Cinderella Puppet Show**
Illustrator: Worcester, Retta Scott
411  1949  8-1/8 x 11-1/4  12 pp.  **$125**

**Cinderella**
Illustrator: Dias, Ron
Author: Walt Disney Studios
10200  1986  8-1/4 x 11  20 pp.  **$5**

**Cinderella**
Open-Door Book
Illustrator: De Santis, George
Author: Chase, Alice
10757  1965  9-3/8 x 12-1/4  **$15**

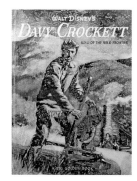

**Davy Crockett**
Illustrator: Schmidt, Al
Author: Beecher, Elizabeth
435  1955  8-3/8 x 10-7/8  48 pp.  **$16**

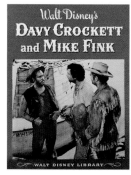

**Davy Crockett and Mike Fink**
Illustrator: Photographs
Author: Shapiro, Irwin
439  1955  8-1/2 x 11-1/4  44 pp.  **$26**

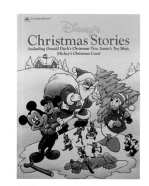

**Disney's Christmas Stories**
Illustrator: Various
Author: Various
15750  1989  8-1/2 x 11  68 pp.  **$6**

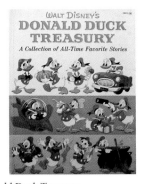

**Donald Duck Treasury**
Illustrator: Various
Author: Bedford, Annie North
12517   1960   7-1/8 x 9-1/4   118 pp.   **$16**

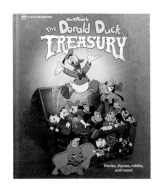

**Donald Duck Treasury, The**
Illustrator: Various
Author: Various
15580   1984   8-3/4 x 10-1/4   62 pp.   **$8**

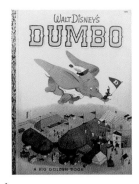

**Dumbo**
Illustrator: Kelsey, Dick
Author: Bedford, Annie North
428   1955   9 5/16 x 12-1/2  32 pp.   **$25**

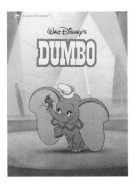

**Dumbo**
Illustrator: Dias, Ron & Guenther, Annie
Author: Slater, Teddy
11994   1988   8-1/4 x 11   20 pp.   **$5**

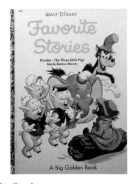

**Favorite Stories**
Illustrator: Various
Author: Various
8007   1957   7-3/4 x 10-7/8   48 pp.   **$8**

**Fox and the Hound, The**
Illustrator: Walt Disney Productions
Author: Walt Disney Productions
16802-21981   8 5/8 x 11-1/4   34 pp.   **$10**

**Great Locomotive Chase, The**
Illustrator: Kaye, Graham
Author: Verral, Charles Spain
447   1956   8-3/8 x 10-7/8   48 pp.   **$18**

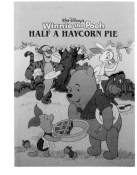

**Half a Haycorn Pie**
Illustrator: Baker, Darrell
Author: Birney, Betty
12338   1992   8 x 10-3/4   24 pp.   **$5**

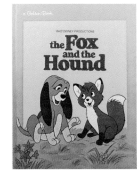

**Hunchback of Notre Dame, The**
Illustrator: Willims, Don
Author: Korman, Justine
10378-01996   8-1/4 x 11   20 pp.   **$5**

**Jungle Book, The**
Illustrator: Walt Disney Studios
Author: Lewis, Jean
10863   1967   9-1/4 x 12-1/2   32 pp.   **$8**

**Jungle Book, The**
Illustrator: Walt Disney Studios
Author: Bedford, Annie North
15613   1967   10 x 12-3/4   80 pp.   **$25**

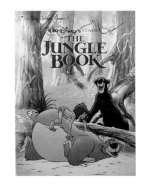

**Jungle Book, The**
Illustrator: Walt Disney Company
Author: Walt Disney Company
12107   1990   8-1/4 x 11   24 pp.   **$5**

**Lady and the Tramp**
Illustrator: Armstrong, Samuel
Author: Greene, Ward
427    1955    9 5/16 x 12-1/2  32 pp.   **$18**

**Lady and the Tramp**
Illustrator: Langley, Bill, Dias, Ron
Author: Slater, Teddy
12367   1993   8 x 10-3/4    24 pp.   **$6**

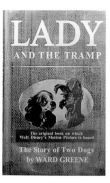

**Lady and the Tramp**
Illustrator: Rinaldi, Joe G.
Author: Green, Ward
830   1955   5-1/4 x 8-3/8   142 pp. **$550**
Without Dust Jacket **$325**

**Legends of America**
Illustrator: Crawford, Mel
Author: Bedford, Annie North
12296   1969   9-1/4 x 11-1/2  48 pp.   **$8**

**Little Mermaid, The**
Illustrator: SiCicco, Sue
Author: Teitelbaum. Michael
12335-11989   8-1/4 x 11   20 pp.   **$5**

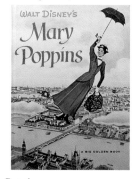

**Mary Poppins**
Illustrator: Clarke, Grace
Author: Bedford, Annie North
10850   1964   9-1/2 x 12-3/4  28 pp.   **$9**

**Mary Poppins**
Look-Inside Book
Illustrator: Walt Disney Productions
Author: Walt Disney Productions
11031   1964   9-1/2 x 13      **$16**

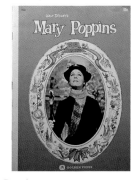

**Mary Poppins**
Pictures from movie
Illustrator: Fraser, Betty & Pineo, Craig
Author: McHargue, Georgess
7600   1964   9-1/8 x 12-3/8  48 pp.   **$8**

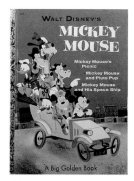

**Mickey Mouse**
Illustrator: Various
Author: Various
8014   1953   7-3/4 x 10-7/8  48 pp.   **$8**

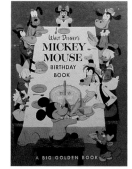

**Mickey Mouse Birthday Book**
Illustrator: Grant, Campbell
Author: Bedford, Annie North
482   1953   8-1/2 x 11   64 pp.   **$22**

**Mickey Mouse Club Annual**
Illustrator: Various
Author: Various
549   1956   8-3/8 x 11-3/4  120 pp.   **$18**

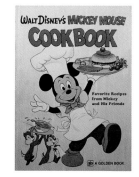

**Mickey Mouse Cookbook**
Illustrator: Cover: Dias, Ron
Author: Walt Disney Productions
16812   1990   8-1/8 x 11-1/4  94 pp.   **$6**

**Mickey Mouse in the Wild West**
Illustrator: Walt Disney Studio
Author: Walt Disney Studios
15778    1973    10-1/2 x 12-1/8 46 pp.    **$6**

**Mickey's Christmas Carol**
Illustrator: Dias, Ron
Author: Walt Disney Company
12179    1990    8-1/4 x 11        24 pp.    **$5**

**New Walt Disney Treasury, The**
Illustrator: Various
Author: Various
15546    1971    10-1/2 x 12-1/8 94 pp.    **$6**

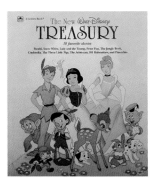

**New Walt Disney Treasury, The**
Illustrator: Various
Author: Various
No #    1971    10-1/2 x 12-1/4 94 pp.    **$4**

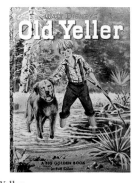

**Old Yeller**
Illustrator: Doremus, Robert
Author: Lindquist, Willis
394    1958    9-1/2 x 12-3/4    28 pp.    **$18**

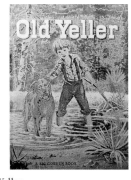

**Old Yeller**
Illustrator: Doremus, Robert
Author: Lindquist, Willis
10394    1958    9-1/4 x 12-1/2    28 pp.    **$16**

**Oliver & Company**
Illustrator: Ito, Willy & Dias, Ron
Author: Korman, Justine
11995    1988    8-1/2 x 11-1/4    28 pp.    **$10**

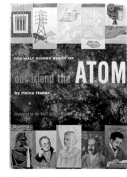

**Our Friend the Atom**
Illustrator: Various
Author: Haber, Heinz
606    1956    8 x 11        166 pp.    **$18**

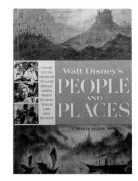

**People and Places**
Illustrator: Various
Author: Watson, Jane Werner
743    1959    8 x 11        168 pp.    **$8**

**Perri**
Illustrator: Kelsey, Dick
Author: Broun, Emily
415    1957    9-1/2 x 12-3/4    28 pp.    **$18**

**Perri**
Illustrator: Kelsey, Dick
Author: Broun, Emily
10415    1957    9-1/4 x 12-1/2    28 pp.    **$15**

**Peter Pan**
Illustrator: Hench, John & Dempster, Al
Author: Barrie, Sir James M.
570    1952    9 5/8 x 13-1/4    28 pp.    **$25**
570    1952    9 5/16 x 12-1/2 28 pp.    **$12**

**Peter Pan**
Illustrator: Dias, Ron
Author: Coco, Eugene Bradley
12081   1989   8-1/4 x 11       20 pp.       **$5**

Pinocchio
Illustrator: Dempster, Al
Author: Collodi
580       1953   9 5/8 x 13-1/4   28 pp.       **$12**

Pinocchio
Illustrator: Dempster, Al
Author: Fletcher, Steffi
10580   1953   9-1/4 x 12-1/2   32 pp.       **$7**

Pinocchio
Illustrator: Walt Disney Studio
Author: Walt Disney Studios
10381   1953   8 x 10-3/4       24 pp.       **$5**

Pinocchio
Illustrator: Dias, Ron
Author: Coco, Eugene Bradley
12109   1990   8-1/4 x 10-3/4   24 pp.       **$5**

Pinocchio
Giant Punch-outs.
Story of Pinocchio on the left side of every page.
Illustrator: Buettner, Carl & McGary, Norman
10605   1961   10 x 12-3/4   15 pp.       **$75 - $125**

**Plot to Capture Robin Hood, The**
Illustrator: Walt Disney Studio
Author: Walt Disney Studios
13754   1973   10-1/2 x 12-1/8 46 pp.       **$15**

**Rescuers Down Under**
Author: Tietelbaum, Michael
12344   1991   8 x 10-3/4       24 pp.       **$5**

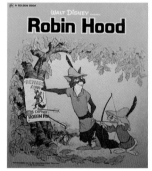

Robin Hood
Illustrator: Walt Disney Studio
Author: Walt Disney Studio
10492   1973   9-3/8 x 12-1/2   20 pp.       **$6**

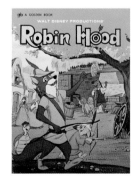

**Robin Hood**
Illustrator: Walt Disney Studio
Author: Walt Disney Studio
16816   1973   10-1/2 x 12-1/8 24 pp.       **$6**

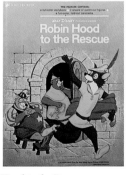

**Robin Hood to the Rescue**
Illustrator: Walt Disney Studio
Author: Walt Disney Studio
15004   1973   8-1/4 x 10-3/4   34 pp.       **$15**

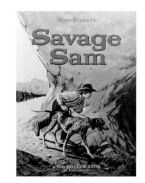

**Savage Sam**
Illustrator: Crawford, Mel
Author: Memling, Carl
10359   1963   9-1/2 x 12-3/4   28 pp.       **$18**

**Sleeping Beauty**
Illustrator: Eyvind, Earl & Svendsen, Julius
Author: Watson, Jane Werner
757    1957    10-1/8 x 13    58 pp.    **$45**

**Sleeping Beauty**
Illustrator: Eyvind, Earl & Svendsen, Julius
Author: Watson, Jane Werner
390    1958    9-3/8 x 12-1/2    28 pp.    **$10**

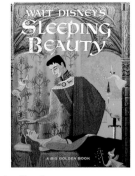

**Sleeping Beauty**
Illustrator: Eyvind, Earl & Svendsen, Julius
Author: Watson, Jane Werner
10390    1958    9-3/8 x 12-1/2    28 pp.    **$7**

**Sleeping Beauty**
Illustrator: Dias, Ron
Author: Walt Disney Studios
10408    1986    8-1/4 x 11-1/4    20 pp.    **$5**

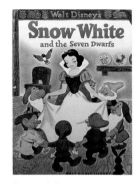

**Snow White and the Seven Dwarfs**
Illustrator: Grant, Campbell
Author: Werner, Jane
566    1952    9-3/8 x 12-3/4    28 pp.    **$25**

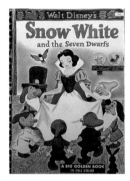

**Snow White and the Seven Dwarfs**
Illustrator: Grant, Campbell
Author: Werner, Jane
10451    1952    9-1/4 x 12-1/2    32 pp.    **$7**

**Snow White and the Seven Dwarfs**
Illustrator: Dias, Ron
Author: Walt Disney Studios
10205    1984    8 x 10-3/4    24 pp.    **$5**

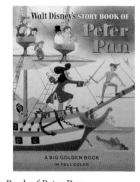

**Story Book of Peter Pan**
Illustrator: Grant, Campbell
Author: Bedford, Annie North
571    1953    8-1/2 x 11-1/4    50 pp.    **$25**

**Surprise Package**
Illustrator: Walt Disney Studios
Author: Palmer, H. Marion
No #    1944    10-1/8 x 13    94 pp.    **$18**

**Sword in the Stone, The**
Illustrator: White, Al
Author: Memling, Carl
10360    1963    9-1/2 x 12-3/4    28 pp.    **$8**

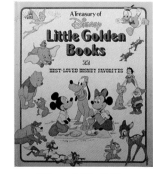

**Treasury of Disney Little Golden Books®, A**
Illustrator: Various
Author: Various
17865    1978    9-7/8 x 10-1/4    94 pp.    **$12**

**Two-Minute Classics**
Illustrator: Dias, Ron
Author: Packard, Mary
12180    1988    8-1/4 x 11    32 pp.    **$4**

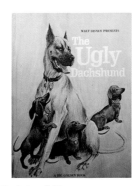

**Two-Minute Good Night Stories**
Illustrator: Langley, Bill; Wakeman, Diane
Author: Packard, Mary
12181   1988   8-1/4 x 11        32 pp.      **$3**

**Ugly Dachshund, The**
Illustrator: Crawford, Mel
Author: Memling, Carl
10860   1965   9 5/8 x 12-3/4   28 pp.      **$22**

**Uncle Remus Stories**
Illustrator: Dempster, Al & Justice, Bill
Author: Palmer, Marion
No #    1947   10-1/4 x 13      94 pp.      **$75**
554     1947   10-1/4 x 13      94 pp.      **$65**

**Uncle Remus Stories**
Illustrator: Dempster, Al & Justice, Bill
Author: Palmer, Marion
15551   1946   10-1/4 x 13      94 pp.      **$50**

**Uncle Remus Stories**
Illustrator: Dempster, Al & Justice, Bill
Author: Palmer, Marion
15551   1986   10-1/4 x 13      94 pp.      **$45**

**Walt Disney Song Book, The**
16825   1979   10-1/2 x 12-1/8 94 pp.      **$16**

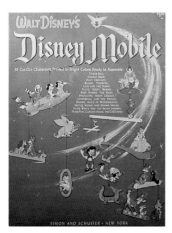

**Walt Disney's Disney Mobile**
36 Cut-Out Pieces
437     1955   10-1/4 x 13-3/8 pp.        **$450**

**Walt Disney's Mother Goose**
Author: Dempster, Al
422     1949   8-1/8 x 13-1/4   28 pp.     **$55**

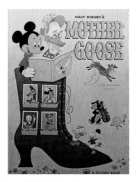

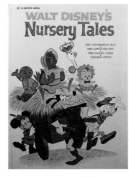

**Walt Disney's Mother Goose**
Illustrator: Walt Disney Studios
Author: Walt Disney Studios
10878   1970   9-3/8 x 12-1/2   28 pp.     **$5**

**Walt Disney's Nursery Tales**
12068   1965   9-3/8 x 12-3/4   64 pp.     **$15**

**Walt Disney's Story Land**
Illustrator: Walt Disney Studio
Author: Walt Disney Studios
16547   1987   7-3/8 x 10-1/4   322 pp.    **$6**

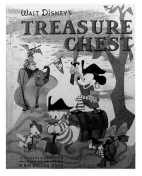

**Walt Disney's Treasure Chest**
Illustrator: Walt Disney Studio
No #     1948   9 x 11-1/4        66 pp.     **$45**

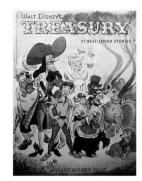

**Walt Disney's Treasury**
Illustrator: Kelsey, Dick & Moores, Dick
Author: Fletcher, Steffi & Werner, Jane
706     1953   10 x 13        142 pp.     **$45**

**Westward Ho the Wagons!**
Illustrator: Schmidt, Al
Author: Coombs, Charles I.
449     1956   8-3/8 x 10-7/8   48 pp.     **$16**

**Winnie-the-Pooh—A Tight Squeeze**
Illustrator: White, Al
Author: Milne, A. A.
10859   1965   9-1/2 x 12-3/4   26 pp.     **$8**

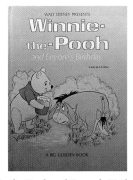

**Winnie-the-Pooh and Eeyore's Birthday**
Illustrator: McGary, Norm & Lorencz, Bill
Author: Milne, A. A.
10861   1965   9-1/2 x 12-3/4   28 pp.     **$8**

**Winnie-the-Pooh and the Missing Pots**
Illustrator: Hicks, Russell
Author: Birney, Betty
12337   1992   8 x 10-3/4   24 pp.     **$5**

**Winnie-the-Pooh Meets Tigger**
Illustrator: Walt Disney Studio
Author: Milne, A. A.
10869   1968   9-1/2 x 12-3/4   24 pp.     **$6**

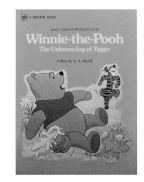

**Winnie-the-Pooh, The Unbouncing of Tigger**
Illustrator: Walt Disney Studio
Author: Milne, A. A.
10504   1974   9-3/8 x 12-1/2   24 pp.     **$8**

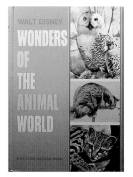

**Wonders of the Animal World**
Illustrator: Walt Disney Studio
Author: Melegari, Vezio
16831   1964   8 x 11        180 pp.     **$15**

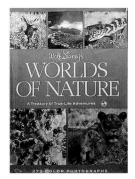

**Worlds of Nature**
Illustrator: Walt Disney Studio
Author: Platt, Rutherford
834     1957   8-1/4 x 11-1/8   168 pp.     **$20**

**Zorro**
Illustrator: Steel, John
Author: Werstein, Irving
398     1958   8 x 11        32 pp.     **$25**

# *Tiny Golden Libraries*

The first of three sets of 12 tiny books, measuring 2-1/8 x 3-1/8 inches, was Tiny Animal Stories released in March 1948. This was followed by Tiny Nonsense Stories in 1949 and Walt Disney's Tiny Movie Stories in 1950. Each of these three sets came in a beautiful lithographed box with a lithographed slipcover. There was a thin piece of plastic attached to the slipcover that allowed the spines of the books to be visible when the box was closed. The front book covers of these original three sets did not have book numbers on them. The books contained 22 pages with full color pictures.

If you are lucky enough to have the box with the slipcover, you'll be able to tell the edition of your set. Look for a letter of the alphabet corresponding with the edition number, which can be found on the bottom of the slipcover. It will look like A100100 or B100100. The "A" means a first edition, and the 100100 means that its suggested retail price was $1. If you have set numbers 401 or 402 and cannot find the A100100, you probably have a first edition.

**Single Book Values:**
Unnumbered   **$3-$6**  •  Numbered   **$1-$5**

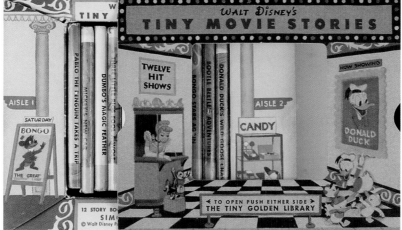

**Tiny Animal Stories**
Why the Little Elephant Got Spanked
"Meow" Said the Fierce Baby Lion
Little Giraffe Wants To Play
Little Leopard and His Fat Stomach

Hop, Hop Little Kangaroo
Shame On You Baby Whale
Baby Hippopotamus's Adventure
Look Out, Baby Bears, Here He Comes

Illustrator: Williams, Garth
Author: Kunhardt, Dorothy
400   1948   **$50-$150**

Two Stuck in the Mud Rhinoceroses
Brave Father Gorilla
Baby Camel and His Naughty Father
Tiger Kitten's Poor, Poor Tail

**Tiny Nonsense Stories**
Cowboy Kitten
Happy Valentine
Easter Bunny
Poor Frightened Mr. Pig
April Fool!
Naughty Little Guest
Little Sheep's Little Lamb
Wonderful Silly Picnic
Uncle Quack
Two Snowbulls
Roger Mouse's Wish
Little Squirrel's Santa Clause

Illustrator: Williams, Garth
Author: Kunhardt, Dorothy
401        1949        $50-$150

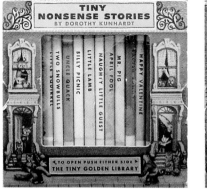

**Walt Disney's Tiny Movie Stories**
(Mickey punches up out of the front cover so that he appears to be sitting on top of the box.)
Bambi Plays Follow the Leader
Bongo Stars Again
Donald Duck's Wild Goose Chase
Mickey's New Car
Dumbo's Magic Feather
Pablo the Penguin Takes a Trip
Three Little Pigs Fool a Wolf
Pinocchio's Surprise
Cinderella's Ball Gown
Dopey and the Wicked Witch
Bootie Beetle's Adventure
Brer Rabbit Plays a Trick

Illustrator: Grant, Campbell
Author: Werner, Jane
402        1950        $100-$200

**The Tiny Golden Library**
Three complete libraries. Thirty-six 24-page books in full color. Box has a slipcover. Contains each of the 12 books from Tiny Animal Stories (numbered 1-12), Tiny Nonsense Stories (numbered 13-24), and Walt Disney's Tiny Movie Stories (25–36). There are no markings on the box to tell a first edition from a reprint.

Baby Camel and His Naughty Father (1)
Little Leopard and His Fat Stomach (2)
Why the Little Elephant Got Spanked (3)
Little Giraffe Wants To Play (4)
Look Out, Baby Bears, Here He Comes (5)
Two Stuck in the Mud Rhinoceroses (6)
Brave Father Gorilla (7)
Baby Hippopotamus's Adventure (8)
Hop, Hop Little Kangaroo (9)
"Meow" Said the Fierce Baby Lion (10)
Shame On You Baby Whale (11)
Baby Camel and His Naughty Father (1)
Tiger Kitten's Poor, Poor Tail (12)
Easter Bunny (13)
Poor Frightened Mr. Pig (14)
Happy Valentine (15)
April Fool! (16)
Uncle Quack (17)
Roger Mouse's Wish (18)
Wonderful Silly Picnic (19)

Little Squirrel's Santa Claus (20)
Little Sheep's Little Lamb (21)
Cowboy Kitten (22)
Two Snowbulls (23)
Naughty Little Guest (24)
Donald Duck's Wild Goose Chase (25)
Pinocchio's Surprise (26)
Bongo Stars Again (27)
Brer Rabbit Plays a Trick (28)
Dumbo's Magic Feather (29)
Bambi Plays Follow the Leader (30)
Three Little Pigs Fool a Wolf (31)

Cinderella's Ball Gown (32)
Dopey and the Wicked Witch (33)
Mickey's New Car (34)
Bootie Beetle's Adventure (35)
Pablo the Penguin Takes a Trip (36)

Illustrator: Williams, Garth
Author: Kunhardt, Dorothy
Disney Books Illustrator: Grant, Campbell
Disney Books Author: Werner, Jane
15505   1965   **$75-$100**

**The Tiny Golden Library**
Three complete libraries. Thirty-six 24-page books in full color. Box has a slipcover that is identical to the face of the box. This set contains each of the 12 books from Tiny Animal Stories (numbered 1-12), Tiny Nonsense Stories (numbered 13-24), and Walt Disney's Tiny Movie Stories (25–36). Slipcover and box both use the A395:395 code for telling box editions. Titles are numbered the same as in the previous set.

Illustrator: Williams, Garth
Author: Kunhardt, Dorothy
Disney Books Illustrator: Grant, Campbell
Disney Books Author: Werner, Jane
15505   1965   **$75-$125**

**The Tiny Golden Library**
Twenty-four, 24-page books in full color. Box and slipcover are identical. Contains each of the 12 books from Tiny Animal Stories (numbered 1-12) and Tiny Nonsense Stories (numbered 13-24). Slipcover and box both use the A395:395 code for telling box editions.

Illustrator: Williams, Garth
Author: Kunhardt, Dorothy
15582   1968   **$50-$100**

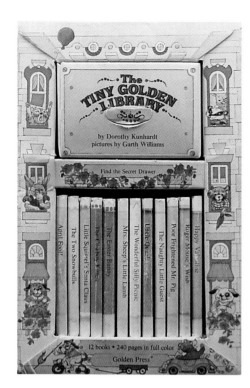

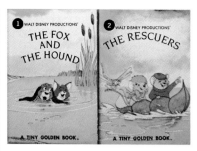

The Tiny Golden Library
Stories are the same as in Tiny
Nonsense Stories
Poor Frightened Mr. Pig (1)
Easter Bunny (2)
Naughty Little Guest (3)
Happy Valentine (4)
Roger Mouse's Wish (5)
Uncle Quack (6)
Wonderful Silly Picnic (7)
Mrs. Sheep's Little Lamb (8)
Cowboy Kitten (9)
Little Squirrel's Santa Claus (10)
Two Snowbulls, The (11)
April Fool (12)

Illustrator: Williams, Garth
Author: Kunhardt, Dorothy
15582   1980   **$25-$35**

**Walt Disney's Tiny Theater**
Open doors at top to see a diorama of Snow
White and the Seven Dwarfs. Books are
renumbered from 1-12.
Bongo and Bootle Beetle are replaced with
Fox and the Hound Friends and Rescuers
Save Penny. Year of printing can be found on
copyright page.
Illustrator: Grant, Campbell
Author: Werner, Jane
13617   1981   **$25-$45**

Fox and the Hound Friends (1)
Rescuers Save Penny (2)
Donald Duck's Wild Goose Chase (3)
Mickey's New Car (4)
Dumbo's Magic Feather (5)
Pablo the Penguin Takes a Trip (6)
Three Little Pigs Fool a Wolf (7)
Pinocchio's Surprise (8)
Cinderella's Ball Gown (9)
Dopey and the Wicked Witch (10)
Bambi Plays Follow the Leader (11)
Brer Rabbit Plays a Trick (12)

# The Golden Hours Library

The Golden Hours Library
contained twelve 24-page books in a
box shaped like a grandfather clock
with moveable hands. The books
measured 3-1/4 x 5-1/2 inches. The
box, 11-3/4 x 5 x 4-1/4 inches, was
made up of a box and lid. The box
stored the books and had the face
and hands of a clock. The lid had
a thin plastic sheet glued to it that
allowed the books and clock face to
be seen when closed. All of the titles
were originally released as Little
Golden® Books.

15581   1967   **$35-$50**
Single Book Value: **$1-$2**

How to Tell Time   Hop, Little Kangaroo   Heidi

Four Puppies   Big Little Book, The   Littlest Raccoon

Old MacDonald Had   Tommy's Camping   Four Little Kittens   Colors Are Nice   Rumpelstiltskin and   Little Cottontail
a Farm   Adventure   the Princess and the Pea

# Golden Story Books

# and Sandpiper Books

Golden Story Books were published between 1949 and 1951 in a hard cardboard cover measuring 5 inches wide by 7-1/16 inches tall. They were bound with a golden-brown woven pattern paper spine. Almost every one of the 128 pages had a full color picture. The back of each book listed existing titles. Simon & Schuster and Western Printing and Lithographing Company produced them. The Artist and Writers Guild created the art.

The backs of the later titles listed titles to number 20. Numbers 17, *Gene Autry and the Red Shirt*; 18, *Donald Duck and the Hidden Gold*; 19, *The Magic Pot*; and 20, *The Christmas Book*, were not published in this series. Numbers 17 through 19 were published as Sandpiper Books.

Sometime around 1950-1951, *My Weekly Reader* either gave away with a subscription or sold through their paper a boxed set called *New Golden Story Library*. The set consisted of seven titles: *Herbert's Zoo; Christopher Bunny; The Stagecoach Robbery; Tom and Jerry; So Dear to My Heart; The Merry Piper; The Cat Who Went To Sea*.

Value of books and box: **$40-$75**

## Golden Story Books

**Boss of the Barnyard, The**
Illustrator: Scarry, Richard
Author: Hubbard, Joan
GS 4　　　1949　　　　**$6**

**Bugs Bunny's Treasure Hunt**
Illustrator: McKimson, Tom
GS 10　　　1949　　　　**$8**

**Cat Who Went to Sea, The**
Illustrator: Battaglia, Aurelius
Author: Jackson, Kathryn & Byron
GS 16　　　1950　　　　**$6**

**Chatterly Squirrel**
Illustrator: Miller, J. P.
Author: Werner, Jane
GS 13　　　1950　　　　**$6**

**Christopher Bunny**
Illustrator: Scarry, Richard
Author: Werner, Jane
GS 3　　　1949　　　　**$6**

**Circus Stories**
Illustrator: Martin, Charles E.
Author: Jackson, Kathryn & Byron
GS 8　　　1949　　　　**$6**

**Herbert's Zoo**
Illustrator: Julian
Author: Various
GS 1             1949             $6

**Horse Stories**
Illustrator: Dewitt, Cornelius
Author: Bechdolt, Jack
GS 14           1950             $6

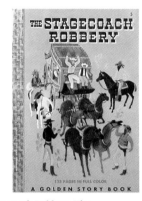

**Magic Wish, The**
Illustrator: Malvern, Corinne
Author: Nast, Elsa Ruth
GS 2             1949             $6

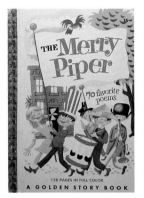

**Merry Piper, The**
Illustrator: Rockwell, Harlow
GS 15           1950             $6

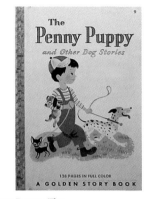

**Penny Puppy, The**
Illustrator: Battaglia, Aurelius
Author: Garfield, Robert
GS 9             1949             $6

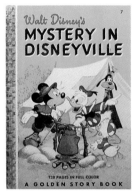

**Stagecoach Robbery, The**
Illustrator: Krush, Beth & Joe
Author: Archer, Peter
GS 5             1949             $6

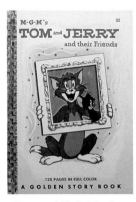

**Tom and Jerry and Their Friends**
Illustrator: Eisenberg, Harvey
GS 11           1950             $8

**Train Stories**
Illustrator: Gergely, Tibor
Author: Garfield, Robert & Knittle, Jessie
GS 6             1949             $8

**Walt Disney's Mystery in Disneyville**
Illustrator: Moores, Richard & Gonzales, Richard
GS 7             1949             $25

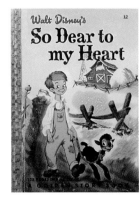

**Walt Disney's So Dear to My Heart**
Illustrator: Peet, Bill
Author: Palmer, Helen
GS 12           1950             $10

# Sandpiper Books

In 1951 Simon & Schuster, Artist and Writers Guild, and Western Printing and Lithographing Company, under the name of Sandpiper Press, produced A Sandpiper Book. A Sandpiper Book, according to the covers, were "Exciting Picture Story Books for new readers." These books contained 80 pages with every page printed in full color.

Each book measured 5-1/4 inches wide by 7-3/8 inches tall.

The book covers were done in a solid color with only a line-drawn picture, title, and "A Sandpiper Book" appearing on the front cover. The covers had either a smooth or meshed type of texture. A full-color dust jacket covered the book. Even though the following two titles were listed on the jackets, I don't believe they were ever printed: *Pirates' Cove and Other Stories* and *The Lost Silver Mine.*

**Airplane Stories**
Illustrator: Rockwell, Harlow
Author: Conger, Marion
S-3      1951      **$8**

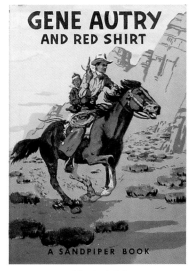

**Gene Autry and the Red Shirt**
Illustrator: Marsh, Jesse
Author: Beecher, Elizabeth
S-1      1951      **$30**

**Lone Ranger's New Deputy, The**
Illustrator: Shearer, Ted
Author: Striker, Fran
S-9      1951      **$30**

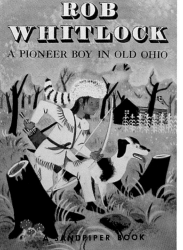

**Rob Whitlock, A Pioneer Boy in Old Ohio**
Illustrator: Dewitt, Cornelius
Author: Jackson, Kathryn & Byron
S-4      1951      **$8**

**Roy Rogers On the Double-R Ranch**
Illustrator: Nordley, Ernest
Author: Beecher, Elizabeth
S-7      1951      **$30**

**Walt Disney's Donald Duck and the Hidden Gold**
Illustrator: Taliaferro, Al
Author: Werner, Jane
S-2      1951      **$40**

**Lost Silver Mine**
S-8      Probably Never Printed
**Pirates' Cove and Other Stories**
S-6      Probably Never Printed
**Walt Disney's Alice In Wonderland**
S-10      Probably Never Printed
**Wishing Stick, The**
S-5      Probably Never Printed

This has to be the shortest-lived series of books produced by Simon and Schuster, Artists and Writers Guild, and Western Printing and Lithographing. All the titles in the series were published in 1952 and never reprinted. The backs of the books mention that new titles were being planned for the future, but none were ever added.

Two of the stories, *Seven Dwarfs Find a House*, S-2, and *Walt Disney's Mother Goose*, S-4, were later reprinted as Little Golden Books. *Mr. Shortsleeves' Great Big Store* was later produced on a Big Golden Record.

**How to determine editions:**
The letter "A" can be found on the last page on the bottom right. All the titles had only one printing.

**Mr. Shortsleeves' Great Big Store**
Illustrator: Myers, Bernice
Author: Hurd, Edith Thacher
6          1952          **$15**

**My Toy Box**
Illustrator: Wilkin, Eloise
Author: Jackson, Kathryn & Byron
1          1952          **$35**

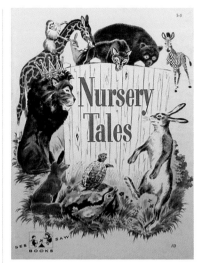

**Nursery Tales**
Illustrator: Medvey, Steve
Author: Archer, Peter
5          1952          **$7**

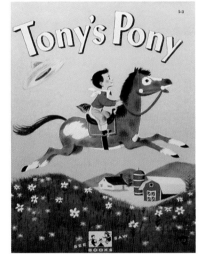

**Tony's Pony**
Illustrator: Kaufman, Van
Author: Schlein, Miriam
3          1952          **$7**

**Walt Disney's Mother Goose**
Illustrator: Walt Disney Studios
Author: Dempster, Al
4          1952          **$20**

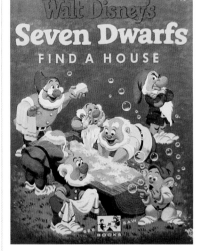

**Walt Disney's Seven Dwarfs Find a House**
Illustrator: Svendsen, Julius
Author: Bedford, Annie North
2          1952          **$15**

# Tell-A-Tale Books

Whitman Publishing Company published the Tell-A-Tale series from 1945 to 1984. Since 1985, the series has been published as A Golden Tell-A-Tale® Book. I have combined the Golden and Whitman Tell-A-Tale Books in this section. Whitman first started printing Tell-A-Tale books with number 850, *Poor Kitty*, in 1945. When the numbers reached 899, someone at Whitman may have questioned why the books had started with 850 and not 800. So around 1952, the company went back to 800 and renumbered until 848. After using up all of the 800 numbers, they numbered the books 900 to 966 from 1953 through 1954. Books numbered 2500 through 2600 were published into the 1970s. Books published since 1955 can have more than one title for the same book number. The numbers on the Golden Tell-A-Tale Books have a dash in the number. The numbers with the dash were not numerical but a book coding system use at Golden Press. If your book has a number like 896:15, the number before the ":" is the book number and the numbers after is the suggested retail price.

**Titles that can be found with dust jackets are:**

855 *Henry the Helicopter*, 857 *Nursery Rhymes*, 850 *Poor Kitty*, 858 *Rainy Day Story on the Farm*, 854 *Sneezer*, 851 *Snooty*, 853 *Snoozey*, 859 *The Three Bears*, 860 *The Three Little Pigs*, and 852 *Wiggletail*.

A dust jacket on a Tell-A-Tale can add $15-$20 to the price of the book.

**How to determine Tell-A-Tale editions:**

There is no sure way to determine a first edition. You can look at the titles on the back of the books and by deduction get an idea of when a book was printed. By using the following information, you can make an educated guess as to the print year of your book. Look at the last title and, in some cases, the first and last titles on the back of your book. If the year I show below matches your copyright or one year before it, you can assume your book is a first edition.

**Example:** Your book lists *Cinderella* as the last title on the back cover and has a copyright date of 1954. I'm showing that the book's back cover was used in 1954. You can make the assumption that your book is a first edition.

When two titles are listed with a slash mark (/) between them, this indicates the first and last titles on the back of the book.

If the back of your book doesn't show a list of available titles, your book was printed between 1945 and 1949.

| Title(s) on Back of Book | Print Year |
|---|---|
| *A Child's Garden of Verses* | 1973 |
| *A Fuzzy Pet* | 1961 |
| *Buster Bulldozer/Christopher John's Fuzzy Blanket* | 1959 |
| *Cinderella* | 1954 |
| *CTW on back cover* | 1978 |
| *Educational books* | 1973-1978 |
| *Franky, the Fuzzy Goat* | 1959 |
| *Fuzzy Friends in Mother Goose* | 1959 |
| *Fuzzy Mittens* | 1963 |
| *Jerry and Dr. Dave/Bugs Bunny* | 1964 |
| *Little Joe's Puppy/Beaver Valley* | 1957 |
| *Nobody's Puppy/Bugs Bunny* | 1964 |
| *Peter Potamus* | 1966 |
| *Pockets/Beaver Valley* | 1956 |
| *Pop-O the Clown* | 1950 |
| *Puffy the Puppy/Woody Woodpecker* | 1953 |
| *Raggedy Ann and Andy on the Farm/Little Red Riding Hood* | 1975 |
| *Socks* | 1950 |
| *That Donkey/Woody Woodpecker* | 1967 |
| *The Elves and the Shoemaker* | 1970 |
| *The More the Merrier/Woody Woodpecker* | 1965 |
| *The Town Mouse and the Country Mouse* | 1969 |
| *The Truck That Stopped at Village Small/Woody Woodpecker* | 1951 |
| *Tom and Jerry* | 1968 |
| *Tommy and Timmy* | 1961 |
| *Train Coming/Christopher John's Fuzzy Blanket* | 1963 |
| *Try Again, Sally!/Little Red Riding Hood* | 1970 |
| *Tweety* | 1953 |
| *Uncle Wiggily* | 1953 |

**How to determine Golden Tell-A-Tale Books:**

A row of letters at the bottom of the copyright page will designate a book's edition. Example: FGKIJ = sixth edition. If there are no letters, there are probably some Roman numerals. If there is an "A" before the Roman numeral date, your book is a first edition. If there is no "A," you can assume the book is a reprint.

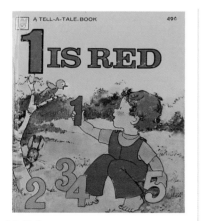

**1 Is Red**
Illustrator: Eugenie
Author: Daly, Eileen
2407-2          1974          **$2**

**1 to 10 Count Again**
Illustrator: Baker, Darrell
2471-47          1988          **$3**

**A B C**
Illustrator: Flory, Jane
896          1949          **$15**

A B C
Illustrator: Flory, Jane
896          1949          **$15**

A B C
Illustrator: Vartanian, Raymond
808          1952          **$12**

A B C
Illustrator: Nugent, Alys
2634         1956          **$10**

**A B C, A Tale of a Sale**
Illustrator: Heckler, William
Author: Hovelsrud, Joyce
2658         1963          **$4**

**Alonzo Purr the Seagoing Cat**
Illustrator: Hafner, Marylin
Author: Carey, Mary
2569         1966          **$6**

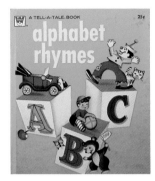

**Alphabet Rhymes**
Illustrator: Nugent, Alys
2430         1956          **$2**

**Amy's Long Night**
Illustrator: Wheeling, Lynn
Author: Carber, Nancy
2512         1970          **$7**

**And So to Bed**
Illustrator: Orville, Oliver
Author: Orville, Oliver
2462-46      1989          **$3**

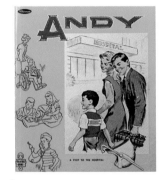

**Andy**
Illustrator: Hoecker, Hazel
Author: Michelson, Florence
2543         1966          **$5**

**Andy and Betsy at the Circus**
Illustrator: Friedel, Violet & Fred
Author: Friedel, Violet & Fred
906          1953          **$15**

**Animal A B C**
Illustrator: Harriett
887          1949          **$15**

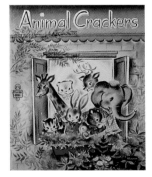

**Animal Crackers**
Illustrator: Peller, Jackie
Author: Georgiana
837          1949          **$20**

**Animal Jingles**
Illustrator: Peller, Jackie
Author: Georgiana
837        1951        **$20**

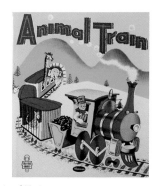

**Animal Train**
Illustrator: Williams, Ben D.
Author: Roberts, Elizabeth
2556        1969        **$7**

**Animals in Mother Goose**
Illustrator: Goldsborough, June
2474        1954        **$4**

**Around and About Buttercup Farm**
Illustrator: Miloche, Hilda; Kane, Wilma
Author: Lynn, Patricia
2524        1951        **$6**

**Baby Goes Around the Block**
Illustrator: Merkling, Erica
Author: Horn, Gladys M.
2493        1973        **$3**

**Baby Moses**
Illustrator: Frost, Bruno
Author: Trent, Robbie
917        1952        **$10**

**Baby's First Book**
Illustrator: Allen, Joan
Author: Swetnam, Evelyn
2422        1952        **$2**

**Barbie and Skipper Go Camping**
Author: Daly, Eileen
2489        1974        **$8**

**Barbie and Skipper Go Camping**
Author: Daly, Eileen
2489        1974        **$8**

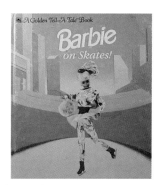

**Barbie On Skates!**
Illustrator: Tierney, Tom
Author: Balducci, Rita
2450-01        1992        **$3**

**Beany — Cecil Captured For the Zoo**
Illustrator: Bradbury, Jack; Wolfe, Gene
Author: Hammer, Barbara
2551        1954        **$25**

**Beany and His Magic Set**
Illustrator: Armstrong, Samuel; Eisenber, Harvey
Author: Clampett, Bob
904        1953        **$25**

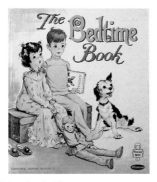

**Bedtime Book, The**
Illustrator: Winship, Florence Sarah
Author: Watts, Mabel
2475-32          1963                    **$3**

**Beloved Son, The**
Illustrator: Winship, Florence Sarah
Author: Watts, Mabel
2518          1963                    **$12**

**Beloved Son, The**
Illustrator: Frost, Bruno
Author: Wagstaff, Blanche Shoemaker
825          1951                    **$15**

**Beloved Son, The**
Illustrator: Winship, Florence Sarah
Author: Watts, Mabel
2518          1963                    **$12**

**Benjamine Brownie and the Talking Doll**
Illustrator: Stang, Judy
Author: Ross, Geraldine
2516          1962                    **$18**

**Benji the Detective**
Illustrator: Willis, Werner
Author: Lewis, Jean
2640          1970                    **$4**

**Benny the Bus**
Illustrator: Vaughan, Eillen Fox
Author: Horn, Gladys M.
846          1950                    **$15**

**Best Surprise of All, The**
Illustrator: D'Amato, Janet & Alex
Author: Pape, Donna Lugg
2521          1961                    **$5**

**Best Surprise of All, The**
Illustrator: D'Amato, Janet & Alex
Author: Pape, Donna Lugg
2601          1961                    **$4**

**Beware of the Dog**
Illustrator: Nagel, Stina
Author: Woyke, Christine
2553          1968                    **$4**

**Big and Little Are Not the Same**
Illustrator: Buckett, George
Author: Ottum, Bob
2474-33          1972                    **$2**

**Big Bark, The**
Illustrator: Nagel, Stina
Author: Woyke, Christine
2510          1968                    **$4**

**Big Bird Follows the Signs**
Illustrator: Delaney, A
Author: Kingsley, Emily Perl
2452-4        1980                    $2

**Big Game Hunter, The**
Illustrator: Read, Isobel
Author: Alexander, Florence Bibo
869          1947                   $12

**Big Game Hunter, The**
Illustrator: Read, Isobel
Author: Alexander, Florence Bibo
2507         1947                   $13

**Big Little Kitty**
Illustrator: Biggers, Jan D.
Author: Biggers, Jan D.
942          1953                   $18

**Big Little Kitty**
Illustrator: Biggers, Jan D.
Author: Biggers, Jan D.
2525         1953                   $15

**Big Red Pajama Wagon, The**
Illustrator: Anderson, Betty
Author: Elting, Mary
840          1949                   $15

**Big Whistle, The**
Illustrator: Myers, Louise
Author: Tompert, Ann
2522         1968                    $4

**Bill's Birthday Surprise**
Illustrator: Hoecker, Hazel
Author: Blair, Irene
966          1954                    $8

**Billy Bunnyscoot—The Lost Bunny**
Illustrator: Tedder, Elizabeth
Author: Smith, Georgia Tucker
888          1948                   $12

**Bingo**
Illustrator: Garris, Norma & Dan
Author: Hogstrom, Daphne
2560         1966                    $5

**Bingo**
Illustrator: Garris, Norma & Dan
Author: Hogstrom, Daphne
2576         1966                    $4

**Box of Important Things, The**
Illustrator: Bradfield, Roger
Author: Hellie, Anne
2510         1968                    $4

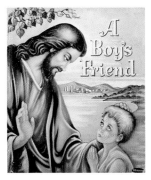

**Boy's Friend, A**
Illustrator: Weiniger, Egon
Author: Trent, Robbie
916        1952        **$10**

**Bozo the Clown: King of the Ring**
Illustrator: White, Al
2552        1960        **$8**

**Breezy the Air Minded Pigeon**
Illustrator: Grider, Dorothy
Author: Grider, Dorothy
870        1947        **$15**

**Bremen-Town Musicians, The**
Illustrator: Mikolaycak, Charles
Author: Zens, Patricia Martin
2610        1964        **$7**

**Brown Puppy and a Falling Star, A**
Illustrator: Winship, Florence Sarah
Author: Ross, Elizabeth
2560        1956        **$6**

**Buffy and the New Girl**
Illustrator: Mode, Nathalee
Author: Bond, Gladys Baker
2526        1969        **$12**

**Bugs Bunny Calling!**
Illustrator: Messerli, Joe
Author: Manuchkin, Fran
2453-48        1988        **$2**

**Bugs Bunny Hangs Around**
Illustrator: Abranz, Alfred; Mcgary, Norm
Author: Hoag, Nancy
2410        1957        **$8**

**Bugs Bunny in Something Fishy**
Illustrator: Abranz, Alfred; Mcgary, Norm
Author: Warner Bros. Cartoons, Inc.
2543        1956        **$8**

**Bugs Bunny Keeps a Promise**
Illustrator: Heimdahl, Ralph; Dempster, Al
2572        1951        **$8**

**Bugs Bunny Party Pest**
Illustrator: Anderson, Al; Mekimson, Thomas J.
Author: Johnston, William
2607        1976        **$2**

**Bugs Bunny Rides Again**
Illustrator: Messerli, Joe
2472-35        1986        **$2**

**Bugs Bunny's Big Invention**
Illustrator: Heimdahl, Ralph
Author: Warner Bros. Cartoons, Inc.
928          1969          **$8**

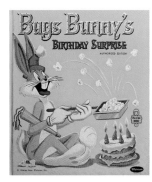

**Bugs Bunny's Birthday Surprise**
Illustrator: Abranza, Alfred; Thomas, Richard
Author: Theresa
2421          1951          **$8**

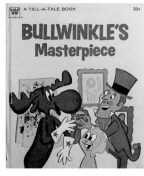

**Bullwinkle's Masterpiece**
Illustrator: Jason, Leon
Author: Lewis, Jean
2594          1976          **$12**

**Bunny Button**
Illustrator: Myers, Bernice
Author: Revena
2526          1953          **$4**

**Bunny Button**
Illustrator: Myers, Bernice
Author: Revena
923          1953          **$7**

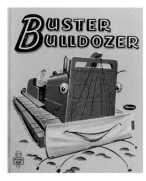

**Buster Bulldozer**
Illustrator: Stoddard, Maru Alice
Author: Danner, Catherine
2615          1952          **$5**

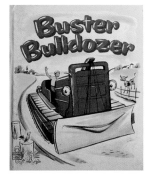

**Buster Bulldozer**
Illustrator: Stoddard, Maru Alice
Author: Danner, Catherine
834          1952          **$10**

**Busy Machines**
Illustrator: Walz, Richard
Author: Harrison, David
2473-42          1985          **$2**

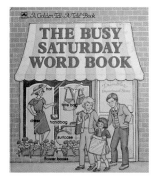

**Busy Saturday Word Book, The**
Illustrator: Dolce, Ellen
2474-42          1985          **$2**

**Butterfly! A Story of Magic**
Illustrator: Winship, Florence Sarah
Author: Daly, Eileen
2559          1969          **$4**

**Buzzy Beaver**
A Fuzzy Wuzzy Book
Illustrator: Hart, Dick
Author: Sankey, Alice
2575          1961          **$15**

**Captain Kangaroo and the Too-Small House**
Illustrator: Crawford, Mel
Author: Haas, Dorothy
2610          1958          **$8**

**Captain Kangaroo Tick Tock Trouble**
Illustrator: Frost, Bruno
Author: Jones, Mary Voell
2610      1961      **$8**

**Captain Kangaroo's Picnic**
Illustrator: Crawford, Mel
Author: Jones, Mary Voell
2547      1959      **$6**

**Chicken Little**
Illustrator: Hartwell, Marjorie
2450      1964      **$4**

**Child's Friend, A**
Illustrator: Weiniger, Egen
Author: Trent, Robbie
2519      1953      **$5**

**Child's Friend, A**
Illustrator: Weiniger, Egen
Author: Trent, Robbie
2519      1953      **$4**

**Child's Ten Commandments, A**
Illustrator: Murray, Marjorie
Author: Regan, Jo B
2624      1959      **$6**

**Child's Garden of Verses, A**
Illustrator: Ruhman, Ruth
Author: Stevenson, Robert Louis
2497      1964      **$6**

**Chitter Chatter**
Illustrator: Read, Isobel
Author: Read, Isobel
889      1948      **$15**

**Christmas Sled, The**
Illustrator: Super, Terri
Author: North, Carol
2487-1      1984      **$2**

**Christopher's Hoppy Day**
Illustrator: Winship, Florence Sarah
Author: Elliot, Edith F.
2601      1967      **$6**

**Christopher John's Fuzzy Blanket**
A Fuzzy Wuzzy Book
Illustrator: Winship, Florence Sarah
Author: Haas, Dorothy
2672      1959      **$15**

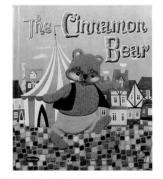

**Cinnamon Bear, The**
A Fuzzy Wuzzy Book
Illustrator: Bakacs, George
Author: Hanson, Alice
2674      1961      **$15**

**Circus Alphabet**
Illustrator: Hudson, Patric
2563          1954          **$4**

**Circus Alphabet ABC**
Illustrator: Hudson, Patric
2505          1959          **$6**

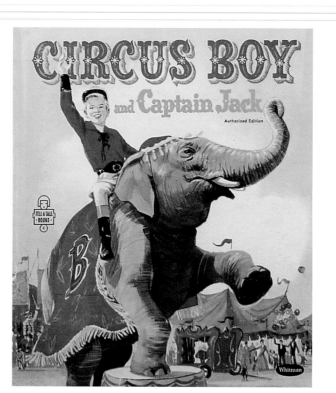

**Circus Boy and Captain Jack**
Illustrator: Boyle, Neil
Author: Snow, Dorothea J
2608          1957          **$18**

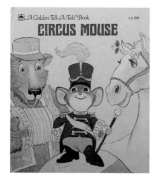

**Circus Mouse**
Illustrator: Horne, Daniel R.
Author: McGuire, Leslie
2466-40          1987          **$3**

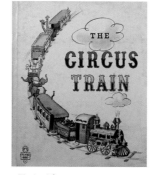

**Circus Train, The**
Illustrator: Dorcas
Author: Knittle, Jessie M.
890          1948          **$16**

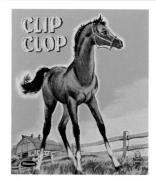

**Clip Clop**
Illustrator: Winship, Florence Sarah
Author: Hoag, Nancy
2492          1958          **$10**

**Columbus, the Exploring Burro**
Illustrator: Koering, Ursula
Author: Brewster, Benjamin
826          1951          **$6**

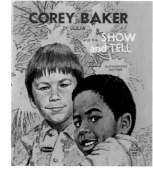

**Corey Baker of Julia and His Show and Tell**
Illustrator: Harris, Larry
Author: Bond, Gladys Baker
2506          1970          **$8**

Count's Poem, The
Illustrator: Cooke, Tom
Author: Sipherd, Ray
2402          1978          **$2**

**Cousin Matilda and the Foolish Wolf**
Illustrator: Osborn, Richard
Author: Cole, Joanna
2530        1970        **$4**

**Cradle Rhymes**
Illustrator: Rachel
Author: Horn, Gladys M.
894        1949        **$18**

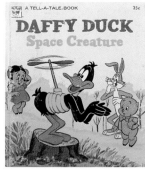

**Daffy Duck Space Creature**
Illustrator: Baker, Darrell
Author: Ingoglia, Gina
2621        1977        **$4**

**Daktari—Judy and the Kitten**
Illustrator: Harris, Larry
Author: Fiedler, Jean
2506        1965        **$7**

**Dale Evans and Buttermilk**
Illustrator: Wegner, Helmuth G.
Author: Welden, Rose
2570        1956        **$25**

**Dally**
Illustrator: Clement, Charles
Author: Julian, Lee
802        1951        **$13**

**Daniel's New Friend**
Illustrator: Wilde, Irma
Author: Bach, Hilda
2433        1968        **$3**

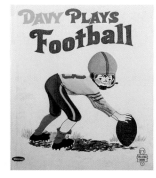

**Davy Plays Football**
Illustrator: Wilde, Carol
Author: Peake, Sylvia
2512        1968        **$5**

**Davy's Wiggly Tooth**
Illustrator: Winship, Florence Sarah
Author: Borden, Marion
2513        1964        **$4**

**Day You Were Born, The**
Illustrator: Wood, Muriel
Author: Swetnam, Evelyn
2524        1972        **$2**

**Dennis the Menace Takes the Cake**
Illustrator: Matchette, Karen
Author: Namm, Diane
2451-4        1955        **$4**

**Diddle Daddle Duckling**
Illustrator: Goldsborough, June
Author: Bennett, Grace Irene
2538        1971        **$3**

**Digger Dan**
Illustrator: Frankel, Simon
Author: Lynn, Patricia
908          1953          **$20**

**Digger Dan**
Illustrator: Frankel, Simon
Author: Lynn, Patricia
2615          1953          **$15**

**Digger Dan**
Illustrator: Frankel, Simon
Author: Lynn, Patricia
2544          1953          **$6**

**Dipsy Donkey**
Illustrator: Laurence, Johnny
Author: Laurence, Johnny
882          1948          **$15**

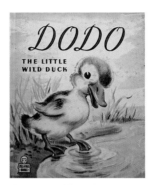

**Dodo the Little Wild Duck**
Illustrator: Grider, Dorothy
Author: Scheinert, Carlton A.
891          1948          **$15**

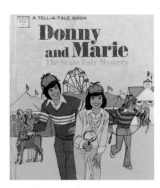

**Donny and Marie, The State Fair Mystery**
Illustrator: Giacomini, Olinda
Author: Daly, Eileen
2635          1977          **$5**

**Dr. Goat**
Illustrator: Clement, Charles
Author: Georgiana
841          1950          **$100**

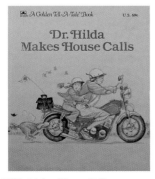

**Dr. Hilda Makes House Calls**
Illustrator: Petruccio, Steven
Author: Watts, Mabel
2463          1988          **$3**

**Dr. Goat**
Illustrator: Clement, Charles
Author: Georgiana
841          1950          **$80**

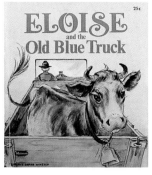

**Eloise and the Old Blue Truck**
Illustrator: Winship, Florence Sarah
Author: Graham, Kennon
2454          1971          **$7**

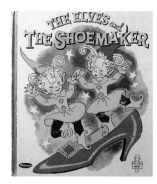

**Elves and the Shoemaker, The**
Illustrator: Miloche, Hilda
2496          1958          **$6**

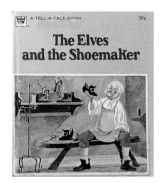

**Elves and the Shoemaker, The**
Illustrator: Robison, Jim
2561          1973          **$3**

**Ernie the Cave King and Sherlock the Smart Person in the Invention of Paper**
Illustrator: Children's Television Workshop
Author: Wilcox, Daniel
2604          1975          **$2**

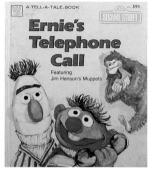

**Ernie's Telephone Call**
Illustrator: Duga, Irra
Author: Sipherd, Ray
2452-34          1978          **$2**

**Especially From Thomas**
Illustrator: Ker, Edith M. Photos By Duesseldorf
Author: Haas, Dorothy
2527          1965          **$6**

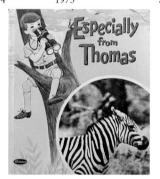

**Especially From Thomas**
Illustrator: Ker, Edith M. Photos by Duesseldorf
Author: Haas, Dorothy
2543          1965          **$6**

**Evening Walk, The**
Illustrator: Durrell, Julie
Author: Ryder, Joanne
2462-43          1985          **$2**

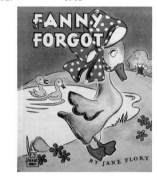

**Fanny Forgot**
Illustrator: Flory, Jane
Author: Flory, Jane
862          1946          **$15**

**Farm A B C**
Illustrator: Michell, Gladys Turlry
Author: Lynn, Patricia
2468          1978          **$3**

**Farm Animals**
Illustrator: Krupp, Marion
Author: Relf, Patricia
2464-50          1992          **$2**

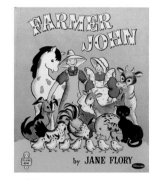

**Farmer John**
Illustrator: Flory, Jane
Author: Flory, Jane
838          1950          **$15**

**Fat Albert and the Cosby Kids
Getting It Together**
Illustrator: Hazelton, Herbert; Willoughby, Jim
Author: French, Laura
2598          1975          **$12**

**Fire Dog**
Illustrator: Clement, Charles
Author: Julian, Lee
2412          1960          **$8**

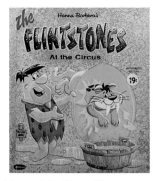

**Flintstones at the Circus, The**
Illustrator: McSavage, Frank; Heiner, Robert
Author: Lewis, Jean
2552          1963          **$15**

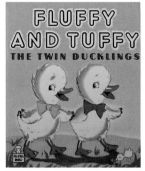

**Fluffy and Tuffy the Twin Ducklings**
Illustrator: McKean, Emma C
Author: McKean, Emma C
872          1947          **$15**

**Flying Sunbeam, The**
Illustrator: Anderson, Betty
Author: Fairbairn, D. N.
820          1950          **$16**

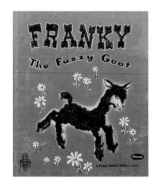

**Franky the Fuzzy Goat**
Illustrator: Suzanne
Author: Horn, Gladys M.
820          1951          **$15**

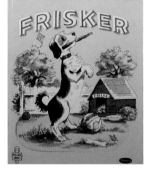

**Frisker**
Illustrator: Shortall, Leonard
Author: Nowak, Mary Lauer
2660          1956          **$6**

**Funny Company**
Illustrator: Fletcher, James
Author: Patrick, Lenore
2567          1965          **$14**

**Funny Friends in Mother Goose Land**
Illustrator: Ford, Pam
2647          1978          **$2**

**Fury**
Illustrator: Bartram, Bob
Author: Haas, Dorothy
2611          1958          **$15**

**Fuzzy Dan**
Illustrator: Biers, Clarence
Author: Whitehead, Jane
821          1951          **$16**

**Fuzzy Duckling**
Illustrator: Banigan, Sharon
912          1952          **$15**

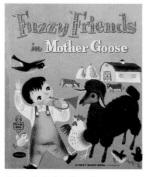

**Fuzzy Friends in Mother Goose**
Illustrator: Cunningham, Dellwyn
914          1952          **$15**

**Fuzzy Joe Bear**
Illustrator: Berry, Anne
Author: Horn, Gladys M.
954          1954          **$15**

**Fuzzy Mittens For Three Little Kittens**
Illustrator: Laqueur, Alys
823          1951          **$15**

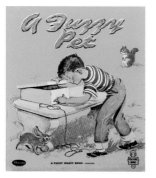

**Fuzzy Pet, A**
Illustrator: Hartwell, Marjorie
Author: Hanson, Alice
2671         1960          **$15**

**Fuzzy Wuzzy Puppy**
Illustrator: Suzanne
Author: Winship, Florence Sarah
915          1954          **$15**

**Gene Autry Makes a New Friend**
Illustrator: Case, Richard
Author: Beecher, Elizabeth
800          1952          **$22**

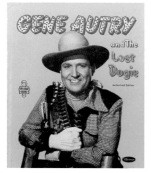

**Gene Autry and the Lost Dogie**
Illustrator: Armstrong, Samuel
932          1953          **$22**

**Gene Autry Goes to the Circus**
Illustrator: Ushler, John
2566         1950          **$22**

**Gentle Ben and the Pesky Puppy**
Illustrator: Harris, Larry
Author: Fiedler, Jean
2552         1969          **$7**

**Getting Ready For Roddy**
Illustrator: Helwig, Hans
Author: Lynn, Patricia
2530         1955          **$8**

**Gingerbread Man, The**
Illustrator: Lesko, Zillah
939          1953          **$12**

**Gingerbread Man, The**
Illustrator: Sari
2504         1958          **$8**

**Gingerbread Man, The**
Illustrator: Mars, W. T.
Author: Zens, Patricia Martin
1581          1963          **$6**

**Gingerbread Man, The**
Illustrator: Giacomini, Olindo
Author: Sukus, Jan
1581          1969          **$5**

**Ginghams, The—The Ice-Cream Parade**
Illustrator: Land, Kate
Author: Bowden, Joan Chase
2619          1976          **$3**

**Goby Goat and the Birthday Gift**
Illustrator: Rutherford, Bonnie & Bill
Author: Russell, Solveig Paulson
2595          1975          **$2**

**Good Night, A Flocked Book**
Illustrator: Paflín, Roberta
Author: Burrowes, Elizabeth
955          1954          **$15**

**Goodnight Book, The**
Illustrator: Karch, Pat & Paul
Author: Well, Lynn & Mandy
2487          1969          **$10**

**Goofy and His Wonderful Cornet**
Illustrator: Alvarado, Peter; Lorencz, William
Author: Brightman, Homer
2477          1973          **$4**

**Grandpa's House**
Illustrator: Stang, Judy
Author: Wright, Betty Ren
2670          1969          **$15**

**Grandpa's Policemen Friends**
Illustrator: Winship, Florence Sarah
Author: Frankel, Bernice
2665          1967          **$4**

**Great Fort, The**
Illustrator: Oechsli, Kelly
Author: Garber, Nancy
2564          1970          **$3**

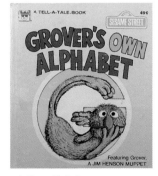

**Grover's Own Alphabet**
Illustrator: Murdocca, Sal
2402-6          1978          **$2**

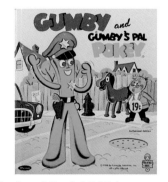

**Gumby and Gumby's Pal Pokey**
Illustrator: DeSantis, George
Author: Biesterveld, Betty
2506          1968          **$15**

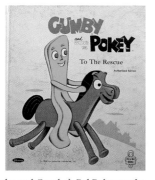

**Gumby and Gumby's Pal Pokey to the Rescue**
Illustrator: DeSantis, George
Author: Lewis, Jean
2552          1969          **$15**

**H.R. Pufnstuf**
Illustrator: Moore, Sparky; Totten, Bob
Author: Lewis, Jean
2624          1970          **$15**

**Handy Andy**
Illustrator: Dreany, E. Joseph
Author: Lynn, Patricia
919          1953          **$8**

**Handy Andy**
Illustrator: Dreany, E. Joseph
Author: Lynn, Patricia
2584          1953          **$6**

**Happiest Christmas, The**
Illustrator: Wilde, Richard
Author: Fairweather, Jessie Home
2482          1950          **$15**

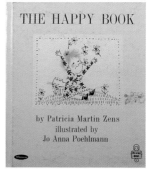

**Happiest Christmas, The**
Illustrator: Wilde, Richard
Author: Fairweather, Jessie Home
2516          1950          **$6**

**Happiest Christmas, The**
Illustrator: Wilde, Richard
Author: Fairweather, Jessie Home
2482          1950          **$10**

**Happy**
Illustrator: Garris, Norma & Dan
Author: Bordon, Marion
2631          1964          **$4**

**Happy Book, The**
Illustrator: Poehlmann, Jo Anna
Author: Zens, Patricia Martin
2555          1965          **$3**

**Have You Seen a Giraffe Hat?**
Illustrator: Storms, Robert
Author: Joyce, Irma
2535          1969          **$4**

**Hello, Joe**
Illustrator: Corrigan, Barbara
Author: Stempel, Ruth
2510          1961          **$6**

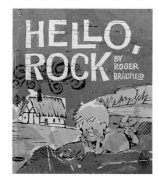

**Hello, Rock**
Illustrator: Bradfield, Roger
Author: Bradfield, Roger
2616          1965          **$30**

**Henrietta and the Hat**
Illustrator: Schweninger, Ann
Author: Watts, Mabel
2472-42          1985          **$2**

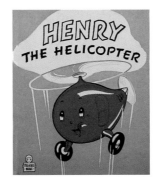

**Henry the Helicopter**
Previously: Little Henry
Illustrator: Williams, Ben D.
Author: Graham, Eleanor
855          1945          **$15**

**Hey There—It's Yogi Bear!**
Illustrator: McSavage, Frank; Young,
Harland
Author: Daly, Eileen
2602          1964          **$12**

**Hi! Cowboy**
Illustrator: Williams, Ben D.
Author: Horn, Gladys M.
847          1950          **$15**

**Hide-Away Henry**
Illustrator: Biers, Clarence
Author: Sankey, Alice
938          1953          **$8**

**Hide-Away Henry**
Illustrator: Biers, Clarence
Author: Sankey, Alice
2601          1953          **$4**

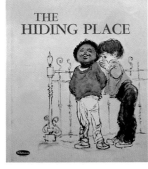

**Hiding Place, The**
Illustrator: O'Sullivan, Tom
Author: Meek, Pauline Palmer
2553          1971          **$4**

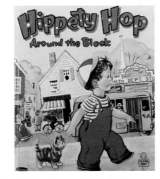

**Hippety Hop Around the Block**
Illustrator: Dorcas
Author: Horn, Gladys M.
924          1953          **$8**

**Ho-Hum**
Illustrator: Myers, Jack & Louise
Author: Lynn, Patricia
2510          1957          **$6**

**Ho-Hum**
Illustrator: Myers, Jack & Louise
Author: Lynn, Patricia
2543          1957          **$12**

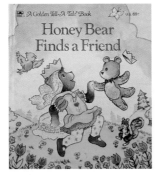

**Honey Bear Finds a Friend**
Illustrator: Orville, Oliver
Author: Pepper, Alice
2466-46          1990          **$2**

**Hooray For Lassie!**
Illustrator: Marshall, Carol
Author: Borden, Marion
2503          1964          **$6**

**Hop, Skippy and Jump**
Illustrator: Vivienne
Author: Vivienne
866          1947          **$15**

**Hoppity Hooper Vs Skippity Snooper**
Illustrator: DeSantis, George
Author: Lewis, Jean
2552          1966          **$12**

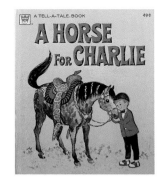

**Horse For Charlie, A**
Illustrator: Elfrieda
Author: Tompert, Ann
2411-1          1970          **$3**

**House My Grandpa Built, The**
Illustrator: Rutherford, Bonnie & Bill
Author: Gohn, Geraldine Everett
2530          1971          **$3**

**House That Jack Built, The**
Illustrator: Suzanne
2480          1961          **$4**

**How Big Is a Baby?**
Illustrator: Garris, Norma & Dan
Author: Holmgren, Virginia C.
2601          1966          **$4**

**How Big Is a Baby?**
Illustrator: Garris, Norma & Dan
Author: Holmgren, Virginia C.
2555          1966          **$4**

**How Can We Get to the Zoo?**
Illustrator: Rutherford, Bonnie & Bill
Author: Joyce, Irma
2660          1966          **$2**

**How Does Your Garden Grow?**
Illustrator: Goldsborough, June
Author: Benton, William & Elizabeth
2521          1969          **$4**

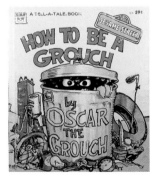

**How to Be a Grouch**
Illustrator: Bathman, Ed
Author: Spinney, Carol
2618          1976          **$2**

**Howdy Doody and the Magic Lamp**
Illustrator: Crawford, Mel
Author: Coppersmith, Jerry
944          1954          **$22**

**Howdy Doody and the Monkey Tale**
902          1953          **$25**

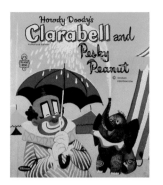

**Howdy Doody's Clarabell and Pesky Peanut**
Illustrator: Kagran Corporation
Author: Kagran Corporation
934          1953          **$20**

**Howdy Doody's Clarabell Clown and the Merry-Go-Round**
Illustrator: Crawford, Mel
Author: Barron, John
2558          1955          **$20**

**Huckleberry Hound, The Rainmaker**
Illustrator: Daly, Eileen
Author: Fletcher, Jim
2611          1963          **$18**

**Huffin Puff Express, The**
Illustrator: Seiden, Art
Author: Harrison, David, L.
2421-2          1974          **$7**

**Hullabaloo**
Illustrator: Weber, Nettie
Author: Georgiana
815          1951          **$12**

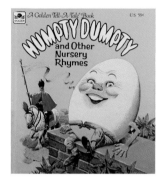

**Humpty Dumpty and Other Nursery Rhymes**
Illustrator: Ruth, Rod
2610          1976          **$3**

**Hungry Lion, The**
Illustrator: Stang, Judy
Author: Fletcher, Steffi
2659          1960          **$7**

**Hurry, Scurry**
Illustrator: Tomes, Jackie
Author: Putnam, Nina; Williams, Gretchen
2616          1963          **$3**

**I Know What a Farm Is**
Illustrator: Crawford, Mel
Author: Fiedler, Jean
2527          1969          **$3**

**I Like the Farm**
Illustrator: Depper, Hertha
Author: Wolf, Nancy Hoag
2522          1961          **$3**

**I Like to Be Little**
Illustrator: Mill, Eleanor
Author: Matthews, Ann
2615          1976          **$2**

**I Like to See: A Book About the Five Senses**
Illustrator: Goldsborough, June
Author: Tymms, Jean
2443          1973          **$2**

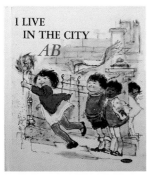

**I Live in the City A B C**
Illustrator: O'Sullivan, Tom
Author: Moore, Lou
2554          1969          **$3**

**I Love My Grandma**
Illustrator: Wilson, Dagmar
Author: Hoag, Florence Jenkins
2671          1960          **$12**

**I Play in the Snow**
Illustrator: Rutherford, Bonnie & Bill
Author: Pape, Donna Lugg
2510          1967          **$4**

**I Walk to the Park**
Illustrator: Nagel, Stina
Author: Schwalj, Marjory
2616          1966          **$4**

**I'm Not Sleepy**
Illustrator: Beylon, Cathy
Author: Ryder, Joanne
2462-42          1986          **$2**

**In Baby's House**
Illustrator: Sherwood, Stewart
Author: Swetnam, Evelyn
2415          1974          **$3**

**In, On, Under, and Through**
Illustrator: Nagel, Stina
Author: Elwart, Joan Potter
2666          1965          **$4**

**Jack and the Beanstalk**
Illustrator: Walz, Richard
Author: Balducci ,Rita
2461-51          1992          **$2**

**Jasper Giraffe**
Illustrator: Myers, Louise W.
Author: Ferrell, Polly
898          1949          **$18**

**Jasper Giraffe**
Illustrator: Myers, Louise W.
Author: Ferrell, Polly
898          1949          **$15**

**Jean Ellen Learns to Swim**
Illustrator: Wilde, Carol
Author: Swetnam, Evelyn
2508          1970          **$3**

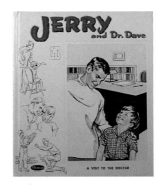

**Jerry and Dr. Dave**
Illustrator: Nankivel, Claudine
Author: Bordon, Marion
2601          1964          **$4**

**Jim Jump**
Illustrator: Banigan, Sharon
Author: Wright, Betty Ren
2527          1954          **$10**

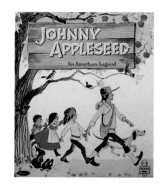

**Johnny Appleseed**
Illustrator: Elfreda
Author: Russell, Solveig Paulson
2679          1967          **$4**

**Johnny Go Round**
Illustrator: Walz, Richard
Author: Wright, Betty Ren
2525          1960          **$12**

**Jolly Jingles**
Illustrator: Williams, Ben
Author: Alexander, Florence Bibo
899          1959          **$14**

**Jumpy, Humpy, Fuzzy, Buzzy Animal Book, The**
Illustrator: Stone, David K.
Author: Davis, Douglas
2488          1974          **$4**

**Katy's First Day**
Illustrator: Aliki
Author: Soule, Jean Conder
2512          1972          **$4**

**Kobo the Koala Bear**
Illustrator: Sampson, Katherine
Author: Schwaljé, Marjory
2521          1968          **$5**

**Lambikin, The**
Illustrator: Myers, Jack & Louise
Author: Hansen, Helen S.
2617          1962          **$8**

**Land of the Lost, The Dinosaur Adventure**
Illustrator: Purtle, John
Author: Godfry, Jane
2607          1975          **$5**

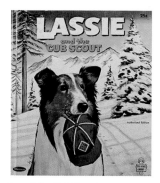

**Lassie and the Cub Scout**
Illustrator: Anderson, Al
Author: Michelson, Florence
2503          1966          **$8**

**Lassie and the Fire Fighters**
Illustrator: Harris, Larry
Author: Michelson, Florence
2462          1968          **$6**

**Lassie and the Kittens**
Illustrator: Grant, Ena Klenetti
2503          1956          **$8**

**Lassie Finds a Friend**
Illustrator: Anderson, Al
Author: Thresa
2406          1960                    **$6**

**Lassie, The Busy Morning**
Illustrator: Harris, Larry
Author: Lewis, Jean
2412-2        1973                    **$4**

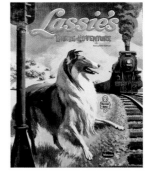

**Lassie's Brave Adventure**
Illustrator: Bartram, Bob
2571          1958                    **$10**

**Lazy Fox and Red Hen**
Illustrator: Suzanne
2485          1957                    **$5**

**Lazy Fox and Red Hen**
Illustrator: Hauge, Carl & Mary
Author: Dwyer, Jane
2603          1969                    **$2**

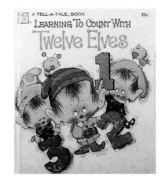

**Learning to Count With Twelve Elves**
Illustrator: Giordano, Joe
Author: Wylie, Joanne
2555          1972                    **$2**

**Let Me See**
Illustrator: Stang, Judy
Author: Hilt, Mary L.
2615          1963                    **$5**

**Let's Count All the Animals!**
Illustrator: Wickart, Terry
Author: Lulas, Jim E.
2407-4        1979                    **$2**

**Let's Play**
Illustrator: Gavy
Author: Georgiana
907           1952                    **$10**

**Let's Play**
Illustrator: Gavy
Author: Georgiana
2601          1952                    **$6**

**Let's Visit the Farm**
Illustrator: Keyser, Evelyn
Author: Cunningham, Virginia
876           1948                    **$15**

**Linus, A Smile For Grouse**
Illustrator: Carleton, James F.
Author: Patrick, Lenore
2567          1966                    **$15**

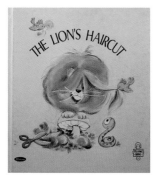

**Lion's Haircut, The**
Illustrator: Eugenie
Author: Giddings, Jennifer
2519          1969          **$5**

**Little Bear and the Beautiful Kite**
Illustrator: Depper, Hertha
Author: Udry, Janice
2548          1955          **$6**

**Little Bear and the Beautiful Kite**
Illustrator: Depper, Hertha
Author: Udry, Janice
2559          1955          **$6**

**Little Beaver**
Author: Beecher, Elizabeth
935          1954          **$15**

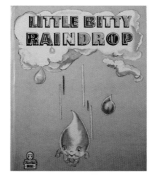

**Little Bitty Raindrop**
Illustrator: Hanson, Marguerite
Author: Usher, Peggy
875          1948          **$17**

**Little Bitty Raindrop**
Illustrator: Hanson, Marguerite
Author: Usher, Peggy
875          1948          **$17**

**Little Black Sambo**
Illustrator: Suzanne
812          1950          **$50**

**Little Black Sambo**
Illustrator: Michell, Gladys Turley
2661          1953          **$42**

**Little Black Sambo**
Illustrator: Lamont, Violet
2661          1959          **$25**

**Little Black Sambo**
Illustrator: Lamont, Violet
2661          1959          **$30**

**Little Boy in the Forest, The**
Illustrator: Osborne, Richard N.
Author: Harrison, David
2553          1969          **$4**

**Little Caboose, The**
Illustrator: Flory, Jane
Author: O'Hearn, Nila
817          1951          **$15**

**Little Chuff Chuff and Big Streamliner**
Illustrator: Barr, Catherine
Author: Barr Jr., Robert
843          1950          **$15**

**Little Folks in Mother Goose**
Illustrator: Rachel
863          1946          **$15**

**Little Gray Rabbit**
Illustrator: Cauley, Lorinda Bryan
Author: Bowden, Joan Chase
2651          1979          **$2**

**Little Hank**
Illustrator: Williams, Ben
Author: Sankey, Alice
883          1948          **$15**

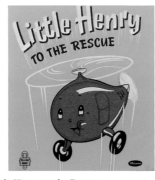

**Little Henry to the Rescue**
Illustrator: Williams, Ben D.
Author: Graham, Eleanor
2604          1945          **$15**

**Little Joe's Puppy**
Illustrator: Winship, Florence Sarah
Author: Haas, Dorothy
2560          1957          **$12**

**Little Lulu and the Birthday Mystery**
Illustrator: Baker, Darrell; Jason Studios
Author: Drake, Arnold
2502          1974          **$8**

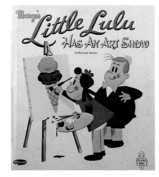

**Little Lulu Has an Art Show**
Illustrator: Buell, Marjorie Henderson
Author: Buell, Marjorie Henderson
2622          1964          **$10**

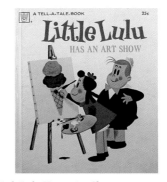

**Little Lulu Has an Art Show**
Illustrator: Buell, Marjorie Henderson
Author: Buell, Marjorie Henderson
2622          1964          **$6**

**Little Lulu—Lucky Landlady!**
2437　　　　1960　　　　**$8**

**Little Lulu Uses Her Head**
Illustrator: Buell, Marjorie Henderson
Author: Buell, Marjorie Henderson
2552　　　　1955　　　　**$17**

**Little Miss Muffet and Other Nursery Rhymes**
Illustrator: Wallace, Lucille
2483　　　　1958　　　　**$3**

**Little Pony, The**
Illustrator: Hartwell, Marjorie
Author: Hawley, Mary Alice
806　　　　1952　　　　**$5**

**Little Red Bicycle, The**
Illustrator: King, Dorothy Urfer
Author: King, Dorothy Urfer
922　　　　1953　　　　**$6**

**Little Red Bicycle, The**
Illustrator: King, Dorothy Urfer
Author: King, Dorothy Urfer
2543　　　　1953　　　　**$5**

**Little Red Bicycle, The**
Illustrator: King, Dorothy Urfer
Author: King, Dorothy Urfer
2508　　　　1953　　　　**$4**

**Little Red Hen**
Illustrator: Wilson, Beth
930　　　　1953　　　　**$6**

**Little Red Riding Hood**
Illustrator: Dolce, Ellen J.
2461-44　　　　1989　　　　**$2**

**Little Red Riding Hood**
Illustrator: Dettmer, Mary Lou
2507　　　　1971　　　　**$2**

**Little Red Riding Hood**
Illustrator: Lesko, Zillah
2606　　　　1957　　　　**$10**

**Little Red Riding Hood**
Illustrator: Depper, Hertha
2651　　　　1959　　　　**$4**

**Little Red Riding Hood**
Illustrator: Stella
937             1953        **$8**

**Little Red Riding Hood**
Illustrator: Goldsborough, June
2507          1964        **$3**

**Little Red Riding Hood**
A Fuzzy Wuzzy Book
Illustrator: Carroll, Nancy
2670          1960        **$15**

**Little Tweet**
Illustrator: Gehr, Mary
Author: Holloway, Charles W.
814            1951        **$15**

**Lone Ranger and the Ghost Horse, The**
Illustrator: Totten, Bob
Author: Sankey, Alice
2561          1955        **$20**

**Lone Ranger Desert Storm, The**
Illustrator: Wenzel, Paul
Author: Revena
2622          1957        **$18**

**Longest Birthday, The**
Illustrator: Leiner, Alan
Author: Garber, nancy
2418-1        1975        **$2**

**Look For Boats**
Illustrator: Nez, John
Author: Bell, Sally
2473-46      1991        **$2**

**Look For Trucks!**
Illustrator: LaPadu La, Thomas
Author: Weiner, Gina (Ingoglia)
2473-25      1989        **$2**

**Loopy de Loop Odd Jobber**
Illustrator: Frost, Bruno
Author: Hagen, Patrick
2611          1964        **$16**

**Lucky Four Leaf Clover**
Illustrator: Peller, Jackie
Author: Antonie, Rosalind Lane
893            1949        **$12**

**Maggie to the Rescue**
Illustrator: Hunt, Judith
Author: Hill, Ari
2476-39      1986        **$2**

Magic Clothes Basket, The
Illustrator: Rutherford, Bonnie & Bill
Author: Thomas, Sharon
2544          1969          $4

Magic Zoo, The
Illustrator: Wylie, Joanne
Author: Mowers, Patricia
2565          1972          $3

Magilla Gorilla Takes a Banana Holiday
Illustrator: Jason Studios
Author: Johnston, William
2552          1965          $15

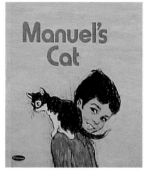

Manuel's Cat
Illustrator: Stone, David K.
Author: Fein, Dorothy A.
2521          1971          $6

Marvelous Monster, The
Illustrator: Ruth, Rod
Author: Joyce, Carolyn
2632          1977          $3

Mary Poppins
Illustrator: Neely, Jan
Author: Brightman, Homer
2606          1964          $8

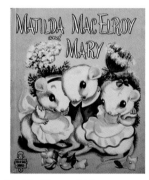

Matilda MacElroy and Mary
Illustrator: Robison, I. E.
Author: Fairweather, Jessie Home
836          1950          $15

Me Too!
Illustrator: Zemsky, Jessica
Author: Nathan, Stella Williams
2616          1962          $6

Merton and His Moving Van
Illustrator: Seiden, Art
Author: Watts, Mabel
2633          1970          $2

Mimi the Merry-Go-Round Cat
Illustrator: Winship, Florence Sarah
Author: Haas, Dorothy
2467          1958          $7

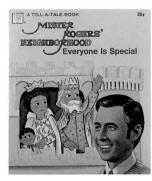

Mister Rogers' Neighborhood, Everyone
Is Special
Illustrator: Jason Art Studio
Author: Rogers, Fred M.
2599          1975          $4

Monsters Come in Many Colors!
Illustrator: McLean, Sammis
Author: Stevenson, Joyce
2452-39          1980          $3

**More the Merrier, The**
Illustrator: Magagna, Anna Marie
Author: Michelson, Florence
2523          1964          **$4**

**Mother Goose**
Illustrator: Scott, Marguerite K.
2417          1960          **$6**

**Mother Goose**
Illustrator: Wallace, Lucille
2511          1958          **$8**

**Mother Goose**
Illustrator: Clement, Charles
2511          1955          **$12**

**Mother Goose**
Illustrator: Vaughan, Eillen Fox
925          1950          **$15**

**Mother Goose**
Illustrator: Lesko, Zillah
2511          1961          **$10**

**Mother Goose On the Farm**
Illustrator: Aitken, Amy
2464-44          1989          **$3**

**Mother Goose On the Farm**
Illustrator: Goldsborough, June
2587          1975          **$3**

**Mother Goose Rhymes**
Illustrator: Nez, John
2464-36          1985          **$3**

**Mr. Grabbit**
Illustrator: Charlie
Author: Hoff, Virginia
2526          1952          **$16**

**Mr. Grabbit**
Illustrator: Charlie
Author: Hoff, Virginia
816          1952          **$20**

**Mr. Jolly**
Illustrator: Spicer, Jesse
Author: Mathison, Jane
868          1948          **$15**

**Mr. Moggs' Dogs**
A Fuzzy Wuzzy Book
Illustrator: Frankel, Si
Author: Revena
958          1954          **$15**

**Mushmouse and Punkin Puss, The Country Cousins**
Illustrator: Alvarado, Peter; Jacobs, Raymond
Author: Freman, Jay
2552          1964          **$18**

**My Little A B C**
Illustrator: Ericksen, Barbara
Author: Vogels, Mary Prescott
2536          1971          **$2**

**My Little Book About Flying**
Illustrator: Irvin, Fred
Author: Graham, Kennon
2414-4          1978          **$2**

**My Little Book About Our Flag**
Illustrator: Karch, Pat & Paul
Author: Mrowski, Jan
2578          1975          **$2**

**My Little Book of Big Animals**
Illustrator: Burridge, Marge Opitz
Author: Kulas, Jim E.
2466-4          1978          **$2**

**My Little Book of Big Machines**
Illustrator: Anderson, Al
Author: Ottum, Bob
2589          1975          **$3**

**My Little Book of Birds**
Illustrator: Solomon, Rosiland
Author: Ingoglia, Gina
2475-50          1991          **$2**

**My Little Book of Birds**
Illustrator: Dunnington, Tom
Author: Ray, Ora
2490          1973          **$2**

**My Little Book of Boats**
Illustrator: Dunnington, Tom
Author: Hanrahan, Mariellen
247332          1974          **$2**

**My Little Book of Bugs**
Illustrator: Solomon, Rosiland
Author: Silverman, Maida
24750          1993          **$2**

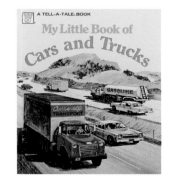

**My Little Book of Cars and Trucks**
Illustrator: Korta, Bob
Author: Graham, Kennon
2473          1974          **$2**

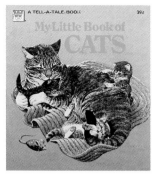

**My Little Book of Cats**
Illustrator: Ruth, Rod
Author: Greiner, N. Gretchen
2626        1976        **$2**

**My Little Book of Dinosaurs**
Illustrator: Ruth, Rod
Author: Daly, Eileen
2482        1972        **$2**

**My Little Book of Dogs**
Illustrator: Stone, David K.
Author: Draper, Delores
2476-93        1976        **$2**

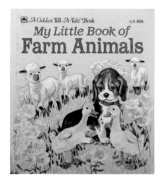

**My Little Book of Farm Animals**
Illustrator: Hauge, Carl & Mary
Author: Hogstrom, Daphne
2559        1972        **$3**

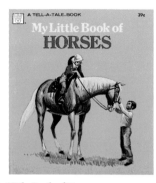

**My Little Book of Horses**
Illustrator: Dunnington, Tom
Author: Walrath, Jane Dwyer
2537        1974        **$2**

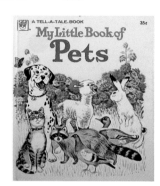

**My Little Book of Pets**
Illustrator: Hauge, Carl & Mary
Author: Sukus, Jan
2401        1972        **$2**

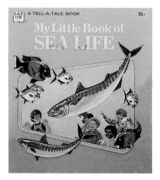

**My Little Book of Sea Life**
Illustrator: Ruth, Rod
Author: Michener, Lucille
2602        1976        **$2**

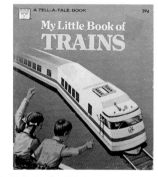

**My Little Book of Trains**
Illustrator: Seward, James
Author: Manrahan, Mariellen
2643        1978        **$2**

**My Little Counting Book**
Illustrator: Ruhman, Ruth
Author: Yerian, Margaret
2407-3        1967        **$2**

**Nancy and Sluggo, The Big Surprise**
Illustrator: Nofziger, Edward; Totten, Robert
Author: Lewis, Jean
2525        1974        **$8**

**Nibbler**
Illustrator: Winship, Florence Sarah
Author: Watts, Mabel
2538        1973        **$5**

**Night Before Christmas**
Illustrator: Newton, Ruth E.
Author: Moore, Clement C.
839        1937        **$18**

**Night Before Christmas, The**
Illustrator: Lesko, Zillah
Author: Moore, Clement C.
839          1953          **$10**

**Night Before Christmas, The**
Illustrator: Lesko, Zillah
Author: Moore, Clement C.
2517          1953          **$10**

**Night Before Christmas, The**
Illustrator: Munshi, Carol
Author: Moore, Clement C.
2517          1963          **$6**

**Night Before Christmas, The**
Illustrator: Winship, Florence Sarah
Author: Moore, Clement C.
2517          1969          **$6**

**Night Before Christmas, The**
Illustrator: Winship, Florence Sarah
Author: Moore, Clement C.
2517          1969          **$6**

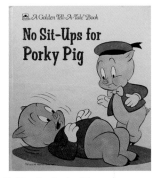

**No Sit-Ups for Porky Pig**
Illustrator: Messerli, Joe
Author: Ingolia, Gina
2453-46          1985          **$2**

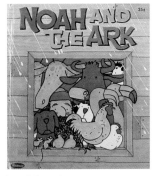

**Noah and the Ark**
Illustrator: Gray, Leslie
Author: Ramsay, Devere
2558          1967          **$5**

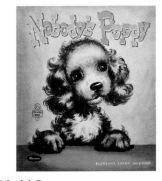

**Nobody's Puppy**
Illustrator: Winship, Florence Sarah
Author: Lynn, Patricia
920          1953          **$6**

**Not Quite Three**
Illustrator: Castagnoli, Martha
Author: Wolf, Helen
962          1954          **$7**

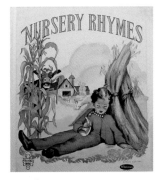

**Nursery Rhymes**
Illustrator: Altson, Louise
857          1945          **$8**

**Oh, Look!**
Illustrator: Myers, Jack & Louise
Author: Haas, Dorothy
2672          1961          **$10**

**Old MacDonald Had a Farm**
Illustrator: Hauge, Carl & Mary
2589          1975          **$3**

**Old Woman and Her Pig, The**
Illustrator: Mars, W. T.
2610          1964          **$4**

**Once I Had a Monster**
Illustrator: Rutherford, Bonnie & Bill
Author: Hellie, Anne
2512          1969          **$4**

**Once Upon a Windy Day**
Illustrator: Flory, Jane
Author: Flory, Jane
865          1947          **$15**

**One Two Buckle My Shoe**
Illustrator: Kaula, Edna M.
807          1951          **$12**

**One Two Three**
Illustrator: Charlie
Author: Charlie
2440          1953          **$2**

**One Two Three**
Illustrator: Charlie
Author: Charlie
2616          1953          **$3**

**One Two Three**
Illustrator: Charlie
Author: Charlie
926          1953          **$5**

**Pals**
Illustrator: O'Sullivan, Tom
Author: Funk, Melissa Don
2544          1966          **$4**

**Pamela Jane's Week**
A Story About Days of the Week
Illustrator: Ike, Jane
Author: Robinson, Alberta
2424          1973          **$2**

**Parade For Chatty Baby, A**
Mattel Doll
Illustrator: Mode, Nathalee
Author: Schwalj, Marjory
2562          1965          **$15**

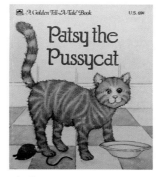

**Patsy the Pussycat**
Illustrator: Super, Terri
Author: Watts, Mabel
2475-4          1986          **$2**

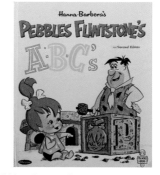

**Pebbles Flintstone's A B Cs**
Illustrator: Lorencz, Bill; Strobl, Anthony
Author: Daly, Eileen
2622          1966          **$18**

**Pebbles Flintstone, Daddy's Little Helper**
Illustrator: Storms, Robert
Author: Hagen, Patrick
2657            1964                    **$18**

Peppermint
Illustrator: Grider, Dorothy
Author: Grider, Dorothy
2502            1950                    **$18**

Peppermint
Illustrator: Burns, Raymond
Author: Grider, Dorothy
848             1966                    **$15**

**Peter Pan and the Tiger**
Illustrator: McNatt Jr., Rich; Totten, Bob
Author: Carey, Mary
2616            1976                    **$8**

**Peter Potamus Meets the Black Knight**
Illustrator: Strobl, Anthony; Jancar, Milli
Author: Freeman, Jane
2506            1965                    **$15**

Peter Rabbit
Illustrator: Wilson, Beth
929             1953                    **$8**

**Peter Rabbit**
Illustrator: Myers, Jack & Louise
2515            1959                    **$6**

Peter Rabbit
Illustrator: Winship, Florence Sarah
2515            1955                    **$6**

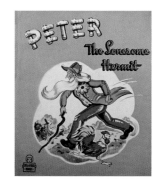

Peter the Lonesome Hermit
Illustrator: Snow, Dorethea J.
Author: Snow, Dorethea J.
884             1948                    **$18**

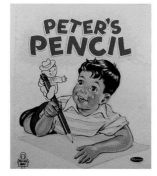

**Peter's Pencil**
Illustrator: Butler, Paula Hurley
Author: Butler, Paula Hurley
927             1953                    **$12**

Peter's Welcome
Illustrator: Schweninger, Ann
Author: Silverman, Maida
2463-38         1985                    **$7**

Petunia
Illustrator: Williams, Ben
Author: Sankey, Alice
885             1948                    **$16**

**Pig and the Witch, The**
Illustrator: Severn, Jeffery
Author: Goldsmith, Howard
2475-48      1990      **$2**

**Pink Panther Rides Again, The**
Illustrator: Jason Art Studios
Author: Graham, Kennon
2628      1976      **$3**

**Pippi Longstocking and the South Sea Pirates**
Illustrator: Baker, Darrell
Author: Carey, Mary
2614      1976      **$15**

**Pitty Pat**
A Fuzzy Wuzzy Book
Illustrator: Winship, Florence Sarah
Author: Horn, Gladys M.
2641      1954      **$15**

**Play School  A B C**
Illustrator: Stellerman, Robbie
2471-46      1985      **$2**

**Playmate For Peter**
Illustrator: Myers, Louise W.
Author: Maritano, Adela Kay
803      1951      **$8**

**Pockets**
Illustrator: Ozone, Lucy
Author: Ozone, Lucy
2504      1955      **$8**

**Pockets**
Illustrator: Ozone, Lucy
Author: Ozone, Lucy
2534      1955      **$8**

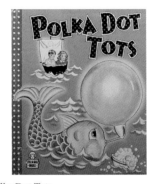

**Polka Dot Tots**
Illustrator: Tedder, Elizabeth
Author: Lieberman, Nina Belle
864      1946      **$16**

**Pony**
Illustrator: Crawford, Mel; Photos: Haas, Arthur
Author: Merow, Erva Loomis
2527      1965      **$5**

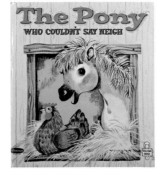

**Pony Who Couldn't Say Neigh, The**
Illustrator: Thomas, Stephen
Author: Schwalje, Marjory
2543      1964      **$7**

**Poor Kitty**
Illustrator: Tedder, Elizabeth
Author: Tedder, Elizabeth
850      1945      **$16**

**Pop-O the Clown**
Illustrator: Cummings, Alison
Author: Whitteberry, Caroline
844          1950          **$15**

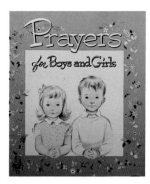

**Prayers For Boys and Girls**
Illustrator: Cummings, Alison
918          1953          **$7**

**Prayers For Boys and Girls**
Illustrator: None Credited
2636          1957          **$6**

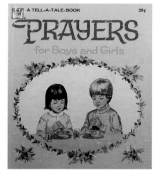

**Prayers For Boys and Girls**
Illustrator: Cummings, Alison
2520          1972          **$2**

**Prickly Tale, A**
Illustrator: Hauge, Carl & Mary
Author: Begley, Evelyn M.
2508          1965          **$5**

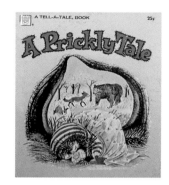

**Prickly Tale, A**
Illustrator: Hauge, Carl & Mary
Author: Begley, Evelyn M.
2519          1965          **$4**

**Princess and the Pea, The**
Illustrator: Herric, Pru
2610          1961          **$7**

**Princess Who Never Laughed, The**
Illustrator: Grunwald, Marcia
2610          1961          **$7**

**Puffy the Puppy**
Illustrator: Porter, Genevieve
Author: Georgiana
819          1952          **$8**

**Puppies on Parade**
Illustrator: Eubank, Mary Grace
Author: Helfand, Karen
2476-45          1989          **$2**

**Purrrt**
A Fuzzy Wuzzy Book
Illustrator: Hartwell, Marjorie
Author: Hartwell, Marjorie
2641          1952          **$15**

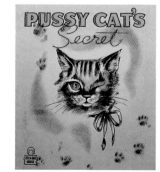

**Pussy Cat's Secret**
Illustrator: Spicer, Jessie
Author: Elting, Mary
895          1949          **$15**

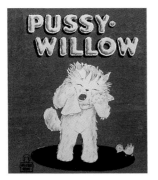

**Pussy-Willow**
Illustrator: MacKean, Emma C.
Author: MacKean, Emma C.
873        1948        **$15**

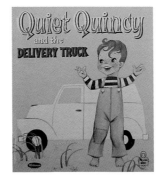

**Quiet Quincy and the Delivery Truck**
Illustrator: Steigerwald, Beverly
Author: Kemp, Polly G.
2615        1961        **$6**

**Quiet Quincy and the Delivery Truck**
Illustrator: Steigerwald, Beverly
Author: Kemp, Polly G.
2541        1961        **$5**

**Rackety-Boom**
Illustrator: Florian
Author: Wright, Betty Ren
893        1953        **$20**

**Rackety-Boom**
Illustrator: Florian
Author: Wright, Betty Ren
2557        1953        **$15**

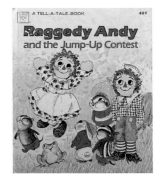

**Raggedy Andy and the Jump-Up Contest**
Illustrator: Goldsborough, June
Author: Schwalj, Marjory
2641        1978        **$6**

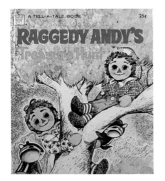

**Raggedy Andy's Treasure Hunt**
Illustrator: Goldsborough, June
Author: Schwaljé, Marjory
2417-2        1973        **$5**

**Raggedy Ann and Andy On the Farm**
Illustrator: Goldsborough, June
Author: Daly, Eileen
2596        1958        **$5**

**Raggedy Ann and the Tagalong Present**
Illustrator: Krehbiel, Becky
Author: Schwaljé, Marjory
2417-1        1978        **$5**

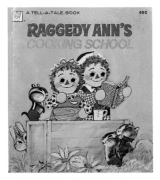

**Raggedy Ann's Cooking School**
Illustrator: Goldsborough, June
Author: Schwaljé, Marjory
2498        1974        **$5**

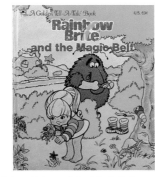

**Rainbow Brite and the Magic Belt**
Illustrator: Costanza, John
Author: Grunewalt, Pine
2451-4        1985        **$4**

**Rainbow Circus Comes to Town, The**
Illustrator: Steadman, Barbara
Author: Ryder, Joann C.
2474-44        1986        **$3**

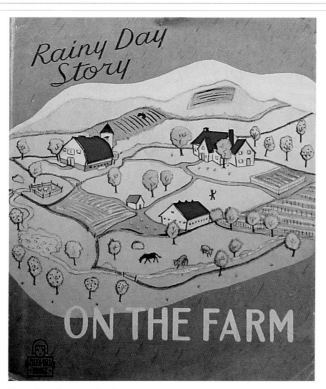

**Rainy Day Story on the Farm**
Illustrator: Matson, Elizabeth
Author: Little, Irene
858             1944                    **$15**

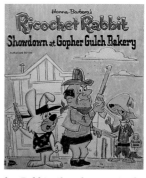

**Ricochet Rabbit, Showdown at Gopher Gulch Bakery**
Illustrator: Anderson, Al; Alvaradom, Peter
Author: Hagen, Patrick
2622             1964                    **$18**

**Rinty and Pals For Rusty**
Illustrator: Bartram, Bob
Author: Francis, Dee
2571             1957                    **$12**

**Road Runner and the Bird Watchers, The**
Illustrator: DeLara, Phil
Author: Lewis, Jean
2408             1968                    **$4**

**Road Runner, The—Tumbleweed Trouble**
Illustrator: Leon Jason Studio
Author: Woolgar, Jack
2466             1971                    **$3**

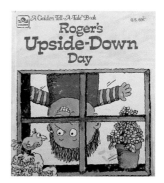

**Roger's Upside-Down Day**
Illustrator: Lee, Jared D.
Author: Wright, Betty Ren
2463-4          1979                    **$3**

**Rootie Kazootie and the Pineapple Pies**
Illustrator: Crawford, Mel
Author: Barrow, John
936             1953                    **$25**

**Roundabout Train**
Illustrator: Clement, Charles
Author: Wright, Betty Ren
2436             1953                    **$5**

**Rowdy**
Illustrator: Scott, Janet Laura
Author: Wyatt, Jane
861             1946                    **$15**

**Roy Rogers at the Lane Ranch**
Illustrator: La Grotta, J. M.
811          1950          **$25**

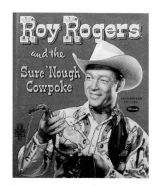

**Roy Rogers and the Sure 'Nough Cowpoke**
Illustrator: Steffen, Randy
Author: Beecher, Elizabeth
801          1952          **$22**

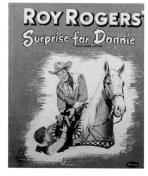

**Roy Rogers' Surprise For Donnie**
Illustrator: Steel, John
Author: Sankey, Alice
943          1954          **$17**

**Roy Rogers' Bullet Leads the Way**
Illustrator: Doe, Bart
Author: Wood, Frances
2567          1953          **$20**

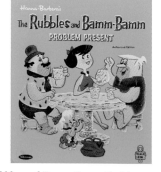

**Rubbles and Bamm-Bamm Problem
Present, The**
Illustrator: Storms, Robert
Author: Carey, Mary
2622          1965          **$18**

**Rudolph the Red-Nosed Reindeer**
Illustrator: Ortiz, Phil; Cuddy, Robbin
Author: Cohen, Robin
2483-02          1993          **$2**

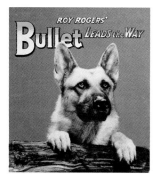

**Rudolph the Red-Nosed Reindeer**
Illustrator: Miyake, Yoshi
Author: Daly, Eileen
2517-2          1980          **$4**

**Ruff and Reddy Go to a Party**
Illustrator: Eisenberg, Harvey; Boyle, Neil
2567          1958          **$20**

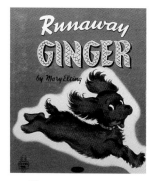

**Runaway Ginger**
Illustrator: Lesko, Zillah
Author: Elting, Mary
2537          1949          **$10**

**Runaway Ginger**
Illustrator: Lesko, Zillah
Author: Elting, Mary
897          1949          **$15**

**Runaway Pancake, The**
Illustrator: Williams, Ben
2465          1956          **$20**

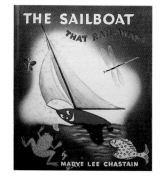

**Sailboat That Ran Away, The**
Illustrator: Chastain, Madye Lee
Author: Chastain, Madye Lee
842          1950          **$15**

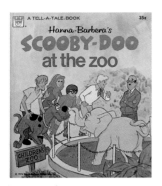

**Scooby-Doo at the Zoo**
Illustrator: Szwejkowski, Adam; Totten, Bob
Author: Nathan, Williams
2570          1974                    **$6**

**See—It Goes!**
Illustrator: Wilde, George & Wilma
Author: Wilde, George & Wilma
805          1953                    **$8**

**See—It Goes!**
Illustrator: Wilde, George & Wilma
Author: Wilde, George & Wilma
2557          1953                    **$5**

**Sesame Street A B C**
Illustrator: Nez, John
Author: Calmenson, Stephanie
2471-43          1987                    **$2**

**Sesame Streets First Times**
Illustrator: Delaney, Toni
Author: Calmenson, Stephanie
2465-43          1987                    **$2**

**Seven Wishes, The**
Illustrator: Miyake, Yoshi
Author: Cowles, Kathleen
2606          1976                    **$3**

**Sherlock Hemlock and the Great
Twiddlebug Mystery**
Illustrator: Children's Television Workshop
Author: Children's Television Workshop
2564          1972                    **$2**

**Sleeping Beauty**
Author: McGary, Norm
2649          1959                    **$10**

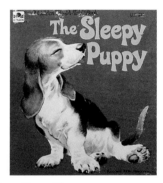

**Sleepy Puppy, The**
Illustrator: Winship, Florence Sarah
Author: Chamberlin, Mary Jo
2462          1961                    **$4**

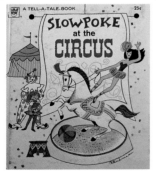

**Slowpoke at the Circus**
Illustrator: Ruhman, Ruth
Author: Richardson, Kay
2457          1973                    **$3**

**Smokey Bear Saves the Forest**
Illustrator: Gantz, David
Author: Graham, Kennon
2463          1971                    **$8**

**Smoky the Baby Goat**
Illustrator: Reed, Veronica
Author: Elting, Mary
867          1947                    **$15**

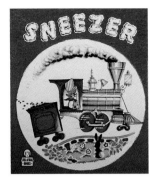

**Sneezer**
Illustrator: Williams, Ben D.
Author: Upson, Estelle McInnes
854          1945          **$15**

**Snooty**
Illustrator: Flory, Jane
Author: Flory, Jane
851          1944          **$15**

**Snoozey**
Illustrator: McKean, Emma C.
Author: McKean, Emma C.
2358         1944          **$12**

**Snoozey**
Illustrator: McKean, Emma C.
Author: McKean, Emma C.
853          1944          **$15**

**Snowball**
A Fuzzy Wuzzy Book
Illustrator: Winship, Florence Sarah
Author: Wright, Betty Ren
2670         1952          **$15**

**Socks**
Illustrator: Winship, Florence Sarah
Author: Ryan, Betty Molgard
886          1949          **$15**

**Somebody Forgot**
Illustrator: Stang, Judy
Author: Horn, Gladys M.
963          1954          **$8**

**Someplace For Sparky**
Illustrator: Walters, Audry
Author: Beatie, Bernadine
2659         1965          **$4**

**Special Pet, A**
Illustrator: Giacomini, Olindo
Author: Schwaljé, Marjory
2521         1968          **$2**

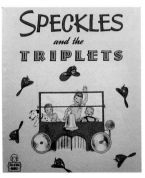

**Speckles and the Triplets**
Illustrator: Stevens, Mary
Author: Elting, Mary
874          1949          **$18**

**Splish, Splash, and Splush**
Illustrator: Wilde, Irma
Author: Pape, Donna Lugg
2526         1962          **$7**

**Spoon Necklace, The**
Illustrator: De Moth, Vivienne
Author: Young, Opal Dean
2472-41      1986          **$3**

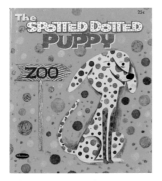

**Spotted Dotted Puppy, The**
Illustrator: Seiden, Art
Author: Fletcher, Steffi
2560          1961          **$4**

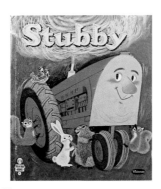

**Stubby**
Illustrator: Seiden, Art
Author: Borden, Marion
2615          1963          **$4**

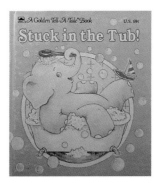

**Stuck in the Tub!**
Illustrator: Orville, Oliver
Author: Hylst, Marguerite Van
2463-44          1988          **$2**

**Sunny, Honey, and Funny**
A Fuzzy Wuzzy Book
Illustrator: Lesko, Zillah
Author: Horn, Gladys M.
824          1951          **$15**

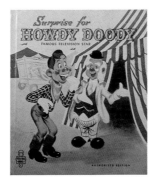

**Surprise For Howdy Doody**
Illustrator: Kean, Edward
2573          1951          **$20**

**Surprise in the Barn**
Illustrator: Flory, Jane
Author: Flory, Jane
2543          1955          **$6**

**Surprise in the Barn**
Illustrator: Flory, Jane
Author: Flory, Jane
2543          1955          **$6**

**Susan and the Rain**
Illustrator: Chastain, Madye Lee
Author: Chastain, Madye Lee
879          1947          **$16**

**Susan and the Rain**
Illustrator: Chastain, Madye Lee
Author: Chastain, Madye Lee
879          1947          **$16**

**Tabitha Tabby's Fantastic Flavor**
Illustrator: Peltier, Phyllis A.
Author: Lewis, Jean
2476-44          1988          **$2**

**Tag-Along Shadow**
Illustrator: Macpherson, Ruth Rosamond
Author: Macpherson, Ruth Rosamond
2601          1959          **$8**

**Tale of Peter Rabbit, The**
Illustrator: Schweninger, Ann
2488-02          1992          **$2**

**Tall Tree Small Tree**
Illustrator: Winship, Florence Sarah
Author: Watts, Mabel
2534          1970          $3

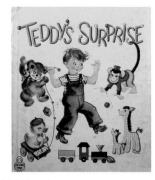

**Teddy's Surprise**
Illustrator: Suzanne
Author: Georgiana
809          1952          $15

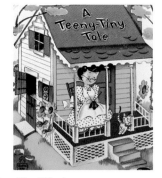

**Teen-Tiny Tale, A**
Illustrator: Williams, Ben D.
2513          1955          $10

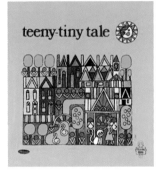

**Teeny-Tiny Tale, A**
Illustrator: Rose, Terry
Author: Sukus, Jan
2558          1969          $5

**Teena and the Magic Pot**
Illustrator: Myers, Louise & Jack
2423          1961          $5

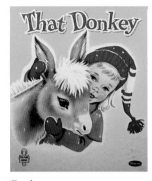

**That Donkey**
Illustrator: Grider, Dorothy
Author: Georgiana
2502          1954          $8

**That Puppy**
Illustrator: Zemsky, Jessica
Author: Haas, Dorothy
2675          1961          $10

**That's Where You Live!**
Illustrator: Fraser, Betty
Author: Vogels, Mary Prescott
2534          1970          $4

**That's Where You Live!**
Illustrator: Fraser, Betty
Author: Vogels, Mary Prescott
2530          1970          $2

**Thin Arnold**
Illustrator: Heckler, Bill
Author: Bacon, Joan Chase
2691          1970          $6

**This Room Is Mine**
Illustrator: Stang, Judy
Author: Wright, Betty Ren
2643          1977          $3

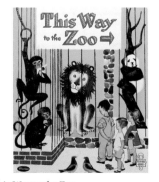

**This Way to the Zoo**
Illustrator: Weber, Nettie
Author: Cunningham, Virginia
2536          1948          $8

**This Way to the Zoo**
Illustrator: Weber, Nettie
Author: Cunningham, Virginia
877            1948            **$12**

**Three Bears, The**
Illustrator: Rowland, Helen
909            1952            **$8**

**Three Bears, The**
Illustrator: Suzanne
2512            1955            **$6**

**Three Bears, The**
Illustrator: Sari
2512            1960            **$5**

**Three Bears, The**
Illustrator: Gordon, Louise
Author: Russell, Solveig Paulson
2462-35            1968            **$3**

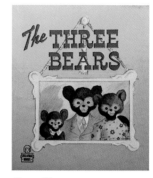

**Three Bears, The**
Illustrator: Yeakey, Carol
859            1945            **$15**

**Three Bears, The**
Illustrator: Yeakey, Carol
859            1945            **$15**

**Three Billy Goats Gruff**
Illustrator: Ames, Lee J.
2515            1954            **$5**

**Three Little Mice**
Matilda MacElroy and Mary
Illustrator: Robison, I. E.
Author: Fairweather, Jessie Home
836            1950            **$10**

**Three Little Pigs, The**
Illustrator: Bracke, Charles
Author: Wood, Jo Anne
2501            1969            **$5**

**Three Little Pigs, The**
Illustrator: Myers, Louise W.
921            1953            **$8**

**Three Little Pigs, The**
Illustrator: Irwin, Josephine
860            1944            **$15**

**Three Little Pigs, The**
Illustrator: Miloche, Hilda
2547          1956          **$6**

**Three Little Pigs, The**
Illustrator: Williams, Ben
2501          1959          **$6**

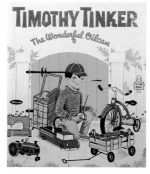

**Timothy Tinker, The Wonderful Oilcan**
Illustrator: Stang, Judy
Author: Watts, Mabel
2522          1968          **$4**

**Timothy's Shoes**
Illustrator: Schad, Helen G.
856          1946          **$15**

**Timothy's Shoes**
Illustrator: Schad, Helen G.
856          1946          **$13**

**Tiny Tots 1-2-3**
Illustrator: Murray, Marjorie
2615          1958          **$6**

**Tiny Tots 1-2-3**
Illustrator: Murray, Marjorie
2435          1958          **$3**

**Tip-Top Tree House, The**
Illustrator: Wilde, Carol
Author: Tucker, Daisy
2555          1969          **$4**

**Toby Bunny's Secret Hiding Place**
Illustrator: Spence, James
Author: Werner, Dave
2465-44          1988          **$2**

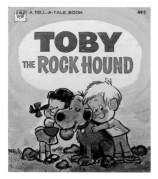

**Toby the Rock Hound**
Illustrator: Bradfield, Roger
Author: Walrath, Jane Dwyer
2408-6          1979          **$3**

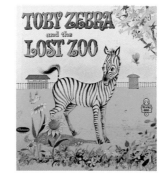

**Toby Zebra and the Lost Zoo**
Illustrator: Garris, Norma & Dan
Author: Pape, Donna Lugg
2505          1963          **$4**

**Tom and Jerry and the Toy Circus**
Illustrator: Armstrong, Samuel; Ray, Tom
913          1953          **$8**

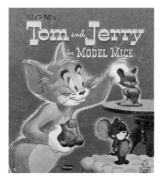

**Tom and Jerry in Model Mice**
Illustrator: Eisenberg, Harvey; Dempster, Al
Author: M-G-M Cartoons, Inc.
2509          1951                    **$10**

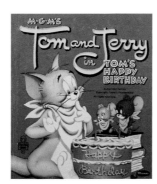

**Tom and Jerry in Tom's Happy Birthday**
Illustrator: Eisenberg, Harvey; Wolfe, Gene
Author: M-G-M Cartoons, Inc.
2611          1955                    **$8**

**Tom and Jerry's Big Move**
Illustrator: Messerli, Joe
Author: Lewis, Jean
2451-38        1985                   **$2**

**Tommy and Timmy**
A Fuzzy Wuzzy Book
Illustrator: Berry, Anne Scheu
Author: Sankey, Alice
822          1951                    **$15**

**Tommy and Timmy**
A Fuzzy Wuzzy Book
Illustrator: Berry, Anne Scheu
Author: Sankey, Alice
2644          1951                    **$15**

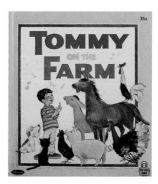

**Tommy On the Farm**
Illustrator: Elfrieda
Author: Russell, Solveig Paulson
2527          1968                    **$3**

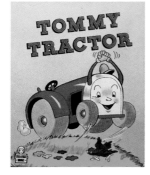

**Tommy Tractor**
Illustrator: Buehrig, Rosemary
Author: Mcpherson, Ge
881          1947                    **$12**

**Too Many Kittens**
Illustrator: Suzanne
Author: Watts, Mabel
2525          1963                    **$8**

**Too Many Names**
Illustrator: Eugenie
Author: Peterson, Jeri
2614          1970                    **$3**

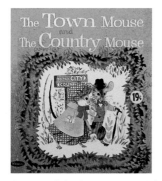

**Town Mouse and the Country Mouse, The**
Illustrator: Stang, Judy
Author: Horn, Gladys M.
2561          1954                    **$7**

**Toy Party, The**
Illustrator: Wysse
Author: Christopher, Til B.
878          1948                    **$15**

**Toy That Flew, The**
Illustrator: Depper, Hertha
Author: Smaridge, Nora
2518          1974                    **$5**

**Train Coming!**
Illustrator: Florian
Author: Wright, Betty Ren
2556          1954                      **$6**

**Truck That Stopped at Village Small, The**
Illustrator: Dorcas
Author: Knittle, Jessie M.
813          1951                      **$8**

**Trumpet**
Illustrator: Myers, Bernice
Author: Lynn, Patricia
931          1953                      **$6**

**Try Again, Sally!**
Illustrator: Tsambon, Athena
Author: Laughlin, Florence
2460          1969                      **$3**

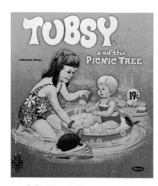

**Tubsy and the Picnic Tree**
Ideal Doll
Illustrator: Sampson, Katherine
Author: Daly, Eileen
2552          1968                      **$12**

**Tuffer**
A Fuzzy Wuzzy Book
Illustrator: Rutherford, Bonnie & Bill
Author: Wright, Betty Ren
2672          1959                      **$13**

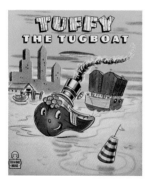

**Tuffy the Tugboat**
Illustrator: Williams, Ben
Author: Sankey, Alice
880          1947                      **$15**

**Tweety**
Illustrator: Abranz, Fred; Maclaughlin
Author: Warner Bros., Inc.
901          1953                      **$10**

**Tweety and Sylvester at the Farm**
Illustrator: Barto, Renzo
Author: Hogan, Cecily Ruth
2453-35          1978                      **$4**

**Tweety and Sylvester, A Visit to the Vet**
Illustrator: Messerli, Joe
Author: Lewis, Jean
2453-47          1988                      **$4**

**Tweety and Sylvester, Picnic Problems**
Illustrator: Leon Jason Studio
Author: Biesterveld, Betty
2448          1970                      **$3**

**Two Kittens**
Illustrator: Zfa-Duesseldorf
Author: Tiffany, Virginia
2525          1966                      **$4**

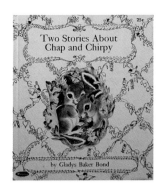

**Two Stories About Chap and Chirpy**
Illustrator: Wilde, Irma
Author: Bond, Gladys Baker
2526        1965        **$4**

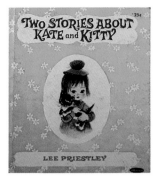

**Two Stories About Kate and Kitty**
Illustrator: Schlesinger, Alice
Author: Priestly, Lee
2510        1968        **$4**

**Two Stories About Lollipop**
Illustrator: Eugenie
Author: Bell, Luann Stull
2683        1969        **$4**

**Two Stories About Ricky**
Illustrator: Goldsborough, June
Author: Frankel, Bernice
2601        1966        **$4**

**Two Stories About Wags**
Illustrator: Garris, Norma & Dan
Author: Biesterveld, Betty
2560        1966        **$4**

**Two Stories About Wendy**
Illustrator: Nagel, Stina
Author: Schwalj, Marjory
2659        1965        **$4**

**Two Too Twins, The**
Illustrator: Goldsborough, June
Author: Priestly, Lee
2543        1966        **$5**

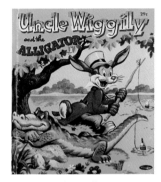

**Uncle Wiggily and the Alligator**
Illustrator: Weaver, William
Author: Turner, Gill; Garis, Howard
903        1953        **$7**

**Under Dog**
Illustrator: Jason Art Studios
Author: Johnston, William
2611        1966        **$10**

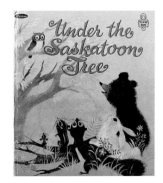

**Under the Saskatoon Tree**
Illustrator: Rutherford, Bonnie & Bill
Author: Russell, Solveig Paulson
2543        1966        **$4**

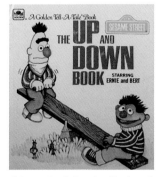

**Up and Down Book Starring Ernie and Bert, The**
Illustrator: Swanson, Maggie
2402-7        1979        **$2**

**Very Best of Friends, The**
Illustrator: Hauge, Carl & Mary
Author: Fletcher, Steffi
2559        1963        **$3**

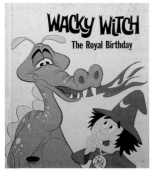

**Wacky Witch: The Royal Birthday**
Illustrator: Arens, Michael; Toten, Bob
Author: Lewis, Jean
2546　　　　1971　　　　**$6**

**Waldo, the Jumping Dragon**
Illustrator: Oechsli, Kelly
Author: Detiege, Dave
2688　　　　1964　　　　**$5**

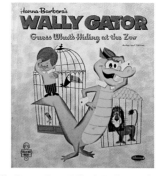

**Wally Gator, Guess What's Hiding at the Zoo**
Illustrator: Crawford, Mel
Author: Daly, Eileen
2506　　　　1963　　　　**$8**

**Waltons, The: Elizabeth and the Magic Lamp**
Illustrator: Neely, Jan
Author: Graham, Charlotte
2579　　　　1975　　　　**$4**

**We Talk With God**
Illustrator: McElwain, Diane
Author: Burdick, Faith Oliver
2404-3　　　1979　　　　**$3**

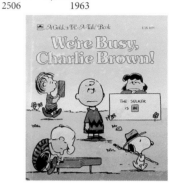

**We're Busy, Charlie Brown!**
Illustrator: Schulz, Charles; Ellis, Art
Author: Namm, Diane
2541-41　　1987　　　　**$3**

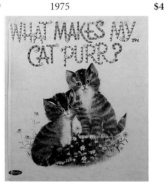

**What Makes My Cat Purr?**
Illustrator: Elfrieda
Author: Tompert, Ann
2425　　　　1965　　　　**$4**

**What Shall I Put in the Hole That I Dig?**
Illustrator: Aliki
Author: Thompson, Eleanor
2563　　　　1972　　　　**$12**

**When I Go to Bed**
Illustrator: Ruhman, Ruth
Author: Yerian, Margaret
2542　　　　1967　　　　**$12**

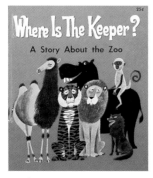

**Where Is the Keeper?**
Illustrator: Seiden, Art
Author: Watts, Mabel
2469　　　　1966　　　　**$4**

**Where Timothy Lives**
Illustrator: Frost, Bruno
Author: Wright, Betty Ren
2505　　　　1958　　　　**$6**

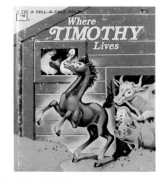

**Where Timothy Lives**
Illustrator: Frost, Bruno
Author: Wright, Betty Ren
2505　　　　1958　　　　**$4**

**Where's Harry?**
Illustrator: Stirnweis, Shannon
Author: Meek, Pauline Palmer
2546            1969            **$4**

**Who Are You?**
Illustrator: Fitch, Winnie
Author: Bradfield, Joan & Rogers
2521            1966            **$4**

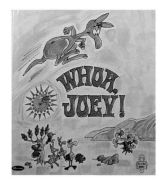

**Whoa, Joey!**
Illustrator: Bracke, Charles
Author: Hogstrom, Daphne
2557            1968            **$4**

**Whoop-Ee, Hunkydory!**
Illustrator: Vaughan, Eillen Fox
Author: Justus, May
884            1952            **$7**

**Whose Baby Is That?**
Illustrator: Nagel, Stina
Author: Jones, Clair
2553            1969            **$4**

**Why Do You Love Me?**
Illustrator: Sampson, Katherine
Author: Watts, Mabel
2428            1970            **$3**

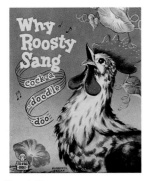

**Why Roosty Sang**
Illustrator: Winship, Florence Sarah
Author: Page, Marguerita
892            1948            **$15**

**Wiggletail**
Illustrator: Charlie
Author: Charlie
852            1944            **$15**

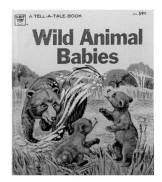

**Wild Animal Babies**
Illustrator: Hauge, Carl & Mary
2475-3            1973            **$2**

**Wild Kingdom, A Trip to a Game Park**
Illustrator: Seward, James/Creative Studios
Author: Dinneen, Betty
2625            1976            **$3**

**Willy Woo-Oo-Oo**
Illustrator: Winship, Florence Sarah
Author: Wright, Betty Ren
818            1951            **$15**

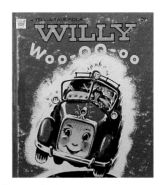

**Willy Woo-Oo-Oo**
Illustrator: Winship, Florence Sarah
Author: Wright, Betty Ren
2444            1951            **$10**

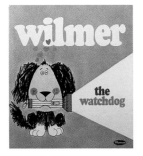

**Wilmer the Watchdog**
Illustrator: Giacomini, Olinda
Author: Kittke, Lael
2627          1970          **$5**

**Wolf and the Seven Kids, The**
Illustrator: Sondern, Ferdinand A.
Author: Hansen, Gretchen
2561          1969          **$4**

**Wonderful Tony**
Illustrator: Berry, Anne Scheu
Author: Page, Marguerita
871          1947          **$15**

**Woody Woodpecker Shoots the Works**
Illustrator: McSavage, Fran;
Armstrong, Samuel
Author: Walter Lantz Studios
2439          1955          **$7**

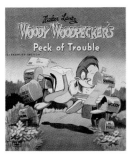

**Woody Woodpecker's Peck of Trouble**
Illustrator: Thompson, Riley;
Armstrong, Sam
Author: Watts, Mabel
831          1951          **$10**

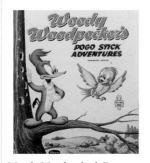

**Woody Woodpecker's Pogo Stick Adventures**
Illustrator: Abranz, Alfred;
Knight, John
Author: Walter Lantz Studios
2562          1954          **$8**

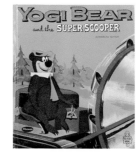

**Wrong-Way Howie Learns to Slide**
Illustrator: Wilde, Carol
Author: Peake, Sylvia
2523          1969          **$4**

**Yellow Cat, The**
A Fuzzy Wuzzy Book
Illustrator: Sari
Author: Wright, Betty Ren
911          1952          **$15**

**Yippie Kiyi**
Illustrator: Munson, Floyd
Author: Rose, Florella
940          1953          **$18**

**Yippie Kiyi and Whoa Boy**
Illustrator: Sari
Author: Rose, Florella
2514          1955          **$15**

**Yogi Bear and the Super Scooper**
Illustrator: Hooper, L ; Thomas, R.
Author: Hoag, Nancy
2642          1961          **$16**

**Yogi Bear's Secret**
Illustrator: Jason, Leon
Author: Jones, Mary Voell
2608          1963          **$18**

**Zoo Friends Are at Our School Today!**
Illustrator: Brewer, Sally King
Author: Watts, Mabel
2423          1979          **$3**

**Beauty and the Beast**
Walt Disney
Illustrator: Kicks, Russell
Author: Korman, Justine
2455-59          1993          **$4**
**Busy Body Book, The**
A First Book About You
Illustrator: Beylon, Catherine
Author: Harrison, David L.
2585          1975          **$6**

**Cookie Monster's Book of Cookie Shapes**
Illustrator: Brown, Richard
2402-8          1979          **$2**
**Little Lulu Has an Art Show**
(Second cover)
Illustrator: Buell, Marjorie
Henderson
Author: Buell, Marjorie
Henderson
2532          1964          **$8**

**Outside With Baby**
Illustrator: Skibinski, Ray
Author: Swetnam, Evelyn
2546          1974          **$3**
**Prayers For Boys and Girls**
Illustrator: Cummings, Alison
2523          1972          **$3**

## Disney Titles

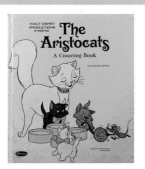

**Aristocats, The, A Counting Book**
Walt Disney
Illustrator: Walt Disney Studios
Author: Walt Disney Studios
2516          1970          **$8**

**Bambi**
Walt Disney
Illustrator: Walt Disney Studios
Author: Walt Disney Studios
2548          1955          **$6**

**Bambi**
Walt Disney
Illustrator: Walt Disney Studios
Author: Walt Disney Studios
2548          1955          **$6**

**Bear Country**
Walt Disney
Illustrator: Godwin, Edward & Stephani
Author: Wright, Betty Ren
2554          1954          **$12**

**Bear Country**
Walt Disney
Illustrator: Godwin, Edward & Stephani
Author: Wright, Betty Ren
2612          1954          **$7**

**Beaver Valley**
Walt Disney
Illustrator: Hartwell, Marjorie
Author: Wright, Betty Ren
2553          1954          **$12**

**Beaver Valley**
Walt Disney
Illustrator: Hartwell, Marjorie
Author: Wright, Betty Ren
2612          1954          **$7**

**Bedknobs and Broomsticks—A Visit to Naboombu**
Walt Disney
Illustrator: Walt Disney Studios
Author: Walt Disney Studios
2541          1971          **$5**

**Big Albert Moves In**
Walt Disney World
Illustrator: Walt Disney Studios
Author: Walt Disney Studios
2533          1971          **$8**

**Cinderella**
Walt Disney
Illustrator: Wheeler, George
Author: Walt Disney Studios
2427-2          1972          **$5**

**Cinderella**
Walt Disney
Illustrator: Wheeler, George
Author: Walt Disney Studios
2604          1954          **$6**

**Cinderella**
Walt Disney
Illustrator: Wheeler, George
Author: Walt Disney Studios
964          1954          **$12**

**Cinderella**
Walt Disney
Illustrator: Wheeler, George
Author: Walt Disney Studios
2456-32 **$4**

**Donald Duck and Chip 'n' Dale**
Walt Disney
Illustrator: Walsh, Stan; Wolfe, Gene
Author: Walt Disney Studios
945 1965 **$8**

**Donald Duck and the New Birdhouse**
Walt Disney
Illustrator: Moores, Dick; Mcgary, Norm
Author: Walt Disney Studios
2516 1955 **$8**

**Donald Duck and the Super-Sticky Secret**
Walt Disney
Illustrator: Kohn, Arnie
Author: Watts, Mabel
2425-6 1979 **$3**

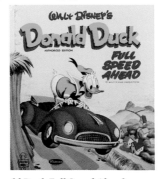

**Donald Duck Full Speed Ahead**
Walt Disney
Illustrator: Banta, Milt; Mac Laughlin, Don
900 1953 **$10**

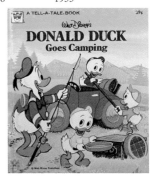

**Donald Duck Goes Camping**
Walt Disney
Illustrator: Walt Disney Studios
Author: Walt Disney Studios
2609 1977 **$4**

**Donald Duck Goes to Disneyland**
Walt Disney
Illustrator: Banta, Milt; Boyle, Neil
Author: Walt Disney Studios
2559 1967 **$15**

**Donald Duck in Frontierland**
Walt Disney
Illustrator: Boyle, Neil
Author: Walt Disney Studios
2520 1969 **$10**

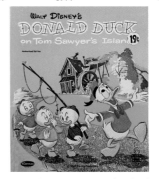

**Donald Duck On Tom Sawyer's Island**
Walt Disney
Illustrator: Strobl, Tony; the Mattinsons
Author: Snow, Dorothea J.
2409 1978 **$8**

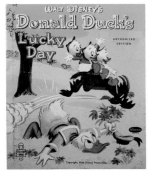

**Donald Duck's Lucky Day**
Walt Disney
Illustrator: Walt Disney Studios
Author: Walt Disney Studios
827 1971 **$7**

**Duck Tales, Silver Dollars For Uncle Scrooge**
Walt Disney
Illustrator: Ito, Willy
Author: Weiner, Gina
2454 1988 **$3**

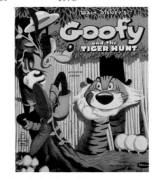

**Goofy and the Tiger Hunt**
Walt Disney
Illustrator: Moores, Dick; Armstrong, Samuel
Author: Walt Disney Studios
2552 1954 **$7**

**Jungle Book, The**
Walt Disney
Illustrator: Walt Disney Studios
Author: Adapted from Rudyard Kipling
2607          1967          **$6**

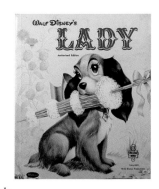

**Lady**
Walt Disney
Illustrator: Hubbard, Allan; Wolfe, Gene
Author: Walt Disney Studios
2456-3          1954          **$8**

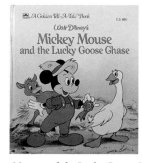

**Mickey Mouse and the Lucky Goose Chase**
Walt Disney
Illustrator: Wilson, Roy; William, Arthur; McGuire
Author: Scooter, M. J.
2454-45          1986          **$3**

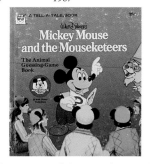

**Mickey Mouse and the Mouseketeers—The Animal Guessing Game Book**
Walt Disney
Illustrator: Walt Disney Studios
Author: Walt Disney Studios
2631          1977          **$3**

**Mickey Mouse and the Pet Show**
Walt Disney
Illustrator: Walt Disney Studios
Author: Walt Disney Studios
2454-2          1976          **$3**

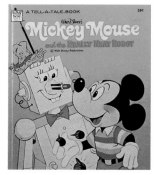

**Mickey Mouse and the Really Neat Robot**
Walt Disney
Illustrator: Walt Disney Studios
Author: Walt Disney Studios
2475          1970          **$3**

**Mickey Mouse and the Second Wish**
Walt Disney
Illustrator: Walt Disney Studios
Author: Walt Disney Studios
2418          1973          **$3**

**Mickey Mouse and the World's Friendliest Monster**
Walt Disney
Illustrator: Walt Disney Studios
Author: Walt Disney Studios
2424-2          1976          **$3**

**Mouseketeers Tryout Time, The**
Walt Disney
Illustrator: Satterfield, Charles
Author: Revena
2649          1956          **$5**

**One Hundred and One Dalmatians**
Walt Disney
Illustrator: Fletcher, James
Author: Walt Disney Studios
2552          1960          **$7**

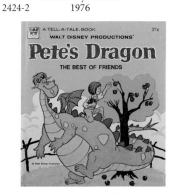

**Pete's Dragon—The Best of Friends**
Walt Disney
Illustrator: Walt Disney Studio
Author: Walt Disney Studios
2637          1977          **$6**

**Pinocchio**
Illustrator: McSavage, Frank; Fisher, Frank
Author: Hass, Dorothy
2428-2          1961          **$6**

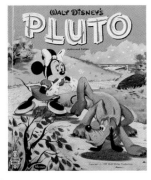

**Pluto**
Walt Disney
Illustrator: Strobl, Tony; Boyle, Neil
Author: Revena
2509          1957          **$6**

**Rescuers, The**
Walt Disney
Illustrator: Walt Disney Studios
Author: Walt Disney Studios
2429-3          1977          **$5**

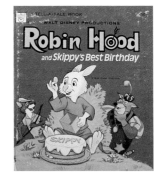

**Robin Hood and Skippy's Best Birthday**
Walt Disney
Illustrator: Walt Disney Studios
Author: Walt Disney Studios
2441          1973          **$5**

**Snow White and the Seven Dwarfs**
Walt Disney
Illustrator: Wegner, Helmuth G.
Author: Walt Disney Studios
2427-4          1957          **$3**

**Snow White and the Seven Dwarfs**
Walt Disney
Illustrator: Wegner, Helmuth G.
Author: Walt Disney Studios
2578          1957          **$12**

**Swiss Family Duck**
Walt Disney
Illustrator: Strobl, Anthony; Irvin, Fred
Author: Hagen, Patrick
2509          1964          **$10**

**Uncle Scrooge, the Winner**
Walt Disney
Illustrator: Strobl, Anthony; Andersen, Al
Author: Carter, Katherine
2552          1964          **$15**

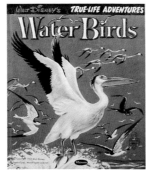

**Water Birds**
Walt Disney
Illustrator: Hartwell, Marjorie
Author: Wright, Betty Ren; Hanson, Alice
2564          1955          **$10**

**Winnie-the-Pooh, The Blustery Day**
Walt Disney
Illustrator: Walt Disney Studios
Author: Milne, A.A.
2577          1975          **$5**

**Winnie-the-Pooh and Eeyore's House**
Walt Disney
Illustrator: Walt Disney Studios
Author: Milne, A.A.
2620          1976          **$5**

**Winnie-the-Pooh and the Unbouncing
of Tigger**
Walt Disney
Illustrator: Walt Disney Studios
Author: Milne, A.A.
2526          1974          **$5**

Whitman Publishing Company produced Top Top Tales from 1960 to 1965. The books measured 6-3/8 x 7-1/2 inches with 36 pages of full-color illustrations. Some of the stories in the series came over form the smaller Tell-A-Tale Book.

**How to determine Top Top Tale editions:**

There is no 100% way to tell a first edition. You can look at the titles on the back of the books and, by deduction, get an idea of when a book was printed. By using the following information, you can make an educated guess as to the print year of your book. Look at the last title and, in some cases, the first and last titles on the back of your book. If the year shown at right matches your copyright or one year before it, you can assume your book is a first edition. Because Top Top Tales didn't start until 1960, and some of the titles were previously published as Tell-A-Tale Books, you will see earlier copyrights. If your book has a pre-1960

copyright and the last title listed is either *Jasper Giraffe* or *Donald Duck*, there's a good chance you have a first edition.

**Example:** Your book lists *Scary Harry* as the last title on the back of the book. Your book has a copyright date of 1964, and I'm showing that the book's back cover was used in 1964. You can assume that your book is a first edition.

| Title(s) on Back of Book | Print Year |
| --- | --- |
| *Cappy* | 1963 |
| *Donald Duck* | 1961 |
| *Jasper Giraffe* | 1960 |
| *Scary Harry* | 1964 |
| *The Three Bears* | 1961 |
| *Uncle Scrooge* | 1962 |
| *Yogi Bear* | 1961 |

**A B C**
Illustrator: Nguyen, Alys
2467          1956                    **$5**

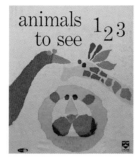

**Animals To See 1 2 3**
Illustrator: Ehlert, Lois
Author: Zens, Patricia Martin
2463          1964                    **$5**

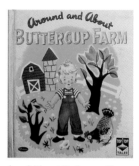

**Around and About Buttercup Farm**
Illustrator: Miloche, Hilda; Kane, Wilma
Author: Lynn, Patricia
2463          1951                    **$6**

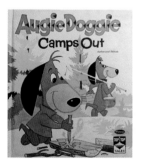

**Augie Doggie Camps Out**
Illustrator: Carey, Joan; Severance, Stan
Author: Wolff, Nancy Hoag
2463          1961                    **$15**

**Benjamin Brownie and the Talking Doll**
Illustrator: Stang, Judy
Author: Ross, Geraldine
2499          1962                    **$15**

**Benjamin Brownie and the Talking Doll**
Illustrator: Stang, Judy
Author: Ross, Geraldine
2499          1962                    **$12**

**Big Red Pajama Wagon, The**
Illustrator: Anderson, Betty
Author: Elting, Mary
2479          1949                    **$6**

**Boy at the Dike, The**
Illustrator: Scott, Marguerite
2471          1961                    **$5**

**Bugs Bunny's Chimney Adventure**
Illustrator: Sgroi, Tony; Wolfe, Gene
Author: Woolgar, Jack
2464          1963                    **$6**

**Busy A B C**
Illustrator: Wilkin, Eloise
2437          1950          **$15**

**Cappy**
Fuzzy Wuzzy Book
Illustrator: Martin, Barry
Author: Hilt, Mary
2457          1963          **$6**

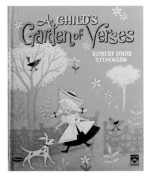

**Child's Garden of Verses, A**
Illustrator: Ruhman, Ruth
Author: Stevenson, Robert Louis
2468          1964          **$6**

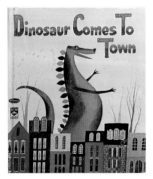

**Cinderella**
Illustrator: Barnes, Catherine
2466          1961          **$8**

**Columbus the Exploring Burro**
Illustrator: Martin, Barry
Author: Hilt, Mary
2480          1951          **$6**

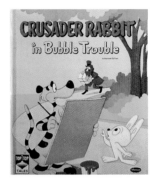

**Crusader Rabbit in Bubble Trouble**
Illustrator: Bemiller, Robert; Neely, Jan
Author: Hoag, Nancy
2468          1960          **$8**

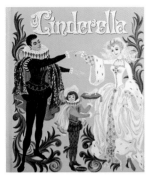

**Dinosaur Comes to Town**
Illustrator: Seiden, Art
Author: Darby, Gene
2452          1963          **$10**

**Dr. Goat**
Illustrator: Clement, Charles
Author: Georgiana
2487          1950          **$150**

**Dragon For Danny Dennis, A**
Fuzzy Wuzzy Book
Illustrator: Stang, Judy
Author: Tostrud, Dorthe
2458          1963          **$12**

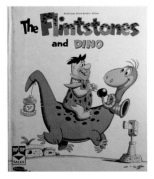

**Flintstones and Dino, The**
Illustrator: Alvarado & Heiner; Robert &
Lorencz
Author: Patrinos, Kay Rausch
2460          1961          **$16**

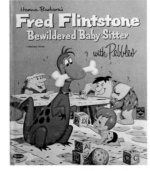

**Fred Flintstone—Bewildered Baby-Sitter
With Pebbles**
Illustrator: Alvarado, Peter; Andersen, Al
Author: Gilbert, Nan
2460          1963          **$16**

**Funny Company and Shy Shrinkin'
Violette, The**
Illustrator: Jason Studios
Author: Hagen, Patrick
2471          1964          **$15**

**Gingerbread Man, The**
Illustrator: Winship, Florence Sarah
2481          1960          **$8**

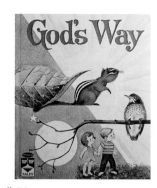

**God's Way**
Illustrator: Hauge, Carl & Mary
Author: McCaw, Mable Niedermeyer
2479          1961          **$5**

**Good, Good Morning, A**
Illustrator: Rutherford, Bonnie & Bill
2466          1963          **$6**

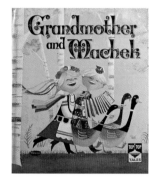

**Grandmother and Machek**
Illustrator: Anders, Frank
Author: Anders, Frank; Anuszkiewicz, Mary
2492          1961          **$7**

**Guess What I Have**
Illustrator: Aliki
Author: Schwalj, Marjory
2461          1964          **$10**

**Happiest Christmas, The**
Illustrator: Wilde, Irma
Author: Fairweather, Jessie Home
2489          1955          **$10**

**Happiest Christmas, The**
Illustrator: Wilde, Irma
Author: Fairweather, Jessie Home
2489          1955          **$10**

**Hi! Cowboy**
Illustrator: Williams, Ben
Author: Horn, Gladys M.
2470          1950          **$6**

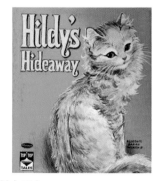

**Hildy's Hideaway**
Illustrator: Winship, Florence Sarah
Author: Watts, Mabel
2473          1961          **$10**

**Huckleberry Hound Helps a Pal**
Illustrator: Alvarado, Peter; Noely, Jan
Author: Jones, Mary Voell
2467          1960          **$7**

**Hullabaloo**
Illustrator: Weber, Nettie
Author: Georgiana
2483          1951          **$15**

**Humm the Singing Hamster**
Illustrator: Stang, Judy
Author: Bing, Catherine
2488          1961          **$15**

**Jasper Giraffe**
Illustrator: Myers, Louise W.
Author: Ferrell, Polly
2472          1949          **$25**

Jetsons, The—The Birthday Surprise
Illustrator: Jason, Leon
Author: Daly, Eileen
2484          1963          **$11**

Katy Did
Illustrator: Aliki
Author: Soule, Jean Conder
2486          1962          **$6**

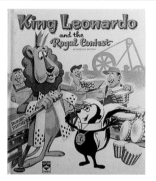

**King Leonardo and the Royal Contest**
Illustrator: Rayburn, Herbert
Author: Daly, Eileen
2472          1962          **$8**

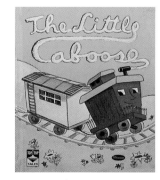

Lassie—The Sandbar Rescue
Illustrator: Lowenbein, Michael
Author: Fiedler, Jean
2475          1964          **$7**

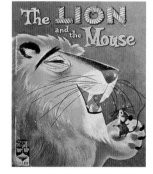

Lion and the Mouse, The
Illustrator: Rutherford, Bonnie and Bill
Author: Watts, Mabel
2483          1961          **$6**

**Little Black Sambo**
Illustrator: Rutherford, Bonnie & Bill
2483          1961          **$40**

Little Caboose, The
Illustrator: Flory, Jane
Author: O'hearn, Nila
2481          1951          **$6**

Little Folks in Mother Goose
Illustrator: Rachel
2471          1946          **$6**

**Little Gray Kitten**
Illustrator: Zemsky, Jessica
Author: Hansen, Helen S.
2451          1964          **$9**

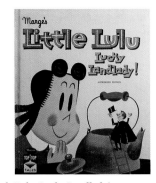

**Little Lulu, Lucky Landlady!**
2476          1960          **$8**

**Little Red Riding Hood**
Illustrator: Zemsky, Jessica
2480          1961          **$8**

**Ludwig Von Drake Dog Expert**
Illustrator: Strobl, Anthony;
Lorencz,William
Author: Daly, Eileen
2482          1962          **$15**

**Mimi**
Illustrator: Winship, Florence Sarah
Author: Haas, Dorothy
2451          1958          **$15**

**Mother Goose**
Illustrator: Scott, Marguerite K.
2478          1960          **$6**

**My Prayers**
Illustrator: Dixon, Rachel Taft
2479          1959          **$5**

**National Velvet**
Illustrator: Anderson, Al
Author: Haas, Dorothy
2465          1962          **$8**

**Night Before Christmas, The**
Illustrator: Winship, Florence Sarah
Author: Moore, Clement C.
2491          1963          **$10**

**Night Before Christmas, The**
Illustrator: Winship, Florence Sarah
Author: Moore, Clement C.
2491          1963          **$10**

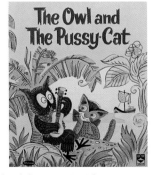

**Owl and the Pussy Cat, The**
Illustrator: Weisner, William
Author: Lear, Edward
2481          1964          **$7**

**Patrick and the Duckling**
Fuzzy Wuzzy Book
Illustrator: Seiden, Art
Author: Haas, Dorothy
2456          1963          **$7**

**Pebbles Flintstone Runaway**
Illustrator: De Santis, George
Author: Daly, Eileen
2465        1964        **$12**

**Penny For Whiffles, A**
Illustrator: Rutherford, Bonnie & Bill
Author: Haas, Dorothy
2476        1962        **$6**

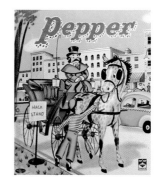

**Pepper**
Illustrator: Williams, Ben
Author: Caplan, Lydia
2495        1955        **$8**

**Peppermint, the Story of a Kitten**
Illustrator: Grider, Dorothy
Author: Grider, Dorothy
2469        1950        **$15**

**Peter Rabbit**
Illustrator: Hauge, Carl & Mary
2493        1961        **$8**

**Petunia**
Illustrator: Williams, Ben D.
Author: Sankey, Alice
2482        1948        **$7**

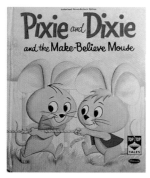

**Pixie and Dixie and the Make-Believe Mouse**
Illustrator: Carey, John; Neely, Jan
Author: Bensen, Mary Windler
2464        1961        **$8**

**Playmate For Peter**
Illustrator: Myers, Louise W.
Author: Maritano, Adela Kay
2475        1951        **$6**

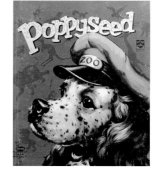

**Poppyseed**
Illustrator: Winship, Florence Sarah
Author: Wright, Betty Ren
2475        1954        **$10**

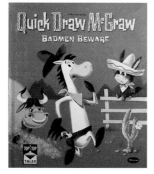

**Quick Draw McGraw**
Illustrator: Fletcher,James; White, Al
Author: Haas, Dorothy
2469        1960        **$8**

**Rocky and Bullwinkle Go to Hollywood**
Author: Daly, Eileen
2494        1961        **$8**

**Scary Harry**
Fuzzy Wuzzy Book
Illustrator: Anders, Frank
Author: Kurtin, Mary Jo
2453        1963        **$7**

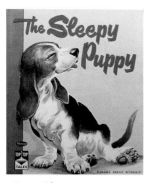

**Sleepy Puppy, The**
Illustrator: Winship, Florence Sarah
Author: Chamberlin, Mary Jo
2462        1961        **$5**

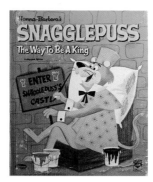

**Snagglepus—The Way To Be King**
Illustrator: Seiden, Art
Author: Johnston, William
2488        1964        **$9**

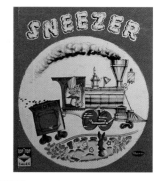

**Sneezer**
Illustrator: Williams, Ben D.
Author: Upson, Estelle McInnes
2461        1955        **$6**

**Somebody Hides**
Fuzzy Wuzzy Book
Illustrator: Wilson, Dagmar
Author: Daly, Eileen
2454        1963        **$5**

**Teddy's Surprise**
Illustrator: Suzanne
Author: Georgiana
2467        1952        **$6**

**Teena and the Magic Pot**
Illustrator: Myers, Jack & Louise
2486        1961        **$8**

**Three Bears, The**
Illustrator: Hauge, Carl & Mary
2474        1961        **$7**

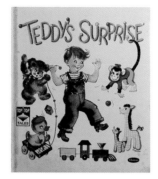

**Three Bears, The**
Illustrator: Yeakey, Carol
2484        1945        **$6**

**Three Little Pigs, The**
Illustrator: Suzanne
2470        1960        **$6**

**Timothy Slept On**
Illustrator: Crawford, Mel
Author: Grant, Eva
2462        1964        **$7**

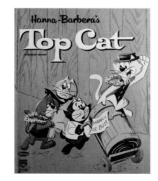

**Top Cat**
Illustrator: Mattinsons, The
Author: Daly, Eileen
2468        1963        **$15**

**Tortoise and the Hare, The**
Fuzzy Wuzzy Book
Illustrator: Rutherford, Bonnie & Bill
Author: Lewis, Jean
2455        1963        **$5**

**Touché Turtle and the Fire Dog**
Illustrator: Crawford, Mel
Author: Lewis, Jean
2485        1963              **$16**

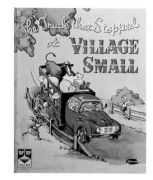

**Truck That Stopped at Village Small, The**
Illustrator: Dorcas
Author: Knittle, Jessie M.
2477        1951              **$6**

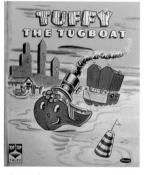

**Tuffy the Tugboat**
Illustrator: Williams, Ben D.
Author: Sankey, Alice
2465        1952              **$6**
2481        1952              **$6**

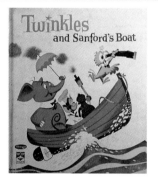

**Twinkles and Sanford's Boat**
Illustrator: Crawford, Mel
Author: Dorfman, Leo
2477        1962              **$8**

**Walt Disney's Babes in Toyland
The Toymaker's Helper**
Illustrator: Anderson, Al
Author: Francis, Dee
2490        1961              **$8**

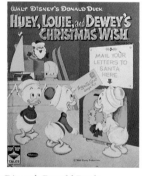

**Walt Disney's Donald Duck
Huey, Louie, and Dewey's Christmas Wish**
Illustrator: Walt Disney Studio
Author: Walt Disney Studios
2497        1962              **$15**

**Walt Disney's Mary Poppins
She's Supercalafragalisticexpialidocious!**
Illustrator: Neely, Jan
Author: Brightman, Homer
2450        1964              **$7**

**Walt Disney's Pinocchio**
Illustrator: McSavage, Frank; Fisher, Frank
Author: Haas, Dorothy
2459        1961              **$6**

**Walt Disney's The Sword In the Stone**
Illustrator: Avlerado,Peter; Andersen, Al
Author: Francis, Dee
2459        1963              **$10**

**What Shall I Put In the Hole That I Dig?**
Illustrator: Aliki
Author: Thompson, Eleanor
2496            1963            **$15**

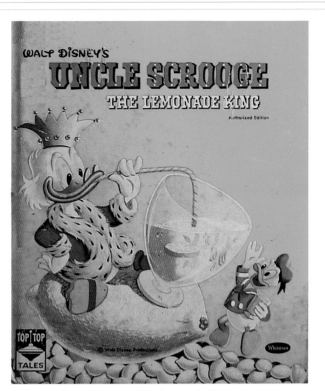

**Walt Disney's Uncle Scrooge—The Lemonade King**
Illustrator: Barks, Carl; Mc Gary, Norm
2465            1960            **$150**

**Where Is the Keeper?**
Illustrator: Seiden, Art
Author: Watts, Mabel
2487            1961            **$15**

**Why Roosty Sang Cock-A-Doodle Doo!**
Illustrator: Winship, Florence Sarah
Author: Page, Marguerita
2468            1958            **$7**

**Wiggletail**
Illustrator: Charlie
Author: Charlie
2474            1944            **$6**

**Willy Woo-Oo-Oo**
Illustrator: Winship, Florence Sarah
Author: Wright, Betty Ren
2469            1951            **$7**

**Yogi Bear, No Picnic**
Illustrator: Mc Savage, Frank; Lorencz,
William
Author: Daly, Eileen
2461            1961            **$8**

**Yogi Bear and the Cranky Magician**
Illustrator: Crawford, Mel
Author: Johnston, William
2494            1963            **$10**

**Yogi Bear Helps Santa**
Illustrator: Branscome, Lee
Author: Daly, Eileen
2498            1962            **$8**

A Cozy Corner Book series began in 1947 and was printed until 1958. The books measured 7-1/2 x 8-1/4 inches with 48 pages of full-color illustrations. Six of the titles were produced with dust jackets. The first title in the series was supposed to be Number 2075, *Flowers for Filbert*. Even though the Whitman catalogs from 1947 show this book, I can't locate one without a 1951 copyright. It may be that the release date was delayed until 1951. The books were produced for 11 years. Two series numberings were used: the 2400 series and the 2000/2100 series.

The first six titles were published with dust jackets: 2076 *Pie Face*, 2077 *Yippee! Cowboy*, 2078 *The Gingerbread Man*, 2079 *Nursery Rhymes and Songs*, 2080 *Mother Goose*, and 2081 *One More Story Please*. A dust jacket on a Cozy Corner Book can add $15-$20 to the price of the book.

**How to determine A Cozy Corner Book editions:**

There is no 100% way to tell a first edition. You can look at the titles on the back of the books and, by deduction, get an idea of when a book was printed. By using the following information, you can make an educated guess as to the print year of your book. Look at the last title and, in some cases, the first and last titles on the back of your book. If the year I show below matches your copyright or one year before it, you can assume your book is a first edition.

**Example:** Your book lists *Mother Goose* as the last title on the back of your book. Your book has a copyright date of 1951, and I'm showing that the book's back cover was used in 1951. You can assume that your book is a first edition.

| Title(s) on Back of Book | Print Year |
|---|---|
| *First Picture Word Book* | 1950 |
| *Lassie (The Famous Movie Dog)* | 1954 |
| *Mother Goose* | 1951 |
| *One More Story, Please* | 1951 |
| *My Big Book/Walt Disney's Ben and Me* | 1955 |
| *Busy Bill/Walt Disney's Ben and Me* | 1956 |
| *Walt Disney's Cinderella* | 1952 |
| *Young MacDonald on the Farm* | 1952 |

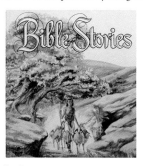

**Bible Stories**
Illustrator: Segner, Lajos
| 2029 | 1952 | $7 |

**Bible Stories**
Illustrator: Segner, Lajos
| 2409 | 1952 | $6 |

**Bugs Bunny, Baker Man**
Author: Heimdahl, Ralph; Armstrong, Samuel
| 2061 | 1952 | $15 |
| 2452 | 1952 | $12 |

**Bugs Bunny and the Big Red Apples**
Illustrator: Heimdahl, Ralph; Dempster, Al
Author: Warner Bros Cartoons Inc.
| 2032 | 1950 | $12 |

**Bugs Bunny, Big Shot of the Big Top**
Illustrator: McGary, Norm
Author: Abranz, Alfred
| 2402 | 1954 | $8 |

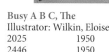

**Busy A B C, The**
Illustrator: Wilkin, Eloise
| 2025 | 1950 | $18 |
| 2446 | 1950 | $15 |

**Busy Bill**
Illustrator: Clement, Charles
Author: Lynn, Patricia
| 2443 | 1954 | $8 |

**First Picture Word Book**
Illustrator: Gehr, Mary
| 2030 | 1950 | $5 |

**Flowers For Filbert**
Illustrator: Lamb, Cecile
Author: Lamb, Cecile
| 2075 | 1951 | $15 |

**Forgotten Little Train, The**
Illustrator: Fabry, Al
Author: Fabry, Sally
2024          1951          **$8**

**Frosting**
Illustrator: Learnard, Rachel
Author: Newton, Ruth E.
2150          1953          **$7**

**Gingerbread Man—The Ugly Duckling**
Illustrator: Kalab, Theresa
2035          1949          **$12**

**Hopalong Cassidy and the Two Young Cowboys**
Illustrator: Higgs, John
Author: Beecher, Elizabeth
2067          1951          **$18**

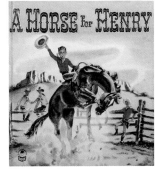

**Horse For Henry, A**
Illustrator: Helwig, Hans
Author: Horn, Gladys M.
2098          1952          **$6**

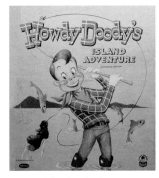

**Howdy Doody's Island Adventure**
Illustrator: Gribbroek, Robert
2410          1955          **$18**

**Hucklebones**
Illustrator: Wilde, Irma
Author: Marks, Mickey Klar
2033          1949          **$6**

**Hurrah For Jonathan!**
Illustrator: Lamont, Violet
Author: Fritz, Jean
2445          1955          **$6**

**In They Go!**
Illustrator: Cummings, Alison
Author: Gerard, Mary
2426          1955          **$6**

**Jenny Wren's New House**
Illustrator: Wilde, Irma
Author: Patton, Kay
2440          1954          **$5**
2442          1954          **$5**

**King and the Princess**
Illustrator: Doremus, Robert
Author: O'Brien, Jack
2034          1949          **$15**

**Kitty Black**
Illustrator: Wilde, Irma
Author: Wilde, Irma
2092          1952          **$8**
2456          1952          **$6**

**Lady the Little Blue Mare**
Illustrator: Winship, Florence Sarah
Author: Elting, Mary
2027          1950          **$10**

**Lassie, Rescue in the Storm**
Illustrator: La Grotta, J. M.; Lenox, August
2039          1951          **$10**
2412          1951          **$8**

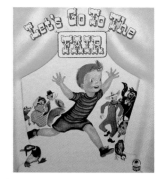

**Let's Go to the Fair**
Illustrator: Wilde, Irma
Author: Marks, Mickey Klar
2071          1951          **$6**

**Little Star**
Illustrator: Myers, Jack & Louise
Author: Myers, Jack & Louise
2094          1952          **$6**

**Lone Ranger and the War Horse, The**
Illustrator: Dreany, E. Joseph
Author: Striker, Fran
2023          1951          **$15**
2411          1951          **$14**

**Lucky Pocket**
Illustrator: Wood, Dorothy F.
Author: Wood, Dorothy F.
2072          1951          **$9**

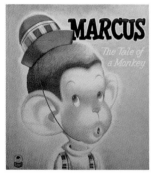

**Marcus—The Tale of a Monkey**
Illustrator: Buehrig, Rosemary
Author: Sankey, Alice
2036          1950          **$10**

**Mother Goose**
Illustrator: Tate, Sally
2080          1947          **$12**

**Mother Goose**
Illustrator: Paschal, Rose
2090          1951          **$10**

**Mother Goose**
Illustrator: Paschal, Rose
2090          1951          **$6**
2447          1951          **$5**

**My Big Book**
Illustrator: Myers, Jack & Louise
Author: Wright, Betty Ren
2422          1954          **$5**

**Nellie**
Illustrator: Chastain, Madye Lee
Author: Chastain, Madye Lee
2082          1948          **$6**

**Night Before Christmas**
Illustrator: Miloche, Hilda; Kane, Wilma
2095          1952          **$25**

**Night Before Christmas, The**
Illustrator: Clement, Charles
2408          1955          **$8**

**Nursery Rhymes and Songs**
Illustrator: Malvern, Corinne
Music: Dallam, Helen
2079          1946          **$8**

**One More Story, Please!**
Illustrator: Miloche, Hilda; Kane, Wilma
2081          1947          **$10**

**Pepper**
Illustrator: Williams, Ben
Author: Caplan, Lydia
2444          1955          **$6**

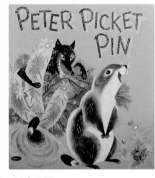

**Peter Picket Pin**
Illustrator: Meyers, Bernice & Lou
Author: Rose, Florella
2062          1953          **$6**

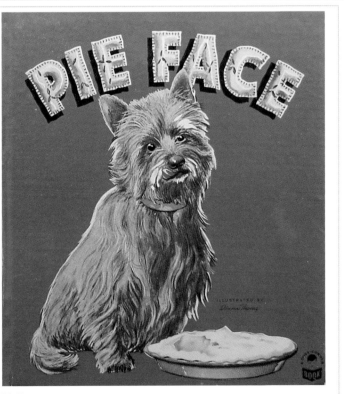

**Pie Face**
Illustrator: Thome, Diane
Author: Doreith, Velma
2076          1947          **$25**

**Poppyseed**
Illustrator: Winship, Florence Sarah
Author: Wright, Betty Ren
2441          1954          **$10**

**Rin Tin Tin: One of the Family**
Illustrator: Armstrong, Samuel
Author: Kearns, Frank
2153          1953          **$15**

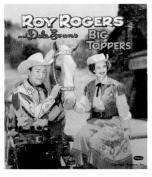

**Roy Rogers and Dale Evans, Big Toppers**
Illustrator: Souza, Paul
2407          1956          **$18**

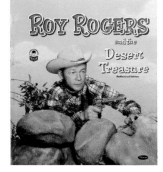

**Roy Rogers and the Desert Treasure**
Illustrator: Souza, Paul
Author: Sankey, Alice
2063          1954          **$18**

**Roy Rogers' Bullet and Trigger**
Illustrator: Lenox, August
Author: Beecher, Elizabeth
2152          1953          **$18**

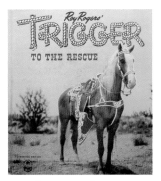

**Roy Rogers' Trigger to the Rescue**
Illustrator: Higgs, John
2038          1950          **$18**

**Scotty's Room**
Illustrator: Myers, Jack & Louise
Author: Wright, Betty Ren
2427          1957          **$6**

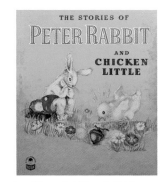

**See the Pictures—Read the Words**
Illustrator: Clement, Charles
Author: Horn, Gladys M.
2151          1953          **$6**

**Sleepytime Stories**
Illustrator: Frommholz, Hilda
Author: Frommholz, Hilda
2087          1948          **$6**

**Stories of Jesus**
Illustrator: Frame, Paul
Author: Trent, Robbie
2401          1954          **$6**

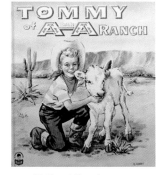

**Stories of Peter Rabbit and Chicken Little, The**
Illustrator: Kalab, Theresa
2086          1949          **$6**

**Susy**
Illustrator: Tiz
2449          1957          **$6**

**Three Friends**
Illustrator: Robinson, J. E.
Author: Robinson, J. E.
2026          1950          **$5**

**Tommy of A-Bar-A Ranch**
Illustrator: Dart, Eleanor
Author: Wood, Frances E.
2028          1951          **$7**

**Walt Disney's Alice in Wonderland**
Illustrator: Armstrong, Samuel
2074          1951          **$16**

**Walt Disney's Ben & Me**
Illustrator: Klein, Earl
2403          1954          **$15**

**Walt Disney's Cinderella**
Illustrator: Scendsen, Julius
Author: Walt Disney Studios
2037          1950          **$15**

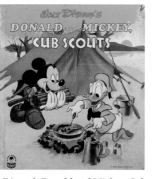

**Walt Disney's Donald and Mickey, Cub Scouts**
2031          1950          **$20**

**Walt Disney's Donald Duck and the Wishing Star**
Illustrator: Gonzales, Manuel; MacLaughlin, Don
2097          1952          **$15**

**Walt Disney's Donald Duck in A Bit of a Hit**
Illustrator: Walt Disney Studios
Author: Strobl, Tony; Boyle, Neil
2414          1956          **$15**

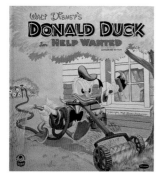

**Walt Disney's Donald Duck in Help Wanted**
Illustrator: Wheeler, George
2406          1955          **$15**

**Walt Disney's Lady**
Illustrator: Armstrong, Samuel
Author: Walt Disney Studios
2218          1954          **$15**
2405          1954          **$12**

**Walt Disney's Peter Pan**
Illustrator: Armstrong, Samuel
2022          1952          **$15**
2415          1952          **$12**

**Walt Disney's Stormy**
Illustrator: Souza, Paul
2404          1954          **$12**

**We Thank Thee**
Illustrator: Blaisdell, Elinore
Author: Emerson, Ralph Waldo
2424          1955          **$5**

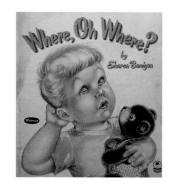

**Where, Oh Where?**
Illustrator: Banigan, Sharon
Author: Banigan, Sharon
2093          1952          **$6**

**Who Am I?**
Illustrator: Fabry, Sally & Al
Author: Fabry, Sally & Al
2088          1952          $6

**Woofus**
Illustrator: Winship, Florence Sarah
Author: Curry, Jane
2084          1944          $6

**Young MacDonald on the Farm**
Illustrator: Kalab, Theresa
Author: Gilbert, Nan
2085          1949          $6

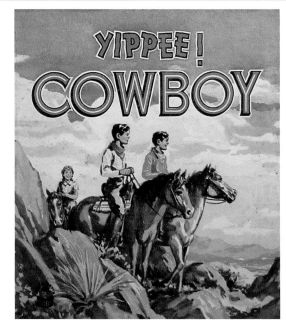

**Yippee! Cowboy**
Illustrator: Wiesman, Robert R.
Author: Wood, Frances
2077          1947          $10

**A B C**
Illustrator: Weihs, Erika
2448          1956          $8
**Boys and Girls From Mother Goose**
Illustrator: Scott, Marguerite K.
2451          1955          $8
**Count With Me**
Illustrator: Wilde, Irma
Author: Fairweather, Jessie Home
2428          1957          $6
**Does Baby Live Here?**
Illustrator: Wilde, Irma
2454          1952          $6
**Gingerbread Man, The**
Illustrator: Tate, Sally
2078          1947          $8
**Hello**
Illustrator: Sari
Author: Hanson, Alice
2425          1955          $6
**Let's Guess**
Illustrator: Stang, Judy
Author: Bane, Sally
2431          1958          $5

**My Picture Book**
Illustrator: Suzanne
Author: Hanson, Alice
2430          1958          $5
**My School**
Illustrator: Suzanne
Author: Hanson, Alice
2429          1958          $5
**Pet For Peter**
Illustrator: Grider, Dorothy
Author: Grider, Dorothy
2096          1952          $6
**Through My Window**
Illustrator: Michell, Gladys Turley
2421          1954          $5
**Who Said It?**
Illustrator: Depper, Hertha
Author: Horn, Gladys M.
2423          1954          $6

The original Tiny Tales had hard covers and measured 3-1/4 x 4 inches. The books contained 22 pages and were illustrated throughout in full color. Series 1030 and 1031 were released around January 1950, and series 1032 followed sometime in the fall. These all had a list of titles on the back inside cover.

In the late 1950s the books were re-released in the 2952 series. This series had covers made of heavy cardboard. The inside color of the cardboard was either blue or yellow. Around 1960 two more series were released: 2934 and 2952. Both of these had thin cardboard covers. *The Mockingbird's Joke, If I Were, The Hound Dog*, and *Fun at the Beach*, which were released in 1960, were the only new titles to be added since 1950.

This makes it easy to know if you own a first edition. If your book is one of the four titles from 1960 or is from the numbered series 1030, 1031, or 1032, it is a first edition.

**Animal 1 2 3**
Illustrator: Meyers, Louise

| | | |
|---|---|---|
| 1031 | 1949 | $5 |
| 2952 | 1949 | $4 |
| 2934 | 1949 | $3 |

**Animal Parade**
Illustrator: McKinley, Clare

| | | |
|---|---|---|
| 1030 | 1949 | $5 |
| 2952 | 1949 | $4 |

**Buddy Bear's Lost Growl**
Illustrator: Cummings, Alison

| | | |
|---|---|---|
| 1031 | 1949 | $5 |
| 2934 | 1949 | $4 |
| 2952 | 1949 | $3 |

**Cowboy Bill**
Illustrator: Dart, Eleanor

| | | |
|---|---|---|
| 1032 | 1950 | $6 |
| 2934 | 1950 | $5 |
| 2952 | 1950 | $4 |

**Five Fat Piggies**
Illustrator: Hartwell, Marjorie

| | | |
|---|---|---|
| 1032 | 1950 | $6 |
| 2934 | 1950 | $5 |
| 2952 | 1950 | $4 |

**Fun at the Beach**
Illustrator: Wilson, Dagmar
Author: Trachtenberg, Gloria

| | | |
|---|---|---|
| 2952 | 1960 | $4 |

**Hide and Seek**
Illustrator: Kendrick, Alcy

| | | |
|---|---|---|
| 1032 | 1950 | $5 |
| 2934 | 1950 | $4 |
| 2952 | 1950 | $3 |

**Hound Dog, The**
Illustrator: Frost, Bruno
Author: Hoag, Nancy

| | | |
|---|---|---|
| 2952 | 1960 | $5 |

**If I Were**
Illustrator: Lesko, Zillah
Author: Trachtenberg, Gloria

| | | |
|---|---|---|
| 2952 | 1960 | $5 |

**Jackie's Airplane Ride**
Illustrator: Stoddart, Mary Alice
1031        1949            $5
2952        1949            $4

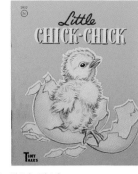

**Little Chick-Chick**
Illustrator: Rachel
1032        1950            $5
2934        1950            $4
2952        1950            $3

**Little Lost Kitten**
Illustrator: Rachel
1030        1950            $5
2934        1950            $4
2952        1949            $4

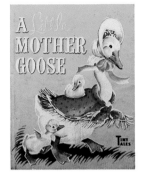

**Little Mother Goose, A**
Illustrator: Scott, Janet Laura
1031        1949            $5
2952        1949            $4

**Mockingbird's Joke, The**
Illustrator: Eleanor
Author: Morton, Virginia
2952        1960            $4

**New Playmate, A**
Illustrator: Doris
1031        1949            $5
2952        1949            $4

**Plush**
Illustrator: Meyers, Louise
1030        1949            $6
2952        1949            $5

**Puff's Vegetable Garden**
Illustrator: Scott, Janet Laura
1031        1949            $8
2934        1949            $6
2952        1949            $5

**Rover**
Illustrator: Scott, Janet Laura
1030        1949            $5
2952        1949            $4

**Sally Squirrel's Wish**
Illustrator: Cummings, Alison
1032        1950            $5
2934        1950            $4
2952        1950            $3

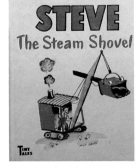

**Steve the Steam Shovel**
Illustrator: Groth, Milt
1032        1950            $5
2934        1950            $4
2952        1950            $3

**Telling Time**
Illustrator: Cummings, Alison
1031        1949            $5
2934        1949            $4
2952        1949            $3

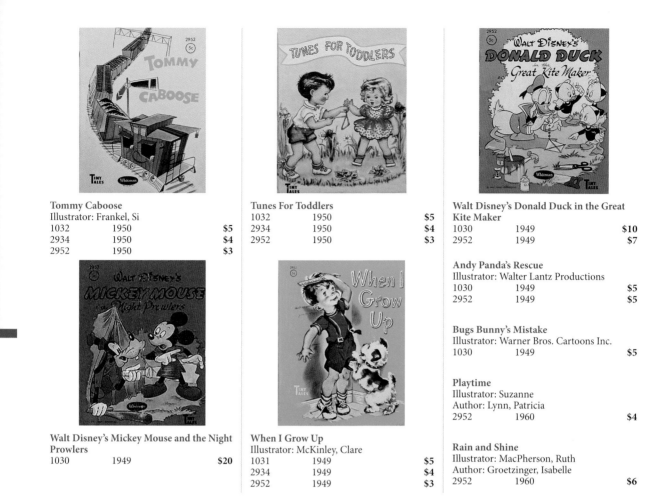

**Tommy Caboose**
Illustrator: Frankel, Si

| | | |
|---|---|---|
| 1032 | 1950 | $5 |
| 2934 | 1950 | $4 |
| 2952 | 1950 | $3 |

**Walt Disney's Mickey Mouse and the Night Prowlers**

| | | |
|---|---|---|
| 1030 | 1949 | $20 |

**Tunes For Toddlers**

| | | |
|---|---|---|
| 1032 | 1950 | $5 |
| 2934 | 1950 | $4 |
| 2952 | 1950 | $3 |

**When I Grow Up**
Illustrator: McKinley, Clare

| | | |
|---|---|---|
| 1031 | 1949 | $5 |
| 2934 | 1949 | $4 |
| 2952 | 1949 | $3 |

**Walt Disney's Donald Duck in the Great Kite Maker**

| | | |
|---|---|---|
| 1030 | 1949 | $10 |
| 2952 | 1949 | $7 |

**Andy Panda's Rescue**
Illustrator: Walter Lantz Productions

| | | |
|---|---|---|
| 1030 | 1949 | $5 |
| 2952 | 1949 | $5 |

**Bugs Bunny's Mistake**
Illustrator: Warner Bros. Cartoons Inc.

| | | |
|---|---|---|
| 1030 | 1949 | $5 |

**Playtime**
Illustrator: Suzanne
Author: Lynn, Patricia

| | | |
|---|---|---|
| 2952 | 1960 | $4 |

**Rain and Shine**
Illustrator: MacPherson, Ruth
Author: Groetzinger, Isabelle

| | | |
|---|---|---|
| 2952 | 1960 | $6 |

# Tiny-Tot Tales

Whitman Publishing Company published Tiny-Tot Tales from 1966 to 1969. These hardcover books measured 4-1/4 x 5-1/2 inches with 20 pages of full-color illustrations. If a title was published with the number 2942 on the back and also published later with another book number, you can assume that the book with 2942 is the first edition. If a title were only printed with a book number other than 2942, you can probably assume that it is a first edition.

The 2942 numbered books were printed from 1966 to 1969. Series 2961 was printed in 1968, and series 2960 and 2964 were printed in 1969.

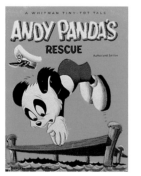

**Andy Panda's Rescue**
Illustrator: Walter Lantz Productions
Author: Walter Lantz Productions

| | | |
|---|---|---|
| 2942 | 1949 | $6 |

**Belonging Book, The**
Illustrator: Myers, Jack & Louise
Author: Watts, Mabel

| | | |
|---|---|---|
| 2942 | 1968 | $5 |
| 2961 H | 1968 | $6 |

**Boys and Girls in Mother Goose**
Illustrator: Oechsli, Kelly

| | | |
|---|---|---|
| 2960 L | 1966 | $5 |

**Bugs Bunny's Mistake**
Illustrator: Warner Bros. Cartoons Inc.
Author: Warner Bros. Cartoons Inc.
2942          1949          **$5**

**Cat Called Cindy, A**
Illustrator: Wilson, Dagmar
Author: Davidson, Alice
2942          1966          **$7**

**Flying Kitten, The**
Illustrator: DeLuna, Tony
Author: Walker, Betty R.
2942          1968          **$7**

**Fun at the Beach**
Illustrator: Wilson, Dagmar
Author: Trachtenberg, Gloria
2960 H          1966          **$5**

**Grandpapa and Me**
Illustrator: Goldsborough June
Author: Haas, Dorothy
2942          1966          **$5**

**Here, Kitty**
Illustrator: Tsambon, Athena
Author: Moore, Margaret
2942          1966          **$5**

**Hound Dog, The**
Illustrator: Frost, Bruno
Author: Hoag, Nancy
2942          1968          **$6**

**I Have a Turtle**
Illustrator: Davidson, R J
Author: Bing, Kathy
No #          1966          **$5**

**Little Things**
Illustrator: Miloche, Hilda
Author: Wright, Betty Ren
2961 K          1968          **$10**

**Michael's Treasure**
Illustrator: Lonette, Reisie
Author: Biesterveld, Betty
2960 A          1969          **$6**
2964 H          1969          **$6**

**Mockingbird's Joke, The**
Illustrator: Eleanor
Author: Morton, Virginia
2942          1966          **$6**

**Most Wonderful Birthday Present, The**
Illustrator: Myers, Jack & Louise
Author: Walker, Betty
2961 B          1968          **$6**

**Mr. McMilikin's Mountain**
Illustrator: DeSantis, George
Author: Klimke, Wilma
2960 B        1969                    **$10**

**Owl and the Pussy-Cat, The**
Illustrator: Rutherford, Bonnie & Bill
Author: Lear, Edward
2961 J        1968                    **$7**

**Patchwork Puppy**
Illustrator: Garris, Norma & Dan
Author: Browne, Katherine
2960 E        1969                    **$10**

**Peter Potamus and the Pirates**
Illustrator: Forsberg, Howard
Author: Lewis, Jean
2942        1968                    **$10**

**Peter's Wagon**
Illustrator: Nagel, Stina
Author: Biesterveld, Betty
2961 A        1968                    **$7**

**Playtime**
Illustrator: Suzanne
Author: Lynn, Patricia
2942        1968                    **$5**

**Quiet Place, A**
Illustrator: Wheeling, Lynn
Author: Wheeling, Lynn
2960 D        1969                    **$6**

**Soda Pop**
Illustrator: Williams, Ben
Author: Haas, Dorothy
2961 F        1968                    **$8**

**Something's in the Backyard**
Illustrator: Garris, Norma; Garris, Dan
Author: Wynn, Ethel
2961 D        1968                    **$6**

**There's a Mouse in Our House**
Illustrator: Winship, Florence Sarah
Author: Wynn, Ethel
2942        1966                    **$15**
2961 L        1966                    **$12**

**They Saw Him Fly**
Illustrator: Rutherford, Bonnie & Bill
Author: Moore, Margaret
2942        1966                    **$5**
2961 N        1966                    **$5**

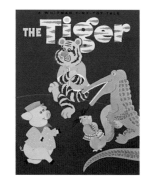

**Tiger, The**
Illustrator: Wallner, Shirley
Author: Hancok, Malcolm
2964 G        1969                    **$7**
2960 F        1969                    **$6**

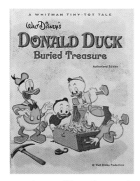

**Walt Disney's Donald Duck Buried Treasure**
Illustrator: Strobl, Anthony; Anderson, Al
Author: Tall, Nick
2942          1968          **$8**

**What Is It?**
Illustrator: Eugenie
Author: Klimke, Wilma F.
2964 H          1969          **$7**
2960 G          1969          **$6**

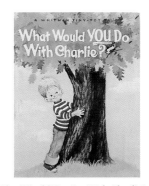

**What Would You Do With Charlie?**
Illustrator: Elfreda
Author: Foley, Joan Ryan
2942          1966          **$7**

# Fuzzy Wuzzy Story Books

Fuzzy Wuzzy Story Books measured 8 x 11-1/4 inches and were Singer sewed. Each of these 36-page books was protected by a full-color dust jacket. There were approximately 11 flocked pages in each book. The books were produced from around 1945 through 1949.

**A Fuzzy Golden Book**

A Fuzzy Wuzzy Golden Book measured 8 x 11-1/4 inches, contained 32 pages, and was covered by a dust jacket. Each book contained 11 or 12 flocked pictures.

**How to determine editions:**

There are no markings for determining editions on the Fuzzy Wuzzy Story Books.

A Fuzzy Golden Book will have a letter of the alphabet corresponding with the edition number on the inside front flap of the dust jacket. It will look like A 100 100 or B 100 100. The "A" means a first edition, and the "100 100" means that it sold for $1. Some reprints had this information on the inside front cover. If your book does not have a dust jacket and you cannot find this information on the cover, then it is probably a first edition.

**Gingerbread Man, The**
Whitman
Illustrator: Tate, Sally
5055          1944          **$35**

**Golden Circus, The**
Golden
Illustrator: Provensen, Alice & Martin
Author: Jackson, Kathryn
444          1950          **$27**

**Miss Sniff**
Whitman
Illustrator: Winship, Florence Sarah
Author: Curry, Jane
5070          1945          **$50**

**Mouse's House**
Golden
Illustrator: Scarry, Richard
Author: Jackson, Kathryn & Byron
442        1949                    **$35**

**Patrick, the Fuzziest Bunny**
Whitman
Illustrator: Werner, Elsa Jane
Author: Lesko, Zillah
5071        1946                    **$35**

**Pom Pom**
Whitman
Illustrator: Barnes, Catherine
Author: Cunningham, Virginia
5074        1947                    **$40**

**Sir Gruff**
Whitman
Illustrator: Winship, Florence Sarah
Author: Gilbert, Nan
5073        1947                    **$35**

**Snowman Who Wanted to Stay, The**
Whitman
Illustrator: Dorcas
Author: Derman, Sarah
5076        1948                    **$45**

**Three Fuzzy Bears, The**
Whitman
Author: Gilbert, Nan
5072        1947                    **$35**

**Walt Disney's Bambi**
Golden
Illustrator: Shaw, Melvin
Author: Salten, Felix
443        1949                    **$40**

**Walt Disney's Circus**
Golden
Illustrator: Walt Disney Productions
Author: Walt Disney Productions
5076        1948                    **$45**

**What Happened to Fluffy**
Whitman
Illustrator: Winship, Florence Sarah
Author: Cunningham, Virginia
5075        1948                    **$40**

**White Bunny and His Magic Nose, The**
Golden
Illustrator: Masha
Author: Duplaix, Lily
441        1945                    **$35**

**Woofus, the Woolly Dog**
Whitman
Illustrator: Winship, Florence Sarah
Author: Curry, Jane
5056        1944                    **$45**

## The Smaller Story Hour Series

The smaller, 4-7/8 x 6-5/8-inch books were comprised of regular titles containing 56 pages and an authorized title that contained 40 pages. They had a cellophane laminated hard cover that was later trademarked as Plasti-Lac. The regular titles started being published around 1947. The authorized books started arriving at stores in January 1949. The books sold for 15 cents and contained both black and white and full-color pictures.

Three titles, *Donald Duck in Bringing Up the Boys*, *Mickey Mouse's Summer Vacation*, and *Bugs Bunny's Adventure*, were given away by Whitman Publishing Company with a subscription to *Walt Disney's Comics & Stories*.

I do not know of any way to determine editions on this series or if the titles ever had more than one printing.

**A B C Book**
Illustrator: Taylor, Kathryn
820           1944           **$10**

**Andy Panda and His Friends**
Illustrator: Walter Lantz Productions
Author: Walter Lantz Productions
805           1949           **$10**

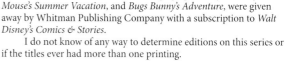

**Bible Stories**
Illustrator: Maloy, Lois
Author: Trent, Robbie
828           1947           **$8**
828           1947           **$8**

**Bugs Bunny's Adventures**
Illustrator: Warner Bros. Cartoons Inc.
Author: Warner Bros. Cartoons Inc.
802           1948           **$8**

**Child's Garden of Verses, A**
Illustrator: Scott, Janet Laura
Author: Stevenson, Robert Louis
826           1947           **$8**

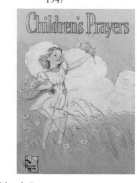

**Children's Prayers**
Illustrator: Segner, Ellen
Author: Cavanah, Frances
822           1945           **$8**

**Nature Stories**
Illustrator: Vivienne
Author: Jolsyn, Dorothy
831           1947           **$8**

**Prayers For Boys and Girls**
Illustrator: Neville, Vera
Author: Cavanah, Frances
833           1945           **$6**

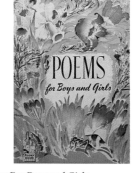

**Poems For Boys and Girls**
Illustrator: Maloy, Lois
Author: Barrows, Marjorie
824           1945           **$8**

**Sleepy Time Stories**
Illustrator: Frommholz, Hilda
823             1944             **$8**

**Stories of Jesus**
Illustrator: Maloy, Lois
Author: Trent, Robbie
835             1950             **$8**

**Stories of Kittens & Puppies**
Illustrator: Taylor, Cathryn
Author: Stoddard, Mary Alice
825             1945             **$15**

**Tom and Jerry**
Illustrator: Loew's Inc.
Author: Loew's Inc.
806             1949             **$10**

**Walt Disney's Bongo**
Illustrator: Walt Disney Productions
Author: Walt Disney Productions
803             1948             **$15**

**Walt Disney's Danny the Little Black Lamb**
Illustrator: Walt Disney Productions
Author: Walt Disney Productions
807             1949             **$25**

**Walt Disney's Corky and White Shadow**
Only published as a soft-cover book.
Illustrator: Haas, Dorothy
Author: Spiegle, Dan
No #             1956             **$16**

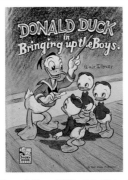

**Walt Disney's Donald Duck in Bringing
Up the Boys**
Illustrator: Walt Disney Productions
Author: Walt Disney Productions
800             1948             **$15**

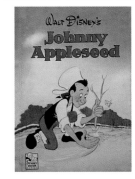

**Walt Disney's Johnny Appleseed**
Illustrator: Walt Disney Productions
Author: Walt Disney Productions
808             1949             **$16**

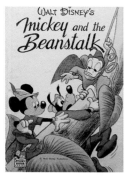

**Walt Disney's Mickey and the Beanstalk**
Illustrator: Walt Disney Productions
Author: Walt Disney Productions
804          1948                    **$16**

**Counting Rhymes**
Illustrator: Rachel
827          1947                    **$8**
**Goldilocks and the Three Bears and Other Stories**
"The Little Red Hen and the Fox," "The Story of Little Black Sambo," "The Elves and the Shoemaker"
Illustrator: Frommholz, Hilda
829          1947                    **$30**
**Mother Goose**
Illustrator: Vaughan, Eileen Fox
834          1950                    **$12**
**Mother Goose**
Illustrator: Weihs, Erika
821          1934                    **$10**

**Walt Disney's Mickey Mouse's Summer Vacation**
Illustrator: Walt Disney Productions
Author: Walt Disney Productions
801          1948                    **$15**

**Walt Disney's The Three Orphan Kittens**
Illustrator: Walt Disney Productions
Author: Walt Disney Productions
809          1949                    **$25**

**Mickey Mouse Club Treasure Mine**
Boxed set contains soft-cover versions of *Bongo, Three Orphans Kittens, Donald Duck in Bringing up the Boys, Mickey and the Beanstalk, Johnny Appleseed, Danny the Little Black Lamb, Mickey Mouse's Summer Vacation,* and *Corky and White Shadow. Corky and White Shadow* was only published in this boxed soft-cover set.
2918          1957                    **$90**

## The Larger Story Hour Series

The larger, 7-1/2 x 8-1/4-inch books were printed from 1958 to 1960. They all contained 36 pages with full-color pictures on heavy paper.

I don't know of any way to determine editions on this series or if the titles ever had more then one printing. My guess is that all of the titles in this larger size series had only one printing.

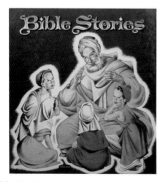

**Bible Stories**
Illustrator: Segner, Lajos
2222          1959                    **$8**

**Busy A B C**
Illustrator: Wilkin, Eloise
2210          1950                    **$12**

**Captain Kangaroo's Super Secret**
Illustrator: Frost, Robert
2206          1959                    **$10**

**First Picture Word Book**
Illustrator: Gehr, Mary
2211          1950          **$8**

**Forgotten Little Train, The**
Illustrator: Fabry, Al
Author: Fabry, Sally
2208          1951          **$8**

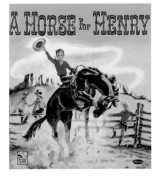

**Horse For Henry, A**
Illustrator: Helweg, Hans H.
Author: Horn, Gladys M.
2211          1952          **$10**

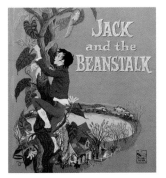

**Jack and the Beanstalk**
Illustrator: Barnes, Catherine
Author: Barnes, Catherine
2218          1958          **$10**

**Mother Goose**
Illustrator: Rutherford, Bonnie & Bill
2214          1960          **$15**

**My Prayers**
Illustrator: Dixon, Rachel Taft
2224          1959          **$8**

**Nursery Rhymes Songs**
Illustrator: Malvern, Corrine
2213          1944          **$8**

**Ship's Dog**
Illustrator: Boyle, Neil
Author: Palmer, Robin
2217          1958          **$10**

**Tale of Peter Rabbit, The**
Illustrator: Drutzu, Anne Marie
2205          1959          **$10**

**Two-in-One Tales**
**Hello! and Who Am I?**
Illustrator: Fabry, Sally & Al; Hanson, Alice
Author: Fabry, Sally & Al & Sari
2207          1958          **$6**

**Two-in-One Tales**
**My Big Book and Scotty's Room**
Illustrator: Rutherford, Bonnie & Bill; Myers,
Jack & Louise
Author: Wright, Betty Ren
2208          1964          **$6**

**Two-in-One Tales**
**My School and In They Go!**
Illustrator: Murray, Marjorie; Cummings,
Alison
Author: Hansen, Mary; Gerard, Mary
2243          1958          **$6**

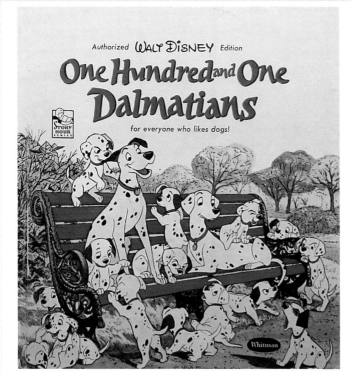

**Walt Disney's One Hundred and One Dalmatians**
Illustrator: Campbell, Collin
Author: Smith, Dodie
2209          1960                    **$18**

A B C
Illustrator: Weihs, Erika
2226          1959                    **$8**
 Gingerbread Man, The
Illustrator: Myers, Jack & Louise
2223          1959                    **$15**
 Hucklebones
Illustrator: Wilde, Irma
Author: Marks, Mickey Klar
2212          1949                    **$12**
 Mimi
Illustrator: Winship, Florence Sarah
Author: Haas, Dorothy
2216          1958                    **$16**
 Night Before Christmas, The
Illustrator: Barnes, Catherine
2221          1959                    **$25**
 Sleepy Time Stories
Illustrator: Frommholz, Hilda
2215          1958                    **$8**

**Two-in-One Tales**
**Where, Or Where? and My Picture Book**
Illustrator: Suzanne; Bannigan, Sharon
Author: Hanson, Alice; Bannigan, Sharon
2212          1958                    **$6**

**Walt Disney's Sleeping Beauty**
Illustrator: Walt Disney Studios
Author: Walt Disney Studios
2219          1959                    **$15**

## Elf & Jr. Elf Books
## Published by Rand McNally

In 1856, William Rand, a young printer from Boston, arrived in Chicago and opened his own print shop. While Rand was starting up his company, another young man was getting ready to leave his homeland in search of his fortune in the United States. Andrew McNally, having finished his seven years as a printer's apprentice, was preparing to leave the county of Armagh in Ireland.

McNally arrived in Chicago and, while looking for work, came upon Rand's business. In just a few years the two men were able to purchase the Chicago Tribune's job printing shop and formed Rand McNally & Company. While looking for new ventures, they started printing passenger tickets, timetables, and guides for railroads. Later they started printing the Railroad Guide, a route map for a single railroad.

By the early 1900s, the automobile started allowing people to move outside of their neighborhoods and see the country. To help people in their travels, the company started producing road maps. In 1907, Andrew McNally II and his wife drove from Chicago to New York, taking pictures of every turn they made on their trip. This was later published as the *Chicago-to-New York Auto Guide*.

As more and more roads crossed the country, Rand McNally, not the government, created the numbering of highways. The first road map to list major roads with numbers was for the state of Illinois. Road maps of the 48 states were available by 1922. *The Rand McNally Road Atlas* that is in print today was first printed in 1924.

The company had been printing children's books since around 1913. In 1949, the company acquired the W.B. Conkey Company and started printing books on a much larger scale. With the proven success of Little Golden Books, the company released the first four titles of its own 6-5/8 x 8-3/4-inch books, Rand McNally Elf Books, around September 1947. Later titles were not released until around the summer or fall of 1948.

Rand McNally sold its low-end children's line to MacMillan Publishing in 1986. Checkerboard Press was formed and became a subsidiary from 1986 to 1990. In 1990, Checkerboard Press became a private company. The name of the company comes from the very popular *Rand McNally Reads Mother Goose*, first printed in 1916. This book has a checkerboard background on the front cover.

When trying to date a Rand McNally Elf or Jr. Elf Book prior to February 1963, look on the last page. You will see a number preceded by the letters "CS." The first number preceding the dash stands for the month, while the next number is the year of printing. For example, CS6-54 means the book was printed in June 1954, and CS12-52 means December 1952. There is no way of telling for sure if a book is a first edition on most books after February 1963.

You will also see two numbers separated by a dash (-) on the last page. These two numbers denote the recommended reading age for that particular book. The first number, divided by 10, is the recommended beginning age. The second number, divided by 10, is the ending age. For example, a book with "50-90" would be for children 5 to 9 years of age.

## Rand McNally Elf Books

The primary construction difference between Elf Books and Little Golden Books is that Elf Books are not flush-cut. A Little Golden Book is put together and then the sides are trimmed, making the pages flush to the cover, but most Elf Books had the cover made separately from the book (although some were done flush-cut between 1954 and 1957). The front and back cover is one piece, which is glued to the cardboard cover backing. The pages are stitched together and are then glued to the cover by the first and last page. With this method, the cover extends past the pages by about one-quarter of an inch. Because the covers on Elf Books did not hold up to use as well as Little Golden® Books covers, they are more difficult to find in nice condition.

From 1947 until around 1954, the books were called Rand McNally Book/Elf Books and had a picture of an elf in a 3/4 x 7/8-inch box in the upper left corner. In 1954 the picture of the elf grew to 1/2 x 1-1/4 inches. In 1955, the books were called Rand McNally Elf Books.

Tip-Top Elf Books, which were first printed around 1959, have a little elf standing on a globe. Start-Right Elf Books were started around 1966. These show an elf sitting down reading a book in the upper left corner, and "Rand McNally Publisher" appears at the bottom of the cover. Rand McNally also printed Ding Dong School Books between July 1953 and June 1956, before they were done as Golden Books.

Quite a few of the books were printed in different numbered series over the years. The first series ran from 425 to as high as 620, but some numbers had no titles before the 8300 period. The second series was from 3800 to around 8460. The fourth series was the Tip-Top Elf Book, which originally went from 1001 to 1038, before it was changed to 8600 and continued to around 8743. The fifth series, the Start-Right Elf Book, began with 8500.

Elf books were originally printed with 36 pages, but books below number 600 could have had 28, 30, or 32 pages. Books numbered higher than 3000 typically had 20 pages, although some had 28.

**A B C Book**
Illustrator: Bryant, Dean

| | | |
|---|---|---|
| 1032 | 1958 | $4 |
| 8364 | 1958 | $5 |
| 8653 | 1958 | $4 |

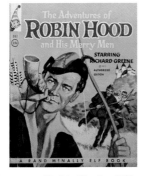

**Adventures of Robin Hood and His Merry Men, The**
Illustrator: Timmins, William
Author: Grant, Bruce, Starring Richard Green

| | | |
|---|---|---|
| 532 | 1955 | **$16** |

**Aesop's Fables**
Illustrator: Leaf, Anne Sellers

| | | |
|---|---|---|
| 463 | 1952 | **$8** |

**Aesop's Fables**
Illustrator: Leaf, Anne Sellers
| | | |
|---|---|---|
| 8440 | 1952 | **$5** |
| 1019 | 1958 | **$6** |
| 8615 | 1952 | **$5** |

**Alice in Wonderland**
Illustrator: Holland, Janice
Author: Carroll, Lewis
| | | |
|---|---|---|
| 451 | 1951 | **$18** |

**Alphabet Walks**
Illustrator: Stahlman, Catherine
Author: Petie, Haris
| | | |
|---|---|---|
| 8553 | 1973 | **$4** |

**Amos Learns to Talk: The Story of a Little Duck**
Illustrator: McKinley, Clare
Author: Bradbury, Bianca
| | | |
|---|---|---|
| 446 | 1950 | **$12** |
| 8352 | 1950 | **$5** |
| 8694 | 1950 | **$5** |

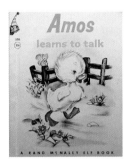

**Amos Learns to Talk: The Story of a Little Duck**
Illustrator: McKinley, Clare
Author: Bradbury, Bianca
| | | |
|---|---|---|
| 576 | 1958 | **$10** |
| 8352 | 1950 | **$5** |

**Angel Child**
Illustrator: Doane, Pelagie
Author: Teal, Val
| | | |
|---|---|---|
| 8373 | 1946 | **$6** |
| 8715 | 1946 | **$5** |

**Animal A B C Book**
Illustrator: Kane, Herbert
| | | |
|---|---|---|
| 8345 | 1964 | **$4** |
| 8658 | 1964 | **$4** |

**Animal Show, The**
Illustrator: Grider, Dorothy
Author: Jackson, Leroy F.
| | | |
|---|---|---|
| 8459 | 1965 | **$4** |
| 8748 | 1965 | **$4** |

**Baby Jesus, The**
Illustrator: Webbe, Elizabeth
Author: Jones, Mary Alice
| | | |
|---|---|---|
| 8556 | 1961 | **$4** |

**Baby Sister**
Illustrator: Cooper, Marjorie
Author: Grayland, Valerie
| | | |
|---|---|---|
| 8443 | 1964 | **$5** |
| 8663 | 1964 | **$4** |

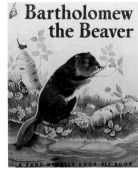

**Bartholomew the Beaver**
Illustrator: Pierce, Alice
Author: Dixon, Ruth
| | | |
|---|---|---|
| 471 | 1952 | **$8** |

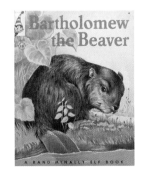

**Bartholomew the Beaver**
Illustrator: Pierce, Alice
Author: Dixon, Ruth
| | | |
|---|---|---|
| 597 | 1952 | **$6** |
| 8423 | 1952 | **$4** |
| 8643 | 1952 | **$4** |

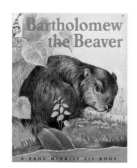

**Bartholomew the Beaver**
Illustrator: Pierce, Alice
Author: Dixon, Ruth
597         1952         $6
8423        1952         $4
8643        1952         $4

**Bartholomew the Beaver**
Illustrator: Pierce, Alice
Author: Dixon, Ruth
8643        1952         $4

**Bedtime Stories**
Illustrator: Clyne, Barbara
Author: Watts, Mabel
499         1955         $7

**Bedtime Stories**
Illustrator: Clyne, Barbara
Author: Watts, Mabel
595         1955         $6
8355        1955         $5
8595        1955         $5

**Bertram and the Ticklish Rhinoceros**
Illustrator: Thompson Van Tellingen, Ruth
Author: Gilbert, Paul
430         1948         $25

**Bible Stories: Old Testament**
Illustrator: Webbe, Elizabeth
Author: Jones, Mary Alice
491         1954         $8
8613        1954         $4

**Billy Whiskers' Twins**
Illustrator: Tamburine, Jean
Author: Wing, Helen
538         1956         $7

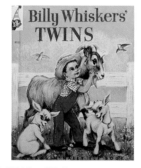

**Billy Whiskers' Twins**
Illustrator: Tamburine, Jean
Author: Wing, Helen
8333        1956         $5
8588        1956         $4

**Billy's Treasure**
Illustrator: Grider, Dorothy
Author: Snow, Dorothea J.
8560        1972         $4

**Bronto the Dinosaur**
Illustrator: Wilde, George
Author: Landis, Dorothy Thompson
8575        1967         $4

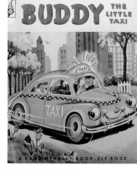

**Buddy the Little Taxi**
Illustrator: Corwin, Elizabeth
Author: Grider, Dorothy
456         1951         $10
8736        1951         $5

**Buddy the Little Taxi**
Illustrator: Corwin, Elizabeth
Author: Grider, Dorothy
564         1951         $8
8351        1951         $6

**Bugle, a Puppy in Old Yorktown**
Illustrator: Lee, Manning De V
Author: Andrews, Mary
1027      1958                    $5
8618      1958                    $4

**Building a Skyscraper**
Illustrator: Frame, Paul
Author: Kozak, Louis Lawrence
8552      1973                    $4

**Bunny Tales**
Illustrator: Endred, Helen; Nebbe, William
Author: Burroes, Peggy
574       1956                    $7
8406      1956                    $5
8417      1956                    $4
8641      1956                    $4

**Bunny Twins, The**
Illustrator: Cooper, Marjorie
Author: Wing, Helen
8676      1964                    $5
8428      1964                    $4

**Burl Ives Sailing on a Very Fine Day**
Illustrator: Myers, Lou
Author: Ives, Burl
497       1954                    $7

**Busy Ants, The**
Illustrator: Street, T.
Author: Farley, Karin Clafford
8551      1973                    $4

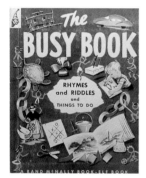

**Busy Book, The**
Illustrator: Szepelak, Helen
Author: Bartlett, Floy; Pease, Josephine
462       1952                    $8

**Busy Book, The**
Illustrator: Szepelak, Helen
Author: Bartlett, Floy; Pease, Josephine
8402      1952                    $4
1038      1952                    $5
8623      1952                    $4

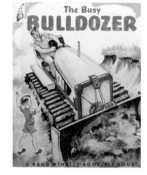

**Busy Bulldozer, The**
Illustrator: Grider, Dorothy
Author: Browning, James
459       1952                    $8

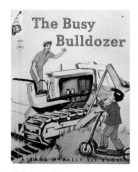

**Busy Bulldozer, The**
Illustrator: Grider, Dorothy
Author: Browning, James
567       1952                    $6
8375      1952                    $4
8732      1952                    $4

**Campbell Kids at Home, The**
Illustrator: G. Schlining Studios
Author: Lach, Alma S.
493       1954                    $22

**Campbell Kids Have a Party, The**
Illustrator: G. Schlining Studios
Author: Lach, Alma S.
494       1954                    $22

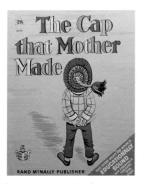

**Cap That Mother Made, The**
Illustrator: Friend, Esther
Author: O'Grady, Alice; Throop, Frances
8579          1967                    **$4**

**Chatterduck**
Illustrator: Evers, Helen & Alf
Author: Evers, Helen & Alf
8576          1967                    **$5**

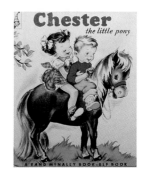

**Chester the Little Pony**
Illustrator: McKinley, Clare
Author: Gunder, Eman
452           1951                    **$10**
8354          1951                    **$6**

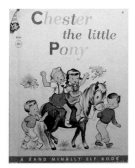

**Chester the Little Pony**
Illustrator: McKinley, Clare
Author: Gunder, Eman
581           1951                    **$8**
8354          1951                    **$5**

**Chester the Little Pony**
Illustrator: McKinley, Clare
Author: Gunder, Eman
8731          1951                    **$5**

**Child's Thought of God, A**
Illustrator: Grider, Dorothy
Author: Asher, Hellen Drummond
8651          1957                    **$4**

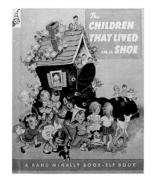

**Children That Lived in a Shoe, The**
Illustrator: Webbe, Elizabeth
Author: Pease, Josephine Van Dolzen
453           1951                    **$10**

**Children That Lived in a Shoe, The**
Illustrator: Webbe, Elizabeth
Author: Pease, Josephine Van Dolzen
8391          1951                    **$4**
8616          1951                    **$4**
1024          1951                    **$5**

**Choo-Choo the Little Switch Engine**
Illustrator: Chase, Mary Jane
Author: Wadsworth, Wallace
485           1954                    **$8**
1034          1954                    **$5**

**Choo-Choo the Little Switch Engine**
Illustrator: Chase, Mary Jane
Author: Wadsworth, Wallace
8394          1954                    **$4**
#8621         1954                    **$4**

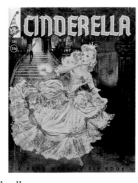

**Cinderella**
Illustrator: Endred, Helen; Nebbe, William
Author: Bates, Katherine Lee
551           1956                    **$7**

**Cinderella**
Illustrator: Endred, Helen; Nebbe, William
Author: Bates, Katherine Lee
8417          1956                    **$4**
8644          1956                    **$4**

**Copy-Kitten**
Illustrator: Evers, Helen & Alf
Author: Evers, Helen & Alf
| | | |
|---|---|---|
| 584 | 1954 | $7 |
| 8370 | 1957 | $5 |
| 8689 | 1957 | $4 |

**Cowboy Eddie**
Illustrator: Grider, Dorothy
Author: Glasscock, Joyce
| | | |
|---|---|---|
| 437 | 1950 | $12 |

**Cowboy Eddie**
Illustrator: Grider, Dorothy
Author: Glasscock, Joyce
| | | |
|---|---|---|
| 599 | 1950 | $10 |
| 8418 | 1950 | $6 |
| 8645 | 1950 | $4 |

**Cowboy Eddie**
Illustrator: Grider, Dorothy
Author: Glasscock, Joyce
| | | |
|---|---|---|
| 8645 | 1950 | $4 |

**Cowboys**
Illustrator: Timmins, William
| | | |
|---|---|---|
| 1004 | 1958 | $5 |
| 8341 | 1958 | $5 |
| 8666 | 1958 | $4 |

**Crosspatch**
Illustrator: Evers, Helen & Alf
Author: Evers, Helen & Alf
| | | |
|---|---|---|
| 8442 | 1964 | $4 |
| 8675 | 1964 | $4 |

**Crybaby Calf**
Illustrator: Evers, Helen & Alf
Author: Evers, Helen & Alf
| | | |
|---|---|---|
| 547 | 1954 | $8 |
| 8426 | 1954 | $6 |

**Crybaby Calf**
Illustrator: Evers, Helen & Alf
Author: Evers, Helen & Alf
| | | |
|---|---|---|
| 8606 | 1954 | $5 |

**Daniel the Cocker Spaniel**
Illustrator: Grider, Dorothy
Author: Watts, Mabel
| | | |
|---|---|---|
| 505 | 1955 | $10 |

**Daniel the Cocker Spaniel**
Illustrator: Grider, Dorothy
Author: Watts, Mabel
| | | |
|---|---|---|
| 8331 | 1955 | $8 |
| 8589 | 1955 | $5 |

**Davy Crockett: American Hero**
Illustrator: Timmons, William
Author: Grant, Bruce
| | | |
|---|---|---|
| 523 | 1955 | $6 |

**Davy's Little Horse**
Illustrator: Dennis, Wesley
Author: Devine, Louise Lawrence
| | | |
|---|---|---|
| 533 | 1956 | $6 |
| 8387 | 1956 | $4 |

**Day on the Farm, A**
Illustrator: Grider, Dorothy
Author: Evers, Alf
432            1948            **$15**

**Day on the Farm, A**
Illustrator: Grider, Dorothy
Author: Evers, Alf
432            1948            **$7**

**Day on the Farm, A**
Illustrator: Grider, Dorothy
Author: Evers, Alf
586            1948            **$6**
8360           1948            **$5**
8586           1948            **$4**

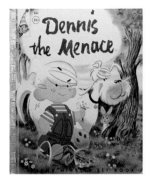

**Dennis the Menace**
Illustrator: Paplo, Bob
Author: Toole, Fred
541            1956            **$10**

**Dennis the Menace Camps Out**
Illustrator: Ketchum, Hank
Author: Toole, Fred
1002           1958            **$8**

**Early One Morning**
Illustrator: Cooper, Marjorie
Author: Graland, Valerie
8436           1963            **$5**
8656           1963            **$4**

**Elephant's Child, The: A Kipling "Just So" Story**
Illustrator: Weihs, Erika
Author: KIpling, Rudyard
508            1955            **$8**

**Elves and the Shoemaker, The**
Illustrator: Lee, Manning De V
8315           1959            **$5**
8682           1959            **$4**

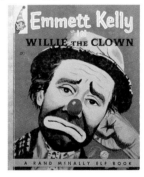

**Emmett Kelly in Willie the Clown**
Illustrator: Timmins, William
Author: Wing, Helen
573            1957            **$16**

**Emperor's New Clothes, The**
Illustrator: Leaf, Anne Sellers
8567           1968            **$7**

**Enchanted Egg, The**
Illustrator: Webbe, Elizabeth
Author: Burrows, Peggy
577            1956            **$7**
8407           1956            **$5**
8640           1956            **$4**

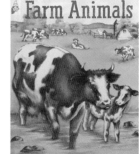

**Farm Animals**
Illustrator: Gayer, Marguerite
Author: Ratzesberger, Anna
467            1952            **$8**

**Farm Animals**
Illustrator: Photographs
Author: Hunter, Virginia
| | | |
|---|---|---|
| 514 | 1956 | $6 |
| 8337 | 1956 | $5 |
| 8735 | 1952 | $4 |

**Farm Babies**
Illustrator: Photographs
Author: Hunter, Virginia
| | | |
|---|---|---|
| 539 | 1956 | $6 |

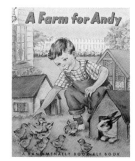

**Farm For Andy, A**
Illustrator: Gayer, Marguerite
Author: Reed, Dorothy
| | | |
|---|---|---|
| 448 | 1951 | $12 |
| 8358 | 1951 | $5 |
| 8741 | 1951 | $5 |

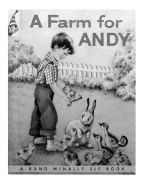

**Farm For Andy, A**
Illustrator: Gayer, Marguerite
Author: Reed, Dorothy
| | | |
|---|---|---|
| 596 | 1951 | $6 |

**Farm Friends**
Illustrator: Photographs
Author: Hunter, Virginia
| | | |
|---|---|---|
| 8329 | 1956 | $5 |
| 8719 | 1956 | $5 |

**Farmer in the Dell, The**
Illustrator: Kane, Sharon
| | | |
|---|---|---|
| 8578 | 1967 | $7 |

**Find the Way Home**
Illustrator: Wilson, Beth
Author: Broderick, Jessica Potter
| | | |
|---|---|---|
| 480 | 1953 | $8 |

**Five Busy Bears, The**
Illustrator: Tamburine, Jean
Author: North, Sterling
| | | |
|---|---|---|
| 8404 | 1955 | $5 |
| 8629 | 1955 | $4 |

**Five Little Bears**
Illustrator: Tamburine, Jean
Author: North, Sterling
| | | |
|---|---|---|
| 498 | 1955 | $10 |

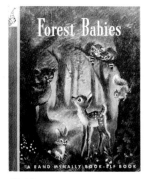

**Forest Babies**
Illustrator: Webbe, Elizabeth
Author: Parrish, Jean J.
| | | |
|---|---|---|
| 435 | 1949 | $15 |

**Forest Babies**
Illustrator: Webbe, Elizabeth
Author: Parrish, Jean J.
| | | |
|---|---|---|
| 546 | 1956 | $6 |

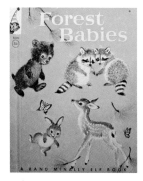

**Forest Babies**
Illustrator: Webbe, Elizabeth
Author: Parrish, Jean J.
| | | |
|---|---|---|
| 8328 | 1956 | $5 |
| 8730 | 1949 | $4 |

**Four Little Kittens**
Illustrator: Frees, Harry Whittier
Author: Dixon, Ruth

| | | |
|---|---|---|
| 566 | 1957 | **$6** |
| 8336 | 1957 | **$5** |
| 8718 | 1957 | **$4** |

**Four Little Puppies**
Illustrator: Frees, Harry Whittier
Author: Dixon, Ruth

| | | |
|---|---|---|
| 578 | 1957 | **$6** |
| 8335 | 1957 | **$5** |

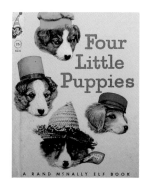

**Four Little Puppies**
Illustrator: Frees, Harry Whittier
Author: Dixon, Ruth

| | | |
|---|---|---|
| 8335 | 1957 | **$5** |
| 8597 | 1957 | **$4** |

**Fraidy Cat**
Illustrator: Tamburine, Jean
Author: Barrows, Marjorie

| | | |
|---|---|---|
| 8319 | 1959 | **$5** |
| 8662 | 1959 | **$5** |

**Freddie's Private Cloud**
Illustrator: Krehbiel, Becky & Evans
Author: Krehbiel, Becky & Evans

| | | |
|---|---|---|
| 8564 | 1971 | **$6** |

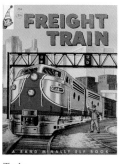

**Freight Train**
Illustrator: Pollard, G.
Author: Reichert, E. C.

| | | |
|---|---|---|
| 534 | 1956 | **$8** |
| 8414 | 1956 | **$6** |
| 8631 | 1956 | **$4** |

**From Tadpoles to Frogs**
Illustrator: Grider, Dorothy
Author: Michener, Lucille

| | | |
|---|---|---|
| 8550 | 1973 | **$4** |

**Funland Party**
Illustrator: Szepelak, Helen
Author: Devine, Louise Lawrence

| | | |
|---|---|---|
| 478 | 1953 | **$8** |

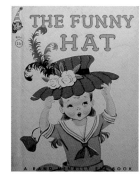

**Funny Hat, The**
Illustrator: Grider, Dorothy
Author: Barrows, Marjorie

| | | |
|---|---|---|
| 8314 | 1959 | **$5** |
| 8677 | 1959 | **$5** |

**Fussbunny**
Illustrator: Evers, Helen & Alf
Author: Evers, Helen & Alf

| | | |
|---|---|---|
| 530 | 1955 | **$6** |
| 8405 | 1955 | **$4** |

**Fuss Bunny**
Illustrator: Evers, Helen & Alf
Author: Evers, Helen & Alf

| | | |
|---|---|---|
| 8642 | 1955 | **$4** |

**Garden Is Good, A**
Illustrator: Cooper, Marjorie
Author: Chaffin, Lillie D.

| | | |
|---|---|---|
| 8438 | 1963 | **$4** |
| 8657 | 1963 | **$4** |

**Gingerbread Man, The**
Illustrator: Leaf, Anne Sellers
| 8457 | 1965 | $7 |
| 8599 | 1965 | $6 |

**Goat That Went to School, The**
Illustrator: Tamburine, Jean
Author: Francis, Sally R.
| 469 | 1952 | $8 |
| 8386 | 1952 | $4 |

**Goat That Went to School, The**
Illustrator: Tamburine, Jean
Author: Francis, Sally R.
| 594 | 1952 | $6 |
| 8594 | 1952 | $4 |

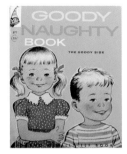

**Goody Naughty Book**
Illustrator: Prickett, Helen
Author: Watts, Mabel
| 572 | 1956 | $6 |
| 8385 | 1956 | $4 |
| 8593 | 1956 | $4 |
| 8693 | 1956 | $4 |

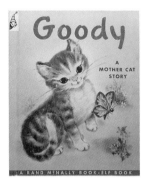

**Goody: A Mother Cat Story**
Illustrator: Leaf, Anne Sellers
Author: Bertail, Inez
| 470 | 1957 | $8 |

**Goody: A Mother Cat Story**
Illustrator: Leaf, Anne Sellers
Author: Bertail, Inez
| 545 | 1957 | $6 |

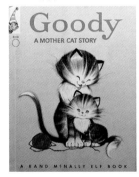

**Goody: A Mother Cat Story**
Illustrator: Leaf, Anne Sellers
Author: Bertail, Inez
| 8310 | 1957 | $5 |
| 8734 | 1957 | $4 |

**Growing Up**
Illustrator: Webbe, Elizabeth
Author: Fritz, Webbe
| 560 | 1956 | $5 |
| 8397 | 1956 | $4 |
| 8634 | 1956 | $4 |

**Hansel and Gretel**
Illustrator: Smith, Kay Lovelace
| 8365 | 1960 | $4 |
| 8638 | 1960 | $4 |

**Happy Holidays**
Illustrator: Bruce, Suzanne
Author: Reichert, E.C.
| 482 | 1953 | $8 |
| 8343 | 1953 | $5 |
| 8596 | 1953 | $5 |

**Happy Twins, The**
Illustrator: Cooper, Marjorie
Author: Wing, Helen
| 8460 | 1956 | $4 |
| 8749 | 1956 | $4 |

**Helpful Henrietta**
Illustrator: Caraway, James
Author: Watts, Mabel
| 8316 | 1959 | $5 |

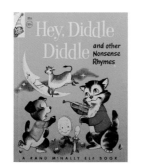

**Hey, Diddle, Diddle and Other Nonsense Rhymes**
Illustrator: Botts, Davi
| | | |
|---|---|---|
| 535 | 1956 | $6 |
| 8304 | 1956 | $5 |
| 8728 | 1956 | $4 |

**Hiawatha**
Illustrator: Wilde, Irma
Author: Gridley, Marion E.
| | | |
|---|---|---|
| 442 | 1950 | $12 |

**Hiawatha**
Illustrator: Wilde, Irma
Author: Gridley, Marion E.
| | | |
|---|---|---|
| 565 | 1950 | $10 |

**Hiawatha**
Illustrator: Wilde, Irma
Author: Gridley, Marion E.
| | | |
|---|---|---|
| 8307 | 1950 | $6 |
| 8686 | 1961 | $4 |

**Hide-Away Puppy**
Illustrator: Dottie
Author: Broderick, Jessica Potter
| | | |
|---|---|---|
| 466 | 1952 | $8 |

**Hide-Away Puppy**
Illustrator: Dottie
Author: Broderick, Jessica Potter
| | | |
|---|---|---|
| 587 | 1952 | $6 |
| 8357 | 1952 | $5 |
| 8587 | 1952 | $4 |

**Homes in the City**
Illustrator: Frame, Paul
Author: Bartkowski, Renee
| | | |
|---|---|---|
| 8554 | 1973 | $4 |

**Honeybee, The**
Illustrator: Street, Theodore
Author: Farley, Karin Clafford
| | | |
|---|---|---|
| 8559 | 1972 | $4 |

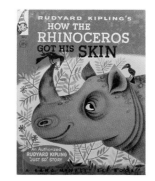

**Hop-Away Joey**
Illustrator: Fleishman, Seymour
Author: Broderick, Jessica Potter
| | | |
|---|---|---|
| 8572 | 1967 | $5 |

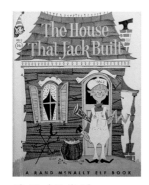

**House That Jack Built, The**
Illustrator: Leaf, Anne Sellers
| | | |
|---|---|---|
| 8681 | 1959 | $7 |
| 8312 | 1959 | $6 |

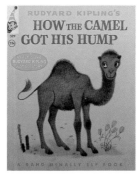

**How the Camel Got His Hump: An Authorized Kipling "Just So" Story**
Illustrator: Weihs, Erika
Author: Kipling, Rudyard
| | | |
|---|---|---|
| 529 | 1955 | $8 |

**How the Rhinoceros Got His Skin: An Authorized Kipling "Just So" Story**
Illustrator: Weihs, Erika
Author: Kipling, Rudyard
| | | |
|---|---|---|
| 540 | 1956 | $7 |

**I Think About Jesus**
Illustrator: Friend, Esther
Author: Smallwood, Kate
8652          1958          **$4**

**Jack and Jill**
Illustrator: Leaf, Anne Sellers
1001          1958          **$7**
8395          1958          **$6**
8625          1958          **$5**

**Jack and the Beanstalk**
Illustrator: Leaf, Anne Sellers
8372          1961          **$6**
8668          1961          **$5**

**Jeepers the Little Frog**
Illustrator: Cooper, Marjorie
Author: Cooper, Marjorie
8733          1965          **$4**
8456          1965          **$4**

**Jo Jo**
Illustrator: Wallace, Ivy L.
Author: Barrows, Marjorie
8450          1964          **$4**
8703          1964          **$4**

**Johnny and the Birds**
Illustrator: Webbe, Elizabeth
Author: Munn, Ian
439          1950          **$12**
8704          1950          **$4**

**Johnny and the Birds**
Illustrator: Webbe, Elizabeth
Author: Munn, Ian
1008          1950          **$5**
8377          1950          **$4**
8704          1950          **$4**

**Johnny the Fireman**
Illustrator: Wood, Ruth
Author: Sprinkle, Rebecca K.
488          1954          **$10**
8412          1954          **$8**
8611          1954          **$6**

**Johnny the Fireman**
Illustrator: Wood, Ruth
Author: Sprinkle, Rebecca K.
8611          1954          **$6**

**Kerry, the Fire-Engine Dog**
Illustrator: Grider, Dorothy
Author: Lewis, Frank; Corchia, Alfred J.
436          1949          **$15**

**Kerry, the Fire-Engine Dog**
Illustrator: Grider, Dorothy
Author: Lewis, Frank; Corchia, Alfred J.
579          1949          **$10**
8353          1949          **$8**
8710          1949          **$6**

**Kitten Twins, The**
Illustrator: Webbe, Elizabeth
Author: Wing, Helen
8422          1960          **$4**
1014          1960          **$5**
8637          1960          **$4**
8722          1960          **$7**

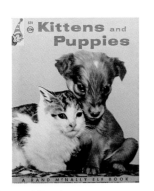

**Kittens and Puppies**
Illustrator: Photographs
Author: Burrows, Peggy
531          1955          **$8**

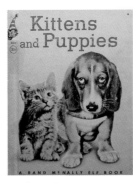

**Kittens and Puppies**
Illustrator: Photographs
Author: Burrows, Peggy
8301         1955          **$6**

**Kittens and Puppies**
Illustrator: Photographs
Author: Burrows, Peggy
8691         1955          **$5**

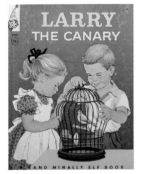

**Larry the Canary**
Illustrator: Koester, Sharon
Author: Wilkie, Ellen
8322         1959          **$6**
8685         1959          **$4**

**Lazy Jack**
Illustrator: Storytoon Express
Author: Storytoon Express
8435         1962          **$8**

**Let's Grow Things**
Illustrator: Wilde, Irma
Author: Comfort, Iris Tracy
8571         1967          **$4**

**Lion and the Mouse, The**
Illustrator: Blake, Vivienne
Author: Duff, Emma Lorne
8569         1968          **$4**

**Little Ballerina**
Illustrator: Grider, Dorothy
Author: Grider, Dorothy
1003         1958          **$8**
8390         1958          **$6**
8614         1958          **$4**

**Little Bobo and His Blue Jacket**
Illustrator: Brice, Tony
Author: Evers, Alf
472          1953          **$10**

**Little Bobo and His Blue Jacket**
Illustrator: Brice, Tony
Author: Evers, Alf
1026         1953          **$6**
8378         1953          **$5**
8654         1953          **$4**

**Little Boy Blue and Other Nursery Rhymes**
Illustrator: Leaf, Anne Sellers
555          1956          **$6**
8366         1956          **$5**
8711         1956          **$5**

**Little Boy Blue and Other Nursery Rhymes**
Illustrator: Leaf, Anne Sellers
8711         1956          **$5**

Little Campers
Illustrator: Grider, Dorothy
Author: Watts, Mabel
| 8439 | 1963 | $4 |
| 8660 | 1963 | $4 |

Little Cub Scout
Illustrator: Timmins, William
Author: Watts, Mabel
| 8445 | 1964 | $6 |
| 8665 | 1964 | $5 |

Little Friends: Kittens, Puppies, Bunnies
Illustrator: Gaddis, Rie
Author: Dixon, Ruth
| 455 | 1951 | $10 |
| 593 | 1951 | $8 |

Little Friends: Kittens, Puppies, Bunnies
Illustrator: Gaddis, Rie
Author: Dixon, Ruth
| 8408 | 1951 | $5 |
| 8737 | 1951 | $5 |

Little Horseman
Illustrator: Grider, Dorothy
Author: Watts, Mabel
| 8347 | 1961 | $4 |
| 8649 | 1961 | $4 |

Little Kittens' Nursery Rhymes, The
Illustrator: Frees, Harry Whittier
| 440 | 1941 | $12 |

Little Kittens' Nursery Rhymes, The
Illustrator: Frees, Harry Whittier
| 8311 | 1941 | $5 |
| 8739 | 1941 | $5 |

Little Little Dog
Illustrator: Adler, Helen
Author: Brailsford, Frances
| 8437 | 1963 | $4 |
| 8661 | 1963 | $4 |

Little Lost Angel
Illustrator: Scott, Janet Laura
Author: Heath, Janet Field
| 483 | 1953 | $12 |
| 8680 | 1953 | $7 |

Little Lost Angel
Illustrator: Scott, Janet Laura
Author: Heath, Janet Field
| 580 | 1953 | $10 |
| 8376 | 1953 | $8 |
| 8680 | 1953 | $7 |

Little Lost Kitten: Story of Williamsburg
Illustrator: Lee, Manning De V
Author: Comfort, Mildred
| 544 | 1956 | $7 |
| 8600 | 1956 | $4 |

Little Mailman of Bayberry Lane, The
Illustrator: Webbe, Elizabeth
Author: Munn, Ian
| 458 | 1952 | $35 |

**Little Mailman of Bayberry Lane, The**
Illustrator: Webbe, Elizabeth
Author: Munn, Ian
| | | |
|---|---|---|
| 590 | 1952 | **$25** |
| 8361 | 1952 | **$15** |
| 8729 | 1952 | **$10** |

**Little Majorette**
Illustrator: Grider, Dorothy
Author: Grider, Dorothy
| | | |
|---|---|---|
| 8410 | 1959 | **$4** |
| 8605 | 1959 | **$4** |

**Little Miss Muffet and Other Nursery Rhymes**
Illustrator: Chase, Mary Jane
| | | |
|---|---|---|
| 556 | 1956 | **$6** |
| 8302 | 1956 | **$5** |

**Little Miss Muffet and Other Nursery Rhymes**
Illustrator: Chase, Mary Jane
| | | |
|---|---|---|
| 8302 | 1956 | **$5** |
| 8709 | 1956 | **$4** |

**Little Red Riding-Hood**
Illustrator: Leaf, Anne Sellers
| | | |
|---|---|---|
| 1037 | 1958 | **$7** |
| 8419 | 1958 | **$6** |

**Little Red Riding-Hood**
Illustrator: Leaf, Anne Sellers
| | | |
|---|---|---|
| 8646 | 1958 | **$5** |

**Little Skater**
Illustrator: Grider, Dorothy
Author: Sherman, Diane
| | | |
|---|---|---|
| 8389 | 1959 | **$6** |
| 8610 | 1959 | **$4** |

**Little Swimmers**
Illustrator: Grider, Dorothy
Author: Grider, Dorothy
| | | |
|---|---|---|
| 8416 | 1960 | **$6** |
| 8633 | 1960 | **$4** |

**Look For a Rainbow**
Illustrator: Cooper, Marjorie
Author: Swetnam, Evelyn
| | | |
|---|---|---|
| 8558 | 1972 | **$4** |

**Looking In and Other Poems**
Illustrator: Grider, Dorothy
Author: Aldis, Dorothy
| | | |
|---|---|---|
| 8568 | 1968 | **$4** |

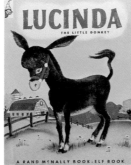

**Lucinda the Little Donkey**
Illustrator: Wilde, George
Author: Wilde, Irma
| | | |
|---|---|---|
| 465 | 1952 | **$8** |
| 8362 | 1952 | **$5** |

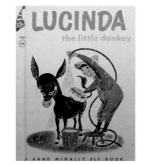

**Lucinda the Little Donkey**
Illustrator: Wilde, George
Author: Wilde, Irma
| | | |
|---|---|---|
| 592 | 1952 | **$6** |
| 8362 | 1952 | **$5** |
| 8584 | 1952 | **$4** |

**Magic Pot, The**
Illustrator: Storytoon Express
Author: Bell, Margie
8433    1962                                    $8

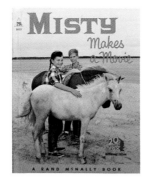

**Misty Makes a Movie**
Illustrator: Photographs
Author: Henry, Marguerite
8655    1961                                    $6

**Misty the Wonder Pony**
Illustrator: McKinley, Clare
Author: Misty, Herself
536    1956                                     $8

**Misty the Wonder Pony**
Illustrator: McKinley, Clare
Author: Misty, Herself
8628    1956                                    $4

**Mommy Cat and Her Kittens**
Illustrator: Rockwell, Eve
Author: Devine, Louise Lawrence
8317    1959                                    $7
8678    1959                                    $5

**Moonymouse**
Illustrator: Evers, Helen & Alf
Author: Evers, Helen & Alf
1021    1958                                    $8
8400    1958                                    $6
8639    1958                                    $5

**Mother Goose**
Illustrator: Friend, Esther
424    1947                                     $15

**Mother Goose**
Illustrator: Friend, Esther
424    1947                                     $7
8300    1947                                    $5
1028    1947                                    $5

**Mother Goose**
Illustrator: Friend, Esther
8647    1947                                    $4

**Mother Goose**
Illustrator: Friend, Esther
8300    1947                                    $5
8723    1947                                    $4

**Moving Day**
Illustrator: Grider, Dorothy
Author: Conmfort, Mildred
588    1958    $6

**Mr. Bear's House**
Illustrator: McKinley, Clare
Author: Rothe, Fenella
475    1953                                     $10
8707    1953                                    $4

**Mr. Bear's House**
Illustrator: McKinley, Clare
Author: Rothe, Fenella
| | | |
|---|---|---|
| 511 | 1953 | $8 |
| 8349 | 1953 | $6 |
| 8707 | 1953 | $4 |

**Mr. Punnymoon's Train**
Illustrator: Phillips, Katherine L.
Author: Hadsell, Alice
| | | |
|---|---|---|
| 557 | 1951 | $12 |
| 8415 | 1951 | $6 |
| 8632 | 1951 | $6 |

**Mr. Punnymoon's Train**
Illustrator: Phillips, Katherine L.
Author: Hadsell, Alice
| | | |
|---|---|---|
| 449 | 1951 | $15 |

**Mr. Punnymoon's Train**
Illustrator: Phillips, Katherine L.
Author: Hadsell, Alice
| | | |
|---|---|---|
| 8632 | 1951 | $6 |

**Mr. Wizard's Junior Science Show**
Illustrator: Bonfils, Robert
Author: Thayer, Ruth Hubley
| | | |
|---|---|---|
| 559 | 1957 | $8 |

**Muggins Becomes a Hero**
Illustrator: Leaf, Anne Sellers
Author: Barrow, Marjorie
| | | |
|---|---|---|
| 8448 | 1965 | $7 |
| 8702 | 1965 | $5 |

**Muggins' Big Balloon**
Illustrator: Leaf, Anne Sellers
Author: Barrow, Marjorie
| | | |
|---|---|---|
| 8447 | 1964 | $7 |
| 8701 | 1964 | $5 |

**Muggins Mouse**
Illustrator: Leaf, Anne Sellers
Author: Barrows, Marjorie
| | | |
|---|---|---|
| 8444 | 1964 | $7 |
| 8673 | 1964 | $5 |

**Muggins Takes Off**
Illustrator: Leaf, Anne Sellers
Author: Barrows, Marjorie
| | | |
|---|---|---|
| 8700 | 1964 | $7 |

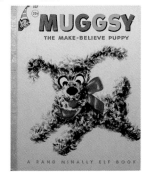

**Muggsy the Make-Believe Puppy**
Illustrator: Webbe, Elizabeth
Author: Lieberthal, Jules M.
| | | |
|---|---|---|
| 537 | 1956 | $10 |

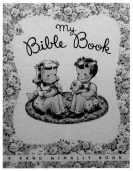

**My Bible Book**
Illustrator: Bryant, Dean
Author: Walker, Janie
| | | |
|---|---|---|
| 8696 | 1946 | $4 |

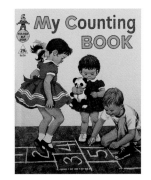

**My Counting Book**
Illustrator: Koester, Sharon
Author: Sherman, Diane
| | | |
|---|---|---|
| 8399 | 1960 | $6 |
| 8636 | 1960 | $4 |

**My Flower Book**
Illustrator: Webbe, Elizabeth
Author: Landis, Dorothy Thompson
| 8382 | 1961 | **$5** |
| 8679 | 1961 | **$4** |

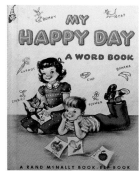

**My Happy Day: A Word Book**
Illustrator: Bruce, Suzanne
Author: Shaw, Thelma
| 450 | 1963 | **$10** |
| 8332 | 1963 | **$5** |

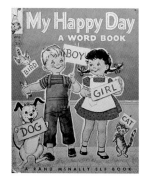

**My Happy Day: A Word Book**
Illustrator: Bruce, Suzanne
Author: Shaw, Thelma
| 8332 | 1963 | **$5** |

**My Prayer Book**
Illustrator: Friend, Esther
Author: Clemens, Margaret
| 8697 | 1947 | **$4** |

**My Truck Book**
Illustrator: Grider, Dorothy
Author: Reichert, E. C.
| 431 | 1948 | **$15** |

**Nancy Plays Nurse**
Illustrator: Grider, Dorothy
Author: Sherman, Diane
| 8726 | 1965 | **$4** |

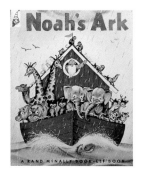

**Noah's Ark**
Illustrator: Webbe, Elizabeth
Author: Briggs, Dorothy Bell
| 461 | 1952 | **$8** |
| 8424 | 1952 | **$4** |
| 8648 | 1952 | **$4** |

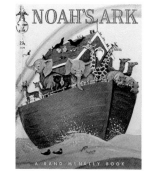

**Noah's Ark**
Illustrator: Webbe, Elizabeth
Author: Briggs, Dorothy Bell
| 1020 | 1952 | **$5** |

**Nonsense A B C's, The**
Illustrator: Endres, Helen; Bonfils, Robert
Author: Lear, Edward
| 550 | 1956 | **$6** |

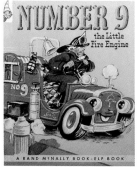

**Number 9 the Little Fire Engine**
Illustrator: Corwin, Eleanor
Author: Wadsworth, Wallace
| 444 | 1950 | **$12** |

**Number 9 the Little Fire Engine**
Illustrator: Corwin, Eleanor
Author: Wadsworth, Wallace
| 585 | 1950 | **$10** |
| 8369 | 1950 | **$6** |
| 8708 | 1950 | **$5** |

**Old Mother Hubbard**
Illustrator: Leaf, Anne Sellers
| 1007 | 1958 | **$7** |
| 8413 | 1958 | **$6** |
| 8624 | 1958 | **$5** |

**Old Woman and Her Pig, The**
Illustrator: Friend, Esther
Author: Wadsworth, Wallace
464          1952          $8

**Old Woman and Her Pig, The**
Illustrator: Friend, Esther
Author: Wadsworth, Wallace
1035         1952          $4
8379         1952          $5
8744         1952          $4

**One, Two, Cock-A-Doodle-Doo**
Illustrator: Wosmek, Frances
Author: Pease, Josephine Van Dolzen
438          1950          $12
8350         1950          $5

**One, Two, Cock-A-Doodle-Doo**
Illustrator: Wosmek, Frances
Author: Pease, Josephine Van Dolzen
512          1950          $6

**One, Two, Cock-A-Doodle-Doo**
Illustrator: Wosmek, Frances
Author: Pease, Josephine Van Dolzen
8570         1950          $4

**Our Animal Friends**
Illustrator: Photographs
Author: Hunter, Virginia
563          1956          $6

**Our Animal Friends**
Illustrator: Photographs
Author: Hunter, Virginia
8403         1956          $4
8630         1956          $4

**Our Auto Trip**
Illustrator: Grider, Dorothy
Author: Edsall, Marian
457          1952          $10
8339         1952          $5

**Our World of Color and Sound**
Illustrator: Cooper, Marjorie
Author: Bartkowski, Renee
8577         1967          $4

**Outdoor Fun**
Illustrator: Tamburine, Jean
Author: Shaw, Thelma & Ralph
479          1953          $8

**Parakeet Peter**
Illustrator: Grider, Dorothy
Author: Sprinkle, Rebecca K.
490          1954          $8

**Parakeet Peter**
Illustrator: Grider, Dorothy
Author: Sprinkle, Rebecca K.
591          1954          $6
8374         1954          $4
8688         1954          $4

**Peaky Beaky**
Illustrator: Oeshsli, Kelly
Author: de Vogue, Bertrand
8598        1967                    $5

**Penny and Pete's Surprise**
Illustrator: McKinley, Clare
Author: Shuman, Ruth Lewis
434         1949                   $15

**Penny and Pete's Surprise**
Illustrator: McKinley, Clare
Author: Shuman, Ruth Lewis
8396        1949                    $4
8627        1949                    $4
1023        1949                    $6

**People Who Work at Night**
Illustrator: Sherman, Diane
Author: Doremus, Robert
8549        1973                    $4

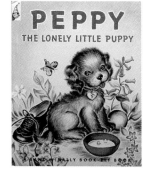

**Peppy the Lonely Little Puppy**
Illustrator: Blake, Vivienne
Author: Friedman, Frieda
425         1947                   $15
8746        1957                    $5

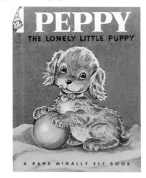

**Peppy the Lonely Little Puppy**
Illustrator: Blake, Vivienne
Author: Friedman, Frieda
553         1957                    $8

**Peppy the Lonely Little Puppy**
Illustrator: Blake, Vivienne
Author: Friedman, Frieda
8305        1957                    $6

**Pets**
Illustrator: Webbe, Elizabeth
Author: Ratzesberger, Anna
486         1954                    $8
8617        1954                    $4
8392        1954                    $4

**Pets**
Illustrator: Webbe, Elizabeth
Author: Ratzesberger, Anna
1025        1954                    $4
8392        1954                    $4

**Pillowtime Tales**
Illustrator: Tamburine, Jean
Author: DeGroot, Marion K.
552         1956                    $6
8338        1956                    $5

**Pillowtime Tales**
Illustrator: Tamburine, Jean
Author: DeGroot, Marion K.
8740        1956                    $4

**Pink Lenonade and Other Peter Patter Rhymes**
Illustrator: Grider, Dorothy
Author: Jackson, Leroy F.
8452        1965                    $4

**Playtime Poodles**
Illustrator: Westelin, Albert; Schmidling, Jack
Author: Wing, Helen

| | | |
|---|---|---|
| 501 | 1955 | **$10** |
| 8330 | 1955 | **$7** |

**Plump Pig**
Illustrator: Evers, Helen & Alf
Author: Evers, Helen & Alf

| | | |
|---|---|---|
| 542 | 1956 | **$7** |

**Plump Pig**
Illustrator: Evers, Helen & Alf
Author: Evers, Helen & Alf

| | | |
|---|---|---|
| 8309 | 1956 | **$7** |
| 8592 | 1956 | **$4** |

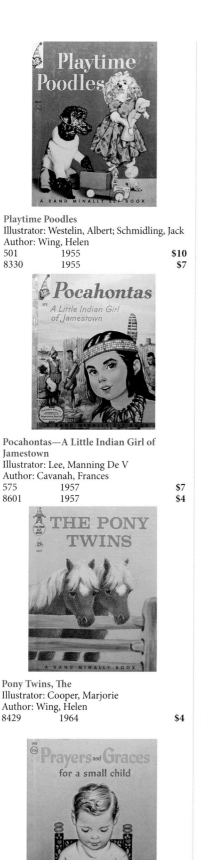

**Pocahontas—A Little Indian Girl of Jamestown**
Illustrator: Lee, Manning De V
Author: Cavanah, Frances

| | | |
|---|---|---|
| 575 | 1957 | **$7** |
| 8601 | 1957 | **$4** |

**Pokey Bear**
Illustrator: Evers, Helen & Alf
Author: Evers, Helen & Alf

| | | |
|---|---|---|
| 8451 | 1965 | **$5** |
| 8720 | 1965 | **$4** |

**Pony Express**
Illustrator: Timmins, William
Author: Grant, Bruce

| | | |
|---|---|---|
| 554 | 1956 | **$6** |
| 8344 | 1956 | **$5** |
| 8659 | 1964 | **$4** |

**Pony Twins, The**
Illustrator: Cooper, Marjorie
Author: Wing, Helen

| | | |
|---|---|---|
| 8429 | 1964 | **$4** |

**Popcorn Party**
Illustrator: Szepelak, Helen
Author: Boyles, Trudy; Macmartin, Louise

| | | |
|---|---|---|
| 468 | 1952 | **$15** |
| 8303 | 1952 | **$10** |
| 8743 | 1952 | **$5** |

**Popcorn Party**
Illustrator: Szepelak, Helen
Author: Boyles, Trudy; Macmartin, Louise

| | | |
|---|---|---|
| 8303 | 1952 | **$8** |

**Prayers and Graces For a Small Child**
Illustrator: Webbe, Elizabeth
Author: Webbe, Elizabeth

| | | |
|---|---|---|
| 502 | 1955 | **$7** |
| 8609 | 1955 | **$4** |

**Prayers For Little Children**
Illustrator: Bruce, Suzanne
Author: Jones, Mary Alice

| | | |
|---|---|---|
| 8557 | 1959 | **$4** |

**Present For the Princess, A**
Illustrator: Webbe, Elizabeth
Author: Paschall, Janie Lowe

| | | |
|---|---|---|
| 8425 | 1959 | **$15** |
| 8602 | 1959 | **$10** |

**Princess and the Pea, The**
Illustrator: Leaf, Anne Sellers
| 8455 | 1965 | $7 |
| 8727 | 1965 | $6 |

**Pudgy the Little Bear**
Illustrator: Tamburine, Jean
Author: Barrows, Marjorie
| 8441 | 1964 | $4 |
| 8674 | 1964 | $4 |

**Puppies to Love**
Illustrator: Lougheed, Robert
Author: Wing, Helen
| 8565 | 1971 | $4 |

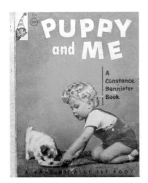

**Puppy and Me**
Illustrator: Bannister, Constance
Author: Ratzesberger, Anna
| 504 | 1955 | $7 |

**Puppy Twins, The**
Illustrator: Bendel, Ruth
Author: Wing, Helen
| 8420 | 1959 | $4 |
| 8603 | 1959 | $4 |

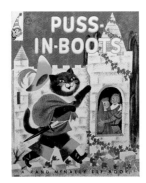

**Puss-In-Boots**
Illustrator: Myers, Bernice & Lou
| 507 | 1955 | $7 |

**Puss-In-Boots**
Illustrator: Myers, Bernice & Lou
| 8356 | 1955 | $5 |
| 8573 | 1955 | $4 |

**Read Me Some Poems**
Illustrator: Cooper, Marjorie
| 8574 | 1968 | $4 |

**Rip Van Winkle**
Illustrator: Leaf, Anne Sellers
Author: Briggs, Dorothy Bell
| 8383 | 1961 | $6 |
| 8671 | 1961 | $4 |

**Rocket For a Cow, A**
Illustrator: Wilde, Irma
Author: Devine, Louise Lawerence
| 8458 | 1965 | $6 |
| 8747 | 1965 | $6 |

**Rumpelstiltskin**
Illustrator: Webbe, Elizabeth
| 8318 | 1959 | $5 |
| 8669 | 1959 | $4 |

**Santa's Rocket Sleigh**
Illustrator: Webbe, Elizabeth
Author: Storch, Florence
| 568 | 1957 | $10 |

**Scalawag the Monkey**
Illustrator: Gaddis, Rie
Author: Dixon, Ruth
477          1953                    **$10**

**Scamper**
Illustrator: Tamburine, Jean
Author: Barrows, Marjorie
8326         1959                    **$5**
8716         1959                    **$4**

**Sergeant Preston and Rex**
Illustrator: Neebe, William
Author: Striker, Fran
569          1956                    **$16**

**Sergeant Preston and the Yukon King**
Illustrator: Neebe, William
Author: Comfort, Mildred H.
500          1955                    **$16**

**Seven Wonderful Cats, The**
Illustrator: Neebe, William
Author: Wadsworth, Wallace C.
548          1956                    **$6**
8411         1956                    **$4**

**Seven Wonderful Cats, The**
Illustrator: Neebe, William
Author: Wadsworth, Wallace C.
8607         1956                    **$4**

**Silly Joe**
Illustrator: Storytoon Express
Author: Storytoon Express
8434         1962                    **$8**

**Sleeping Beauty**
Illustrator: Webbe, Elizabeth
8320         1959                    **$5**
8683         1959                    **$4**

**Sleepy-Time Rhymes**
Illustrator: Szepelak, Helen
Author: Smith, Goldie Capers
8346         1964                    **$5**
8664         1964                    **$4**

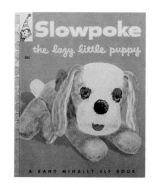

**Slowpoke the Lazy Little Puppy**
Illustrator: Neebe, William
Author: Lieberthal, Jules M.
582          1957                    **$6**

**Smart Little Mouse, The**
Illustrator: Phillips, Katherine L.
Author: Sherwan, Earl
441          1950                    **$12**

**Smart Little Mouse, The**
Illustrator: Phillips, Katherine L.
Author: Sherwan, Earl
1039         1950                    **$5**
8421         1950                    **$4**
8626         1950                    **$4**

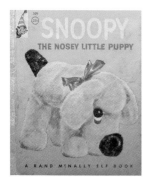

**Snoopy the Nosey Little Puppy**
Illustrator: Neebe, William
Author: Lieberthal, Jules M.
509        1955                    **$10**

**Snow-White and Rose-Red**
Illustrator: Cooper, Marjorie
Author: Bros. Grimm
8580       1967                    **$4**

**Snuggles**
Illustrator: Frees, Harry Whittier
Author: Dixon, Ruth
1005       1958                    **$6**
8340       1958                    **$5**
8650       1958                    **$4**

**So Long**
Illustrator: Evers, Helen & Alf
Author: Evers, Helen & Alf
1036       1958                    **$5**
8342       1958                    **$5**
8622       1958                    **$4**

**Space Ship to the Moon**
Illustrator: Bilder, A. K.
Author: Reichert, E. C.
473        1952                    **$16**

**Sparky the Fire Dog**
Illustrator: Chase, Mary Jane
Author: Browning, James
495        1954                    **$15**

**Squiffy the Skunk**
Illustrator: Neff, George; Brett, Grace Neff
Author: Brett, Grace Neff
476        1953                    **$10**

**Squirrel Twins, The**
Illustrator: Webbe, Elizabeth
Author: Wing, Helen
8381       1961                    **$4**
8670       1961                    **$4**

**Stories of the Christ Child**
Illustrator: Corwin, Eleanor
Author: Jones, Mary Alice
484        1953                    **$8**
8612       1953                    **$4**

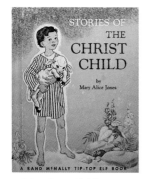

**Stories of the Christ Child**
Illustrator: Corwin, Eleanor
Author: Jones, Mary Alice
8612       1953                    **$4**

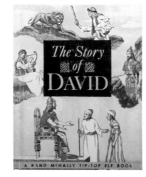

**Story of David, The**
Illustrator: Lee, Manning De V
Author: Richards, Jean H.
8725       1965                    **$4**

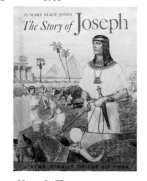

**Story of Joseph, The**
Illustrator: Lee, Manning De V
Author: Jones, Mary Alice
8724       1965                    **$4**

**Story of Our Flag, The**
Illustrator: Wilde, Irma
Author: Devine, Louise Lawrence
| | | |
|---|---|---|
| 8398 | 1955 | $4 |
| 8635 | 1955 | $4 |

**Storybook For Little Tots**
Illustrator: Devine, Louise Lawrence
Author: Hunter, Virginia
| | | |
|---|---|---|
| 1029 | 1958 | $4 |
| 8393 | 1958 | $4 |
| 8619 | 1958 | $4 |

**Sugar Plum Tree, The**
Illustrator: Storytoon Express
Author: Storytoon Express
| | | |
|---|---|---|
| 8432 | 1962 | $8 |

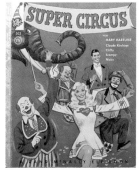

**Super Circus**
Illustrator: Timmins, William
Author: Wing, Helen
| | | |
|---|---|---|
| 503 | 1955 | $16 |

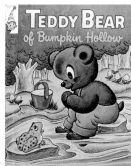

**Superliner United States, The: World's Fastest Liner**
Illustrator: Bilder, A.K.
Author: Ford, J. Duncan
| | | |
|---|---|---|
| 474 | 1953 | $16 |

**Surprise!**
Illustrator: Ozone, Lucy
Author: Ozone, Lucy
| | | |
|---|---|---|
| 562 | 1956 | $6 |
| 8384 | 1956 | $4 |
| 8583 | 1956 | $4 |

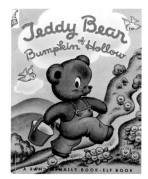

**Teddy Bear of Bumpkin Hollow**
Illustrator: Bryant, Dean
Author: Boucher, Sharon
| | | |
|---|---|---|
| 429 | 1948 | $25 |

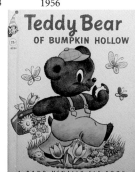

**Teddy Bear of Bumpkin Hollow**
Illustrator: Bryant, Dean
Author: Boucher, Sharon
| | | |
|---|---|---|
| 561 | 1948 | $10 |

**Teddy Bear of Bumpkin Hollow**
Illustrator: Bryant, Dean
Author: Boucher, Sharon
| | | |
|---|---|---|
| 8334 | 1948 | $8 |
| 8693 | 1948 | $8 |

**Teddy Bear Twins, The**
Illustrator: Cooper, Marjorie
Author: Wing, Helen
| | | |
|---|---|---|
| 8453 | 1965 | $7 |
| 8637 | 1965 | $6 |
| 8722 | 1965 | $6 |

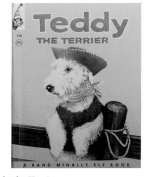

**Teddy the Terrier**
Illustrator: Latimer, Constance; Love, Mary
Author: Hunter, Virginia
| | | |
|---|---|---|
| 558 | 1956 | $9 |

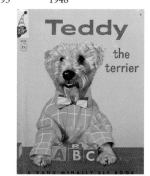

**Teddy the Terrier**
Illustrator: Latimer, Constance; Love, Mary
Author: Hunter, Virginia
| | | |
|---|---|---|
| 8308 | 1956 | $5 |
| 8738 | **$10** | |

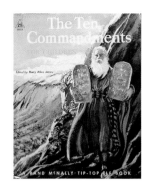

**Ten Commandments For Children, The**
Illustrator: Bonfils, Robert
Author: Jones, Mary Alice
| 543 | 1956 | $6 |
| 8604 | 1956 | $4 |

**Ten Commandments For Children, The**
Illustrator: Bonfils, Robert
Author: Jones, Mary Alice
| 8604 | 1956 | $4 |

**Ten Commandments For Children, The**
Illustrator: Bonfils, Robert
Author: Jones, Mary Alice
| 8604 | 1956 | $4 |

**This is the World**
Illustrator: Wood, Ruth
Author: Pease, Josephine
| 549 | 1957 | $5 |

**Three Bears Visit Goldilocks, The**
Illustrator: McKinley, Clare
Author: Rarick, Carrie
| 445 | 1950 | $12 |

**Three Bears Visit Goldilocks, The**
Illustrator: McKinley, Clare
Author: Rarick, Carrie
| 1031 | 1950 | $10 |
| 8401 | 1950 | $6 |
| 8620 | 1950 | $4 |

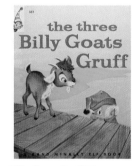

**Three Bears, The**
Illustrator: Webbe, Elizabeth
| 8313 | 1959 | $5 |
| 8706 | 1959 | $4 |

**Three Billy Goats Gruff, The**
Illustrator: Neebe, William
Author: O'Grady, Alice; Throop, Frances
| 583 | 1957 | $6 |
| 8368 | 1957 | $5 |
| 8712 | 1957 | $5 |

**Three Little Bunnies**
Illustrator: Rooks, Dale & Sally
Author: Dixon, Ruth
| 443 | 1950 | $12 |

**Three Little Bunnies**
Illustrator: Rooks, Dale & Sally
Author: Dixon, Ruth
| 589 | 1950 | $6 |
| 8388 | 1950 | $4 |
| 8742 | 1950 | $4 |

**Three Little Kittens**
Illustrator: Cooper, Marjorie
| #8462 | 1966 | $4 |
| #8582 | 1966 | $4 |

**Three Little Puppies**
Illustrator: Rooks, Dale & Sally
Author: Dixon, Ruth
| 447 | 1951 | $12 |

**Three Little Puppies**
Illustrator: Rooks, Dale & Sally
Author: Dixon, Ruth
| | | |
|---|---|---|
| 598 | 1951 | **$6** |
| 8363 | 1951 | **$5** |
| 8745 | 1951 | **$4** |

**Three Pigs, The**
Illustrator: Storytoon Express
Author: Storytoon Express
| | | |
|---|---|---|
| 8430 | 1962 | **$12** |

**Time For Everything**
Illustrator: Kane, Sharon
Author: Smaridge, Norah
| | | |
|---|---|---|
| 8562 | 1972 | **$4** |

**Timothy Tiger**
Illustrator: Wilde, Irma
Author: Barrows, Marjorie
| | | |
|---|---|---|
| 8324 | 1959 | **$5** |
| 8672 | 1959 | **$4** |

**To the Store We Go**
Illustrator: Walker, O.
Author: Reichert, E. C.
| | | |
|---|---|---|
| 460 | 1952 | **$8** |

**Tom Thumb**
Illustrator: Wallace, Lucille
| | | |
|---|---|---|
| 8323 | 1959 | **$5** |
| 8684 | 1959 | **$4** |

**Tom Thumb**
Illustrator: Wallace, Lucille
| | | |
|---|---|---|
| 8684 | 1959 | **$4** |

**Tortoise and the Hare, The**
Illustrator: Storytoon Express
Author: Storytoon Express
| | | |
|---|---|---|
| 8431 | 1962 | **$8** |

**Trip in Space, A**
Illustrator: Fleishman, Seymour
Author: Grant, Bruce
| | | |
|---|---|---|
| 8566 | 1968 | **$6** |

**Trucks**
Illustrator: Wilde, George
Author: Reichert, E.C.
| | | |
|---|---|---|
| 8325 | 1959 | **$5** |
| 8687 | 1959 | **$4** |

**Tubby Turtle**
Illustrator: Adler, Helen
Author: Wing, Helen
| | | |
|---|---|---|
| 8321 | 1959 | **$5** |
| 8692 | 1959 | **$5** |

**Turtles Turn Up on Tuesday**
Illustrator: Frame, Paul
Author: Shaw, Thelma
| | | |
|---|---|---|
| 8561 | 1972 | **$4** |

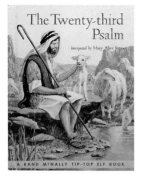

**Twenty-Third Psalm, The**
Illustrator: Lee, Manning De V
Author: Jones, Mary Alice
8698     1964     $4

**Twilight Tales**
Illustrator: Bryant, Dean
Author: Potter, Miriam Clark
426     1947     $15
8427     1947     $4

**Twilight Tales**
Illustrator: Bryant, Dean
Author: Potter, Miriam Clark
8608     1947     $4

**Twilight Tales**
Illustrator: Bryant, Dean
Author: Potter, Miriam Clark
8608     1947     $4

**Ugly Duckling, The**
Illustrator: Opitz, Marge
8327     1959     $5
8590     1959     $4

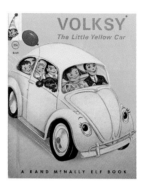

**Volksy the Little Yellow Car**
Illustrator: Chase, Mary Jane
Author: Wing, Helen
8449     1965     $9
8695     1965     $9

**What Happened to George?**
Illustrator: Opitz, Marge
Author: Engebretson, Betty
1006     1958     $45
8409     1958     $35
8667     1958     $25

**When God Imagined a World**
Illustrator: Richards, Jean H.
Author: Goldsborough, June
8699     1964     $4

**Where From?**
Illustrator: Smith, Eunice Young
Author: Smith, Eunice Young
8371     1961     $5
8713     1961     $4

**Who Wants a Pop Can Park?**
Illustrator: Leaf, Anne Sellers
Author: Bartkowski, Renee
8563     1972     $8

**Wild Animals**
Illustrator: Vlasaty, J. L.
Author: Ratzesberger, Anna
454     1951     $10
8348     1951     $5
8717     1951     $5

**Wild Animals**
Illustrator: Vlasaty, J. L.
Author: Ratzesberger, Anna
510     1951     $6
8348     1951     $5
8721     1951     $4

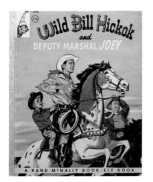

**Wild Bill Hickok and Deputy Marshal Joey**
Illustrator: Timmons, William
Author: Stone, Ethel B.
496          1954                    **$16**

**Wild Bill Hickok and the Indians**
Illustrator: Timmons, William
Author: Stone, Ethel B.
570          1956                    **$16**

**Wonderful Plane Ride, The**
Illustrator: Mastri, Fiore & Jackie
Author: Weir, R. C.
433          1947                    **$15**

**Wonderful Train Ride**
Illustrator: Mastri, Fiore & Jackie
Author: Weir, R. C.
427          1947                    **$15**
427          1947                    **$10**

**Wynken, Blynken and Nod and Other Nursery Rhymes**
Illustrator: McKinley, Clare
Author: Feld, Eugene
571          1956                    **$6**
8367         1956                    **$5**
8714         1956                    **$4**

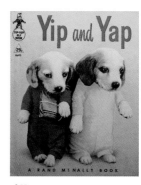

**Yip and Yap**
Illustrator: Frees, Harry Whittier
Author: Dixon, Ruth
1022         1958                    **$5**
8380         1958                    **$4**
8690         1958                    **$4**

**Zippy's Birthday Party**
Illustrator: Ecuyer, Lee
Author: Ecuyer, Lee
506          1955                    **$10**

**Zippy Goes to School**
Illustrator: Westelin, Albert G.; Ecuyer, Lee
Author: Ecuyer, Lee
489          1954                    **$10**

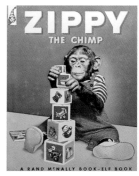

**Zippy the Chimp**
Illustrator: Mitchell, Benn
Author: Ecuyer, Lee
487          1953                    **$10**
8306         1953                    **$7**
8705         1953                    **$4**

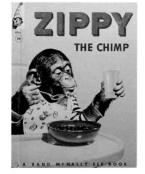

**Zippy the Chimp**
Illustrator: Mitchell, Benn
Author: Ecuyer, Lee
8306         1953                    **$7**

**Clue Club: The Case of the Missing Racehorse**
Illustrator: Franzen, Jim
Author: Brown, Fern G.
1972                                    $8

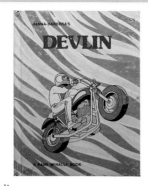

**Devlin**
Illustrator: Carleton, Jim
Author: Daly, Kathleen
1975                                    $8

**Dynomutt and the Pie in the Sky Caper**
Illustrator: Wise, Marilou
Author: Brown, Fern G.
1977                                    $8

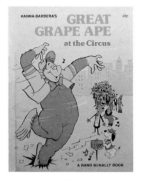

**Great Grape Ape at the Circus**
Illustrator: Wise, Marilou
Author: Lewis, Jean
1976                                    $8

**Hong Kong Phooey and the Bird Nest Snatchers**
Illustrator: Ostapczuk, Phil
Author: Lewis, Jean
1976                                    $8

**Hong Kong Phooey and the Fire Engine Mystery**
Illustrator: Ostapczuk, Phil
Author: Sherman, Diane
1977                                    $8

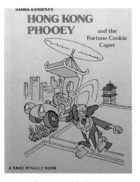

**Hong Kong Phooey and the Fortune Cookie Caper**
Illustrator: Ostapczuk, Phil
Author: Lewis, Jean
1975                                    $8

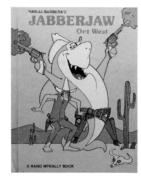

**Jabberjaw Out West**
Illustrator: Franzen , Jim
Author: Lewis, Jean
1977                                    $8

**Josie and the Pussycats
The Bag Factory Detour**
Illustrator: Franzen, Jim
Author: Russell, Solveig Paulson
1976                                    $8

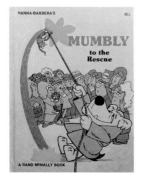

**Mumbly to the Rescue**
Illustrator: Wise, Marilou
Author: Lewis, Jean
1977                                    $8

**Scooby-Doo and the Case of the Counterfeit Money**
Illustrator: Lowe, Richard
Author: Brown, Fern G.
1976                                    $8

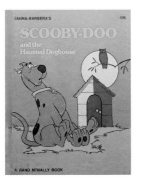

**Scooby-Doo and the Haunted Doghouse**
Illustrator: Lowe, Richard
Author: Lewis, Jean
1975                                    $8

**Scooby-Doo and the Headless Horseman**
Illustrator: Lowe, Richard
Author: Brown, Fern G.
1976                                    $8

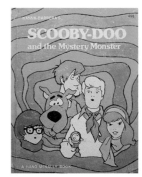

**Scooby-Doo and the Mystery Monster**
Illustrator: Canaday, Ralph
Author: Lewis, Jean
1975                                    $8

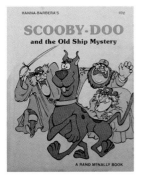

**Scooby-Doo and the Old Ship Mystery**
Illustrator: Ostapczuk, Phil
Author: Russell, Solveig Paulson
1977                                    $8

**Speed Buggy and the Secret Message**
Illustrator: Anderson, Bill & Judie
Author: Warren, Mary Phraner
1976                                    $8

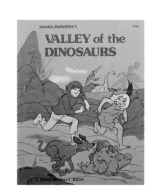

**Valley of the Dinosaurs**
Illustrator: Kantz, Phil
Author: Daly, Kathleen N.
1975                                    $8

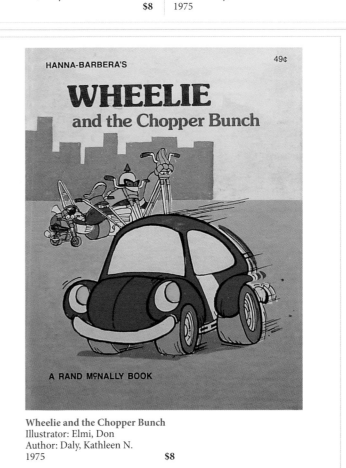

**Wheelie and the Chopper Bunch**
Illustrator: Elmi, Don
Author: Daly, Kathleen N.
1975                        $8

During the early 1940s, Rand McNally was publishing a smaller children's book that measured 5 x 6-3/4 inches. These books were numbered sequentially from 300 and 400. They were only known as "A Rand McNally Book."

In 1947 these books started evolving into the Jr. Elf book series. The size was reduced by 1/8 inch on the width while the height stayed the same. These 36-page books were now numbered starting with 600, and they still stated "A Rand McNally Book." Around 1950 the series name was changed on the books to "A Rand McNally-Elf Junior." Between the middle of 1954 and early 1956, there appears to have been a transition period where either "A Rand McNally-Elf Junior" or "A Rand

McNally Junior Elf Book" appeared at the bottom of the book's front cover.

The cover price of a Jr. Elf Book stayed at 15 cents from 1947 to around 1962, when it was raised to 19 cents. The amount of pages in the original stories was 36. Books can be found with 32 or 36 pages between 1954 and 1955. From 1956 to 1962 each book contained 32 pages. When the cover price changed in the late 1960s to 25 cents, the number of pages dropped to 28.

After the cover price changed to 25 cents, it became impossible to determine a book's printing date. Rand McNally started omitting this information when the book's cover price was 19 cents, so some of these books will not have printing information.

**A B C Book**
Cover: Morey, Jean
Illustrator: Grider, Dorothy
Author: Pease, Josephine
694          1954                    $15
8038         1955                    $6

**Alexander Kitten**
Illustrator: Opitz, Marge
Author: Broderick, Jessica Potter
8003         1959            $10

**Alice in Wonderland**
Illustrator: Bruce, Suzanne
Author: Carroll, Lewis
662          1950          $25

**All Around the City**
Illustrator: Lee, Manning De V
Author: Sherman, Diane
8146         1967        $3

**Animal Fair, The**
Illustrator: Kane, Herbert
Author: Wilkie, Elllen
8107         1964        $3

**Animal Mothers and Babies**
Illustrator: Photos
Author: Ratzesberger, Anna
699          1956                $10
8078         1956                $6

**Animal Mysteries**
Illustrator: Hague, Carl & Mary
Author: Fisher, Dr. Lester E.
8062        1971                    $3
8172        1971                    $2

**Animal Stories We Can Read**
Illustrator: Grider, Dorothy
Author: Carpenter, Flora L.
610         1947                    $12

**Animal Stories We Can Read**
Illustrator: Grider, Dorothy
Author: Carpenter, Flora L.
8031        1947                    $6

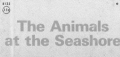

**Animals at the Seashore, The**
Illustrator: Helps, Racey
Author: Wing, Helen
8125        1966                    $3

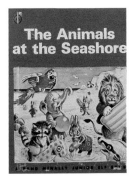

**Animals at the Seashore, The**
Illustrator: Helps, Racey
Author: Wing, Helen
8125        1966                    $2

**Animals Talk To Me**
Illustrator: Robinson, Irma
Author: Mason, Sue
8133        1966                    $3

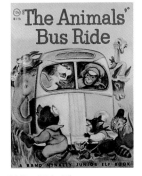

**Animals' Bus Ride, The**
Illustrator: Wilde, Irma
Author: Wing, Helen
8118        1965                    $3

**Animals' Tea Party, The**
Illustrator: Wilde, Irma
Author: Wing, Helen
8116        1965                    $3

**Animals' Train Ride, The**
Illustrator: Corwin, Eleanor
Author: Potter, Miriam Clark
682         1953                    $15

**Animals' Train Ride, The**
Illustrator: Corwin, Eleanor
Author: Potter, Miriam Clark
8040        1953                    $6

**Baby Animal Zoo, The**
Illustrator: Hague, Carl & Mary
Author: Fisher, Dr. Lester E.
8170        1971                    $3

**Baby Animals**
Illustrator: Opitz, Marge
Author: Zimmerman, Naoma
689         1955                    $8
8071        1955                    $4

**Baby Jesus, The**
Illustrator: Webbe, Elizabeth
Author: Jones, Mary Alice
8086        1961        $5

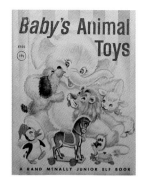

**Baby's Animal Toys**
Illustrator: Chase, Mary Jane
Author: Watts, Mabel
8103        1963        $3

**Baby's Own Mother Goose**
Illustrator: Blake, Vivienne
8162        1969        $4

**Backyard Circus**
Illustrator: Grider, Dorothy
Author: Stanley, Helen Frances
8149        1967        $3

**Bears' Picnic, The**
Illustrator: Carlson, Charlotte
Author: Burrow, Peggy
686        1954        $15

**Bear's Picnic, The**
Illustrator: Carlson, Charlotte
Author: Burrows, Peggy
8084        1954        $6

**Bedtime Stories**
Illustrator: Brice, Tony
Author: Potter, Miriam Clark
669        1951        $12
8035        1951        $6

**Benjie Engie**
Illustrator: Corwin, Eleanor
Author: Devine, Louise Lawrence
656        1950        $15

**Benjie Engie**
Illustrator: Corwin, Eleanor
Author: Devine, Louise Lawrence
8008        1950        $5

**Beth's Happy Day**
Illustrator: Fenwick, Patti
Author: Ochocki, Phyllis
8141        1966        $4

**Bible Stories For Little Children**
Illustrator: Kenndey, Janet Robson
Author: Jones, Mary Alice
643        1949        $10
8013        1949        $6

**Big Helpers: Power Shovels, Trucks, Derricks**
Illustrator: Wilde, George
Author: Wilde, Irma
680        1953        $8
8047        1953        $4

**Big Red Apple, The**
Illustrator: Wilde, Irma
Author: Patch, Kate Whiting
8157          1968                    $3

**Birds**
Illustrator: Opitz, Marge
Author: Watts, Mabel
8090          1957                    $3

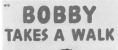

**Bobby Takes a Walk**
Illustrator: Buehrig, Rosemary
Author: Devine, Louise Lawrence
612          1947                    $15

**Bobby's Magic Blanket**
Illustrator: Petrie, Haris
Author: Stanley, Helen Franes
8183          1973                    $3

**Bounce the Jeep**
Cover: Schumacher, J. C.
Illustrator: Peterson, Harold
Author: Snedeker, Barbara Jane
608          1945                    $15

**Bouncing Bear—A Nursey Rhymer**
Illustrator: Brice, Tony
Author: Laing, Dilys Bennet
613          1945                    $15

**Bouncing Bear—A Nursey Rhymer**
Illustrator: Brice, Tony
Author: Laing, Dilys Bennett
8054          1945                    $6

**Bremen Town Musicians, The**
Illustrator: Wilde, Irma
8066          1960                    $5

**Bunny Blue**
Illustrator: Tellingen, Ruth Thompson Van
Author: Stahlmann, Catherine
601          1946                    $25

**Bunny Blue**
Illustrator: Tellingen, Ruth Thompson Van
Author: Stahlmann, Catherine
8023          1946                    $15

**Butterball the Little Chick**
Illustrator: Chase, Mary Jane
Author: Wing, Helen
693          1955                    $15
8032          1955                    $10

**Captain Kitty**
Illustrator: Webbe, Elizabeth
Author: Lynn, Godfrey
665          1951                    $15
8049          1951                    $12

**Child's Garden of Verses, A**
Illustrator: Webbe, Elizabeth
Author: Stevenson, Robert Louis
8095          1962                    $5

**Christmas Joys**
Illustrator: McClain, Mary
Author: Daly, Kathleen
8206          1980                    $4

**Christmas Snowman, The**
Illustrator: Kane, Sharon
Author: Sherman, Diane
8202          1977                    $5

**Cinderella**
Illustrator: Chase, Mary Jane
8005          1966                    $3

**Cock, the Mouse and the Little Red Hen, The**
Illustrator: Adler, Helen
8067          1960                    $5

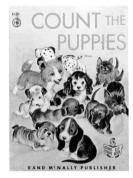

**Count the Puppies**
Illustrator: Whilldin, Mary
Author: Dee, Carolyn
8139          1966                    $3

**Cowboy Dan**
Illustrator: Phillips, Katherine L.
Author: Cobb, Andy
659          1950                    $20
8009          1950                    $15

**Davy Deer's New Red Scarf**
Illustrator: Adler, Helen
Author: Adler, Helen
8129          1966                    $3

**Dinosaurs**
Illustrator: Street, Theodore
Author: Miller, M.R.
8176          1971                    $3

**Disposal Truck, The**
Illustrator: Popp, Walter and Marie
Author: Ratzesberger, Anna
8161          1969                    $3

**Doll House, The**
Illustrator: Adler, Helen
Author: Adler, Helen
8082          1961                    $5

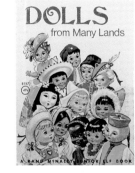

**Dolls From Many Lands**
Illustrator: Grider, Dorothy
Author: Bartkowski, Renee
8187          1975                    $5

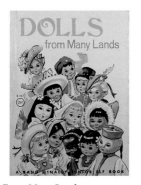

**Dolls From Many Lands**
Illustrator: Grider, Dorothy
Author: Bartkowski, Renee
8787          1975                    $5

**Elves and the Shoemaker, The**
Illustrator: Friend, Esther
Author: Brothers Grimm
8137          1966                    $3

**Farm Animals**
Illustrator: Wilde, Irma
Author: Zimmerman, Naoma
8019          1966                    $3

**Farm Pets**
Illustrator: Phillips, Katherine L.
Author: Ratzesberger, Anna
8041          1954                    $3
684          1954                    $12
8034          1954                    $2

**Feathered Friends**
Illustrator: Opitz, Marge
Author: Watts, Mabel
606          1957                    $10
8090          1957                    $6

**Feeding Time at the Zoo**
Illustrator: Hauge, Carl & Mary
Author: Fisher, Dr. Lester E.
8174          1971                    $3

**Fire Fighters**
Illustrator: Merryweather, Jack
Author: Grant, Bruce
8168          1971                    $3

**Fireman Joe**
Illustrator: Webbe, Elizabeth
Author: Hunter, Virginia
8006          1959                    $6

**Five Beds For Bitsy**
Illustrator: Webbe, Elizabeth
Author: Munn, Ian
661          1950                    $15
8002          1950                    $10

**Flying Sandbox, The**
Illustrator: Wilson, Beth
Author: Cambell, Pauline C.
676          1952                    $15

**Friends Are For Loving**
Illustrator: Grider, Dorothy
Author: Jones, Mary Alice
8143          1968                    $3

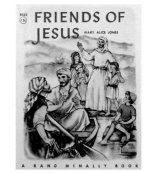

**Friends of Jesus**
Illustrator: Kennedy
Author: Jones, Mary Alice
687          1954                    $8
8022          1954                    $6

**Giant's Shoe, The**
Illustrator: Friend, Esther
Author: North, Jessica Nelson
8148        1967                    $3

**Gingerbread Man, The**
Illustrator: Burrows, Peggy
Author: Wadsworth, Wallace
685         1954                   $15
8021        1954                    $6

**Go-To-Sleep Book**
Cover: Marge Opitz
Illustrator: Wosmek, Frances
Author: Gilbert, Helen Earle
642         1949                   $12
8073        1949                    $5

**God Is Good**
Illustrator: Webbe, Elizabeth
Author: Jones, Mary Alice
692         1955                   $10
8018        1955                    $5

**God Loves Me**
Illustrator: Webbe, Elizabeth
Author: Jones, Mary Alce
8069        1961                    $5

**God's Plan For Growing Things**
Illustrator: Wilde, Irma
Author: Jones, Mary Alice
8112        1964                    $3

**Happy Animals' A B C**
Illustrator: Helps, Racey
Author: Wing, Helen
8131        1966                    $3

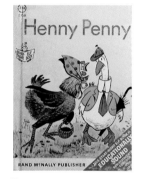

**Henny Penny**
Illustrator: Tweetdale, George
Author: Wadsworth, Wallace C.
8138        1966                    $3

**Henrietta's Ride**
Illustrator: Webbe, Elizabeth
Author: Lynn, Godfrey
651         1949                   $15

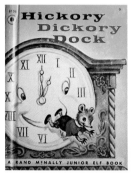

**Hickory Dickory Dock**
Illustrator: Corwin, Eleanor
Author: Wing, Helen
8106        1964                    $3

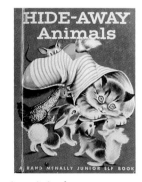

**Hide-Away Animals**
Illustrator: Chase, Mary Jane
Author: Watts, Mabel
604         1957                   $10
8083        1957                    $4

**Hoppity Skip**
Illustrator: Grider, Dorothy
Author: Warren, Mary Phraner
8169        1971                    $3

**House That Jack Built, The**
Illustrator: Brice, Tony
8055        1942        **$6**

**How Chicks Are Born**
Illustrator: Whilldin, Mary
Author: Grant, Bruce
8153        1967        **$3**

**How Seeds Travel**
Illustrator: Cooper, Marjorie
Author: Faber, Robert J.
8192        1976        **$2**

**Humpty Dumpty and Other Mother Goose Rhymes**
Illustrator: Chase, Mary Jane
647        1952        **$10**

**Humpty Dumpty and Other Mother Goose Rhymes**
Illustrator: Chase, Mary Jane
8058        1952        **$5**

**I Like**
Illustrator: Armstrong, George
Author: Saffron, Rose
8120        1965        **$3**

**I Once Knew**
Illustrator: Leaf, Anne Sellers
Author: Sellers, Thelma
8142        1967        **$3**

**Jack and the Beanstalk**
Illustrator: Berry, Anne Scheu
666        1951        **$12**

**Jack and the Beanstalk**
Illustrator: Berry, Anne Scheu
8034        1951        **$6**

**Jack and the Beanstalk**
Illustrator: Leaf, Anne Sellers
8167        1969        **$5**

**Jack Sprat**
Illustrator: Leaf, Anne Sellers
Author: Wing, Helen
8130        1966        **$5**

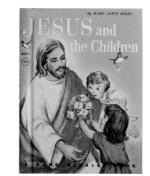

**Jesus and the Children**
Illustrator: Corwin, Eleanor
Author: Jones, Mary Alice
8074        1961        **$5**

**Jesus Who Helped People**
Illustrator: Lee, Manning De V.
Author: Jones, Mary Alice
8113        1964                    $3

**Jiggers**
Illustrator: Breuer, Matilda
Author: Lacey, Joy Muchmore
617        1942                    $15

**Jiggers**
Illustrator: Breuer, Matilda
Author: Lacey, Joy Muchmore
8101        1943                    $6

**Johnny's Secret**
Illustrator: Cooper, Marjorie
Author: Lewis, Frank
8188        1975                    $3

**Jolly Jingle Book, The**
Illustrator: McKinley, Clare
Author: Jackson, Leroy F.
667        1951                    $12

**Jolly Jingle Book, The**
Illustrator: McKinley, Clare
Author: Jackson, Leroy F.
8001        1951                    $4

**Jumping Jack**
Illustrator: Leaf, Anne Sellers
Author: Sherman, Diane
8094        1962                    $5

**Kittens**
Illustrator: Opitz, Marge
Author: Stahlmann, Catherine
679        1953                    $15

**Kittens**
Illustrator: Opitz, Marge
Author: Stahlmann, Catherine
8085        1953                    $6

**Lancelot**
Illustrator: Tamburine, Jean
Author: Barrows, Marjorie
8105        1963                    $4

**Let's Find Koala Bears**
Illustrator: Cooper, Marjorie
Author: Simmons, Ida H.
8160        1969                    $5

**Let's Read About Rocks**
Illustrator: Fleishman, Seymour
Author: Comfort, Iris Tracy
8165        1969                    $3

**Little Bear**
Illustrator: Opitz, Marge
Author: Hunter, Virginia
602     1956     **$15**
8072    1956     **$6**

**Little Beaver**
Illustrator: Hawkinson, John
Author: Di Valentin, Maria M.
8100    1963     **$6**

**Little Bird**
Illustrator: Wilde, Irma
Author: Stahlmann, Catherine
8110    1964     **$4**

**Little Bo-Peep**
Illustrator: Chase, Mary Jane
Author: Wing, Helen
8010    1966     **$3**

**Little Boy Blue's Horn**
Illustrator: Wilde, Irma
Author: Wing, Helen
8117    1965     **$3**

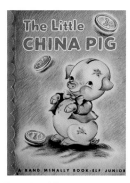

**Little China Pig, The**
Illustrator: Blake, Vivienne
Author: Rawls, Dorothy Dickens
652     1949     **$18**

**Little China Pig, The**
Illustrator: Blake, Vivienne
Author: Rawls, Dorothy Dickens
8059    1949     **$10**

**Little Deer**
Illustrator: Opitz, Marge
Author: Zimmerman, Naoma
696     1956     **$10**
8080    1956     **$6**

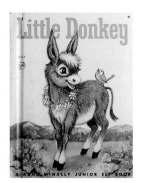

**Little Donkey**
Illustrator: Tamburine, Jean
Author: Broderick, Jessica Potter
8111    1964     **$3**

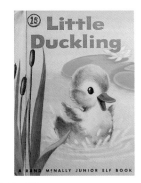

**Little Duckling**
Illustrator: Ozone, Lucy
Author: Wing, Helen
603     1956     **$10**
8029    1956     **$5**

**Little Elephant**
Illustrator: Ozone, Lucy
Author: Broderick, Jessica Potter
8007    1959     **$6**
8011    1959     **$5**

**Little Fox**
Illustrator: Wilde, Irma
Author: Watts, Mabel
8077    1961     **$5**

**Little Lamb's Hat**
Illustrator: Corwin, Eleanor
Author: Phillips, Mary G.
675        1952                    **$15**
8024       1952                    **$7**

**Little Lost Angel**
Illustrator: Scott, Janet Laura
Author: Heath, Janet Field
8205       1953                    **$5**

**Little Penguin**
Illustrator: DeMuth, Vivienne Blake
Author: Rarick, Carrie
8057       1960                    **$5**
8028       1960                    **$5**

**Little Rabbit's Bath**
Illustrator: Blake, Vivienne
Author: Potter, Miriam Clark
624        1948                    **$15**
8063       1948                    **$6**

**Little Racoon**
Illustrator: Tamburine, Jean
Author: Watts, Mabel
8081       1961                    **$5**

**Little Red Boot, The**
Illustrator: Grider, Dorothy
Author: Dixon, Ruth
8134       1966                    **$3**

**Little Red Hen, The**
Illustrator: Bendel, Ruth
605        1957                    **$12**
8030       1957                    **$6**

**Little Red Riding-Hood**
Illustrator: Friend, Esther
658        1950                    **$12**
8004       1950                    **$3**
8048       1950                    **$5**

**Little Red Wagon, The**
Illustrator: Mc Kinley, Clare
Author: Cederborg, Hazel P.
650        1949                    **$8**

**Little Red Wagon, The**
Illustrator: Mc Kinley, Clare
Author: Cederborg, Hazel P.
8075       1949                    **$3**

**Little Tiger**
Illustrator: Tamburine, Jean
Author: Watts, Mabel
8097       1962                    **$5**

**Little Toy Train**
Illustrator: Bryant, Dean
Author: Stahlmann, Catherine
8031       1965                    **$3**

**Little Yellow Chick**
Illustrator: Adler, Helen
Author: Munn, Ian
8087        1961                    $5

**Look! A Parade**
Illustrator: Timmons, William
Author: Barrows, Marjorie
8135        1966                    $3

**Magician's Counting Book, The**
Illustrator: Grider, Dorothy
Author: Stanley, Helen Frances
8179        1973                    $3

**Mailman Mike**
Illustrator: Tamburine, Jean
Author: Watts, Mabel
8005        1959                    $6

**Mary Had a Little Lamb**
Illustrator: Gavy
8045        1955                    $5
690         1955                    $10
8088        1955                    $3

**Me, Myself and God**
Illustrator: Grider, Dorothy
Author: Jones, Mary Alice
8115        1965                    $3

**Milkman Bill**
Illustrator: Tamburine, Jean
Author: Broderick, Jessica Potter
8056        1960                    $5

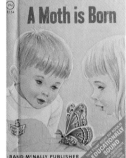

**Moth is Born, A**
Illustrator: Dottig
Author: Walker, Herbert B.
8154        1967                    $3

**Mother Goose**
Illustrator: Brice, Tony
600         1946                    $15
8012        1946                    $6

**Mr. Flopears**
Illustrator: Helps, Racey
Author: Helps, Racey
8163        1969                    $5

**Mr. Snitzel's Cookies**
Illustrator: Flory, Jane
Author: Flory, Jane
653         1950                    $18

**Mr. Snitzel's Cookies**
Illustrator: Flory, Jane
Author: Flory, Jane
8046        1950                    $10

**Mrs. Duck's Lovely Day**
Illustrator: Blake, Vivienne
Author: Blake, Vivienne
| 691 | 1955 | $12 |
| 8003 | 1955 | $4 |
| 8091 | 1955 | $6 |

**Mrs. Hen Goes to Market**
Illustrator: Webbe, Elizabeth
Author: Lynn, Godfrey
| 663 | 1949 | $15 |

**Mrs. Hen Goes to Market**
Illustrator: Webbe, Elizabeth
Author: Lynn, Godfrey
| 8036 | 1949 | $5 |

**Mulberry Bush, The**
Illustrator: Grider, Dorothy
| 8159 | 1969 | $6 |

**Mumpsy Goes to Kindergarten**
Illustrator: Grider, Dorothy
Author: Devine, Louise Lawrence
| 607 | 1945 | $15 |

**Mumpsy Goes to Kindergarten**
Illustrator: Grider, Dorothy
Author: Devine, Louise Lawrence
| 8052 | 1945 | $6 |

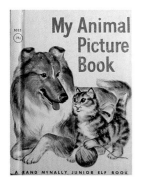

**My Animal Picture Book**
Illustrator: Opitz, Marge
Author: Hunter, Virginia
| 8025 | 1959 | $5 |

**My Birthday Book**
Illustrator: Leaf, Anne Sellers
Author: Stenstrom, Lois
| 8195 | 1967 | $20 |

**My Cowboy Book**
Illustrator: Merryweather, J.
| 8150 | 1967 | $3 |

**My First Picture Book of Christmas Carols**
Illustrator: McClain, Mary
| 8196 | 1979 | $3 |

**My First Zoo Book**
Illustrator: Phillips, Katherine
Author: Cobb, Andy
| 677 | 1952 | $8 |
| 8020 | 1952 | $5 |

**My Indian Book**
Illustrator: Merryweather, Jack
Author: Grant, Bruce
| 8158 | 1968 | $3 |

**My Magic Telephone**
Illustrator: Kane, Sharon
Author: Hogstrom, Daphne Doward
8190          1975                    $5

**My Oak Tree**
Illustrator: George, Pricilla
Author: Sherman, Diane
8181          1973                    $3

**My Toys**
Illustrator: Friend, Esther
Author: Goldin, Augusta R.
688           1955                   $10
8051          1955                    $3

**My Toys**
Illustrator: Friend, Esther
Author: Goldin, Augusta R.
8026          1955                    $4

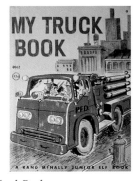

**My Truck Book**
Illustrator: Wilde, George
Author: Watts, Mabel
8062          1960                    $5

**Myrtle Turtle**
Illustrator: Tamburine, Jean
Author: Sherman, Diane
8076          1961                    $5

**Night Before Christmas, The**
Illustrator: Webbe, Elizabeth
Author: Moore, Clement Clark
657           1950                   $15

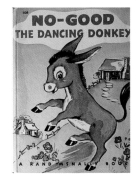

**No-Good the Dancing Donkey**
Illustrator: Friend, Esther
Author: Snow, Dorothea J.
606           1944                   $12

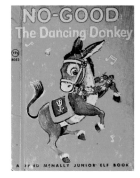

**No-Good the Dancing Donkey**
Illustrator: Friend, Esther
Author: Snow, Dorothea J.
8053          1944                    $6

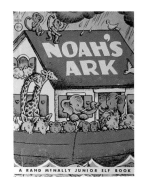

**Noah's Ark**
Illustrator: Brice, Tony
Author: Briggs, Dorothy Bell
8026          1946                    $6

**Noah and His Ark**
Illustrator: Brice, Tony
Author: Briggs, Dorothy Bell
698           1946                   $15

**Noni the Christmas Reindeer**
Illustrator: Goldsborough, June
Author: Hogstrom, Daphne Doward
8197          1979                    $4

**Nubbins and the Tractor**
Illustrator: Mc Kinley, Clare
Author: Sinnickson, Freda
670          1951                    $12

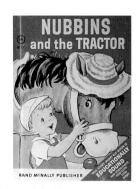

**Nubbins and the Tractor**
Cover: Barbara Clyne
Illustrator: McKinley, Clare
Author: Sinnickson, Freda
8027         1951                    $5

**Old Woman and Her Pig, The**
Illustrator: Brice, Tony
Author: Wadsworth, Wallace C.
629          1944                    $20

**Once Upon a Time**
Illustrator: Webbe, Elizabeth
8068         1950                    $6

**Owl and the Pussy-Cat and Calico Pie, The**
Illustrator: Wilde, Irma
Author: Lear, Edward
8096         1962                    $6

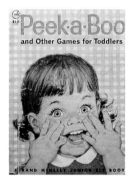

**Peek-A-Boo and Other Games For Toddlers**
Illustrator: Kane, Sharon
8119         1965                    $5

**Penny For Candy, A**
Cover: Marge Oplitz
Illustrator: Reppy, Nell
Author: Devine, Louise Lawrence
602          1946                    $15

**Penny For Candy, A**
Cover: Marge Oplitz
Illustrator: Reppy, Nell
Author: Devine, Louise Lawrence
8093         1946                    $6

**Pet For Peter, A**
Illustrator: Werber, Adele; Laslo, Doris
Author: Vandevere, J. Lilian
655          1950                    $15

**Pet For Peter, A**
Cover: Barbara Clyne
Illustrator: Werber, Adele; Laslo, Doris
Author: Vandevere, J. Lillian
8043         1950                    $6

**Pet Parade, The**
Illustrator: Kane, Sharon
Author: Warren, Mary Phraner
8156         1969                    $5

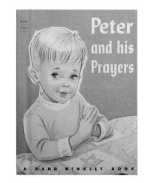

**Peter and His Prayers**
Illustrator: Grider, Dorothy
Author: Dowd, Susan Bromley
8122         1966                    $4

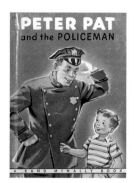

**Peter Pat and the Policeman**
Illustrator: Grider, Dorothy
Author: Stahlmann, Catherine
625     1948     **$10**
8042    1948     **$6**

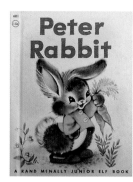

**Peter Rabbit**
Illustrator: Leaf, Anne Sellers
Author: Wadsworth, Wallace
681     1953     **$12**
8017    1953     **$5**

**Picnic in the Park, A**
Illustrator: Grider, Dorothy
Author: Miller, Malinda R.
8177    1973     **$3**

**Pillowtime Tales**
Illustrator: Taylor, Ethel Bonney
Author: DeGroot, Marion K.
627     1943     **$12**

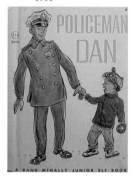

**Policeman Dan**
Illustrator: Wilde, George
Author: Hunter, Virginia
8098    1962     **$5**

**Ponies**
Illustrator: Webbe, Elizabeth
Author: Ratzesberger, Anna
683     1953     **$8**
8089    1953     **$4**

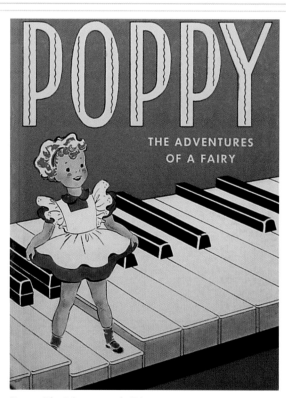

**Poppy –The Adventures of a Fairy**
Illustrator: Barclay, Betty
Author: Pérez-Guerra, Anne
621     1942     **$20**

**Prayers For Little Children**
Illustrator: Bruce, Suzanne
Author: Jones, Mary Alice
644     1949     **$8**
8014    1949     **$4**

**Puddle Jumper**
Illustrator: Snow, Dorothea J.
Author: Snow, Dorothea J.
626     1948     **$15**

**Puppies**
Illustrator: Wilde, Irma
Author: Stahlmann, Catherine
8037        1952                    $5
673         1952                    $10

**Puppy That Found a Home, The**
Illustrator: Grider, Dorothy
Author: Francis, Sally R.
609         1947                    $12

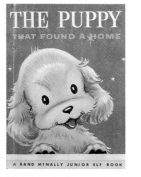

**Puppy That Found a Home, The**
Illustrator: Grider, Dorothy
Author: Francis, Sally R.
8033        1947                    $5

**Pussy Cat Talks To Her Kittens**
Cover: Elizabeth Webb
Illustrator: Smock, Nell
Author: Mead, Elizabeth
8060        1942                    $10

**Pussy Cat Talks To Her Kittens**
Illustrator: Smock, Nell
Author: Mead, Fannie E.
631         1942              $25

**Raggedy Goat and Other Verses, The**
Illustrator: Blake, Vivienne
8152        1967                    $4

**Road Builders**
Illustrator: Doremus, Robert
Author: Bartkowski, Renee
8193        1976              $3

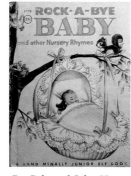

**Rock-a-Bye Baby and Other Nursery Rhymes**
Illustrator: Chase, Mary Jane
697         1956                    $10
8079        1956                    $5

**Runaway Airplane, The**
Cover: Esther Friend
Illustrator: Brice, Tony
Author: Graham, Hugh
639         1943                    $15

**Runaway Kangaroos, The**
Illustrator: Rockwell, Eve
Author: Lewis, Eliza
8004     1959     **$4**
639     1959     **$8**

**Safe All Day With the Happies**
Illustrator: Friend, Esther
Author: Van Dolzen Pease, Josephine
636     1949     **$15**

**Santa's Runaway Elf**
Illustrator: Cooper, Marjorie
Author: Lewis, Jean
8203     1977     **$4**

**Sally's Lost Shoe and Other Stories**
Illustrator: Salter, Florence
Author: Laughlin, Florence
648     1944     **$15**

**Scooby-Doo and the Santa Claus Mystery**
Illustrator: Franzen, Jim
Author: Brown, Fern G.
8201     1977     **$10**

**Seashells For Katie and Andy**
Illustrator: Cooper, Marjorie
Author: Russell, Solveig Paulson
8182     1973     **$3**

**See My Toys**
Illustrator: Brice, Tony
Author: Garfield, Lillian B.
611     1947     **$15**

**See My Toys**
Illustrator: Brice, Tony
Author: Garfield, Lillian E. B.
8092     1947     **$6**

**Sleeping Beauty, The**
Illustrator: Blake, Vivienne
668     1951     **$12**
8050     1951     **$6**

**Sleeping Tree Mystery, The**
Illustrator: Goldsborough
Author: Lewis, Jean
8191     1975     **$4**

**Snow-White and the Seven Dwarfs**
Illustrator: Wilde, Irma
8027     1959     **$4**

**Sparrows' Nest, The**
Illustrator: Wilde, Irma
Author: Stanley, Helen Frances
8164     1969     **$3**

**Story of Jesus, The**
Illustrator: Pointer, Priscilla
Author: Glover, Gloria Diener
645     1949     **$10**
8015    1935     **$4**

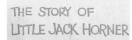

**Story of Little Jack Horner, The**
Illustrator: Leaf, Anne Sellers
Author: Wing, Helen
8104    1963     **$5**

**Story of Old King Cole, The**
Illustrator: Leaf, Anne Sellers
Author: Hogstrom, Daphne Doward
8037    1975     **$5**
8186    1975     **$4**

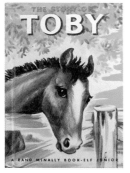

**Story of Toby, The**
Illustrator: Grider, Dorothy
Author: Moore, Jane Shearer
654    1950     **$10**

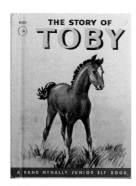

**Story of Toby, The**
Illustrator: Grider, Dorothy
Author: Moore, Jane Shearer
8000    1950     **$4**

**Sunny Meadow Stories**
Illustrator: Wilde, Irma
Author: Cory, David
605    1963     **$15**

**Sunny Meadow Stories**
Illustrator: Taylor, Ethel Bonney
Author: Cory, David
8102    1963     **$3**

**Surprise in the Barnyard**
Illustrator: Chase, Mary Jane
Author: Cranford, Martha
671    1952     **$12**

**Surprise in the Barnyard**
Illustrator: Chase, Mary Jane
Author: Cranford, Martha
8010    1952     **$4**

**Teeny Teeny Tiny Giraffe**
Illustrator: Goldsborough, June
Author: Russell, Solveig Paulson
8184    1975     **$3**

**Ten Commandments, The**
Illustrator: Grider, Dorothy
Author: Jones, Mary Alice
672    1952     **$10**
8016    1952     **$5**

**Ten Little Monkeys**
Illustrator: Pillips, Katherine L.
Author: Broderick, Jessica Potter
678    1953     **$15**
8044    1953     **$5**

**Thousand Candy Santas, A**
Illustrator: Wise, Marilou
Author: Hogstrom, Daphen Doward
8200        1977                    $4

**Three Bears, The**
Illustrator: Brice, Tony
Author: Wadsworth, Wallace C.
621        1942                    $15

**Three Bears, The**
Illustrator: Brice, Tony
Author: Wadsworth, Wallace C.
8036        1942                    $6
8065        1942                    $6

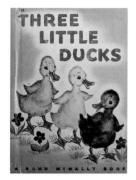

**Three Little Ducks**
Illustrator: Shusie
Author: Woodstock, Rhoda Wyatt
633        1945                    $10

**Three Little Ducks**
Cover: Elizabeth Webbe
Illustrator: Shusie
Author: Woodstock, Rhoda Wyatt
8064        1945                    $4

**Three Little Pigs, The**
Illustrator: Bendel, Ruth
637        1956                    $12
8039        1956                    $5
8006        1956                    $4

**Three Wishes, The**
Illustrator: Friend, Esther
Author: Wadsworth, Wallace C.
603        1945                    $15

**Three Wishes, The**
Cover: Barbara Clyne
Illustrator: Friend, Esther
Author: Wadsworth, Wallace C.
8061        1945                    $6

**Tie My Shoe**
Illustrator: Kane, Sharon
Author: Wing, Helen
8109        1964                    $6

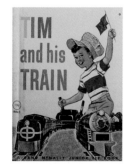

**Tim and His Train**
Cover: Jackie Mastri
Illustrator: Mastri, Fiore & Jackie
Author: Reichert, E.C.
635        1949                    $12
8045        1949                    $6

**Time For a Rhyme**
Illustrator: Kane, Sharon
Author: Wilkie, Ellen
#8132        1966                    $5

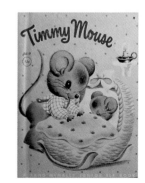

**Timmy Mouse**
Illustrator: Brice, Tony
Author: Potter, Miriam Clark
664        1951                    $12
8019        1951                    $6

**Timothy the Little Brown Bear**
Illustrator: Flory, Jane
Author: Flory, Jane
634          1949                    **$15**

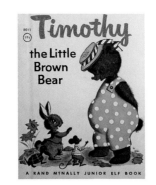

**Timothy the Little Brown Bear**
Illustrator: Flory, Jane
Author: Flory, Jane
8011         1949                    **$8**

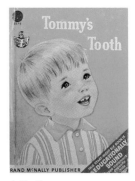

**Tommy's Tooth**
Illustrator: Fenwick, Patti
Author: Russell, Solveig Paulson
8155         1967                    **$3**

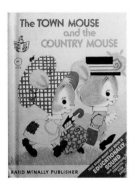

**Town Mouse and the Country Mouse, The**
Illustrator: Leaf, Anne Sellers
8058         1973                    **$4**
8180         1973                    **$3**

**Treasure Trunk, The**
Illustrator: Kane, Sharon
Author: Warren, Mary Phraner
8145         1967                    **$5**

**Walk in the Zoo, A**
Illustrator: Hague, Carl & Mary
Author: Fisher, Dr. Lester E.
8173         1971                    **$3**

**Walk With Grandpa, A**
Illustrator: Wilde, Irma & George
Author: Stanley, Helen Frances
8126         1967                    **$3**

**We Love America**
Illustrator: Friend, Esther
Author: Pease, Josephine Van Dolzen
632          1941                    **$10**

**What Are Daisies For?**
Illustrator: Drescher, Joan E.
Author: Drescher, Joan E.
8185         1975                    **$3**

**What Can I Do?**
Illustrator: Adler, Helen
Author: Conarroe, Lewis, H.
8070         1961                    **$5**

**What's in the Bakery Truck**
Illustrator: Drescher, Joan E.
Author: Wells, Tilden
8151         1967                    **$3**

**Wild Babies**
Illustrator: Hauge, Carl & Mary
Author: Fisher, Dr. Lester E.
8175         1971                    **$4**
8047         1971                    **$3**

Around 1898 Alexander Grosset and George T. Dunlap, with combined capital of $1,350, formed the partnership of Grosset & Dunlap. The company was created to sell and distribute books.

While using the works of authors like Rudyard Kipling, the company moved into the business of rebinding paperbacks with hard covers. This method was used for a few years before the company started producing its own reprints of books. The company's reprints sold for around 50 cents each at this time.

1908 saw Grosset & Dunlap publishing its own line of children's books after the purchase of the Chatterton & Peck Company, which was already successful with the Rover Boys and the Bobbsey Twins. Around 1910 the company was publishing the adventures of Tom Swift, and by the 1920s, it was producing popular book series like Zane Grey's westerns and the Hardy Boys mysteries. With the success of the Hardy Boys, the company gave girls their own sleuth, Nancy Drew, in the 1930s.

A paper shortage during World War II pushed the selling price of reprinted books up to around $1, but when the war ended, the price went back to 50 cents.

In 1944 the Book-of-the-Month Club, Harper, Little, Brown, Scribners, and Random House purchased Grosset & Dunlap. A year later Bantam Books was formed—the Curtis Company owned 30 percent. Bantam was to eventually become one of the largest paperback publishers.

Wonder Books, Inc. was formed in 1947 with a joint Curtis-Grosset distribution. Random House distributed the first Wonder Books. Wonder Books later became a subdivision of Grosset & Dunlap.

The first 17 Wonder Book titles originally measured 7-1/2 x 9-3/4 inches and contained 46 pages, with 20 pages in full color. This size was around for only a short while. The size of the books changed to 6-1/2 x 8-1/8 inches around 1948.

Of the first 17 titles, most were reprinted in the smaller size except for the following titles:

#508 *How the Rabbit Fooled the Whale and the Elephant and Other Stories* became *Why the Bear Has a Short Tail and Other Stories*.

#511 *Animal Stories* became *The Shy Little Horse and Other Stories*. *The Little Cat That Could Not Sleep* was dropped from the book when the title was changed.

#515 *How the Baby Hippo Found a Home* was never reprinted as a Wonder Book.

Bound in dirt-resistant "Durasheen," Wonder Books became known as the books with the washable covers. Even though their covers were washable, their spines did not hold up very well. With a glossy paper cover that went from front to back, the more the book was opened, the more chances there were of the spine falling off because of splitting or tearing.

Filmways purchased Grosset & Dunlap in 1974. Grosset & Dunlap purchased Platt & Munk in 1977. The Putnam Publishing Group purchased Grosset & Dunlap in 1982. The last company that I know of owning the rights to Wonder Books was Price Stern Sloan. Because of changes in ownership through the years, it is difficult to pinpoint accurate historical Wonder Books information.

Those of you familiar with the Treasure Books will notice that some their titles were later published as Wonder Books.

**How to determine Wonder Book editions:**

There are no markings on Wonder Books that will tell you exactly what edition you own, but you should be able to narrow down the time period of publication by using a little deductive reasoning.

The earlier book had a listing of titles in print either on the back cover or on the last page of the book. You can use this list to approximate the time of a book's printing. For example, you own #557, *Billy and His Steam Roller*, with a copyright of 1951. The last title listed is #742, *Whose Hat Is That*. When you look up #742, you find that it has a copyright of 1960, so your copy of #557 must have been published around 1960. If the last title number had been #560 instead of #742, the book probably would be a first edition. Unfortunately, this method of dating Wonder Books cannot guarantee that you have a first edition. Once the company stopped listing the books in print, one is only able to approximate the date of printing by using the cover price. Prices stayed steady for years at a time, so this method will only give you a period of printing.

Wonder Books, like most Elf Books, had a one-piece wraparound cover. This makes it very difficult to find nice early copies with their spines intact. Some titles, like those by certain illustrators and books based on cartoon and TV characters, will continue to increase in value.

---

## Original Larger Size Wonder Books

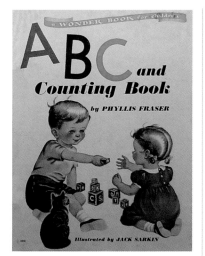

**A B C and Counting Book**
Illustrator: Sarkin, Jack
Author: Fraser, Phyllis
506          1946          **$15**

**Animal Stories**
Illustrator: Robinson
Author: Scott, Therese
511          1947          **$15**

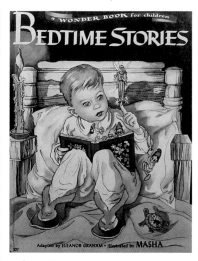

**Bedtime Stories**
Illustrator: Masha
Author: Graham, Eleanor
507          1946          **$15**

**Child's First Picture Dictionary, A**
Illustrator: Weber, Nettie; Clement, Charles
Author: Moore, Lilian
517      1948      **$15**

**Cozy Little Farm, The**
Illustrator: Angela
Author: Bonino, Louise
502      1946      **$15**

**Favorite Nursery Tales**
Illustrator: Dixon, Rachel Taft
Author: Graham, Eleanor
503      1946      **$15**

**Famous Fairy Tales**
Illustrator: Jules, Mervin
Author: Graham, Eleanor
505      1946      **$15**

**How the Baby Hippo Found a Home**
Illustrator: Gannett, Ruth
Author: Thomas, Dorothy
515      1942      **$12**

**How the Rabbit Fooled the Whale and
the Elephant**
Illustrator: Sari
Author: Williams, Louise B.
508      1946      **$25**

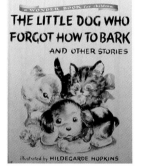

**Little Dog Who Forgot How to Bark, The**
Illustrator: Hopkins, Hildegard
Author: Bailey, Carolyn S.
504      1946      **$15**

**Little Train That Won a Medal, The**
Illustrator: Loeb, Anton
Author: Geis, Darlene
512      1947      **$15**

**Magic Bus, The**
Illustrator: Gergely, Tibor
Author: Dolbier, Maurice
516      1948      **$35**

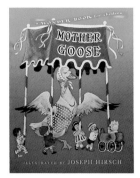

**Mother Goose**
Illustrator: Hirsch, Joseph
501      1946      **$15**

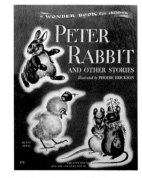

**Peter Rabbit and Other Stories**
Illustrator: Erickson, Phoebe
Author: Potter, Beatrix
513      1947      **$15**

**Race Between the Monkey and the Duck,
The**
Illustrator: Hurd, Clement
Author: Hurd, Clement
510      1940      **$35**

**Randolph: The Bear Who Said No**
Illustrator: Walker, Nedda
Author: Nelson, Faith
509          1946                    **$50**

**Storytime Favorites**
Illustrator: Leob, Anton
Author: Scott, Theresa Ann
514          1947                    **$15**

## Regular Size Wonder Books

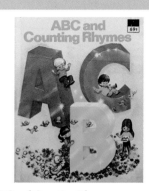

**10 Rabbits**
Illustrator: Dixon, Rachel Taft
Author: Potter, Miriam Clark
648          1957          **$7**

**A B C and Counting Book**
Illustrator: Sarkin, Jack
Author: Fraser, Phyllis
506          1946          **$15**

**A B C and Counting Rhymes**
Illustrator: Horton, Mary
823          1963          **$6**

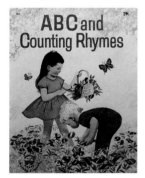

**A B C and Counting Rhymes**
Illustrator: Horton, Mary
823          1963          **$3**

**Aesop's Fables**
Illustrator: Seiden, Art
706          1958          **$6**

**Alice in Wonderland**
Illustrator: Matulay, Laszlo
Author: Martin, Marcia
574          1951          **$15**

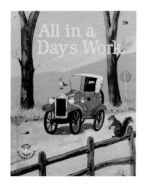

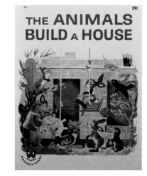

**All in a Day's Work**
Illustrator: Leone, Sergio
Author: Emerson, Caroline D.
807          1964          **$6**

**Alvin's Lost Voice**
Illustrator: Kurtz, Bob
Author: Kurtz, Bob
824          1963          **$16**

**Animals Build a House, The**
Illustrator: Marsia, Robert
Author: Marsia, Robert; Delahaye, Gilbert
817          1963          **$6**

**Animals' Party, The**
Illustrator: Brozowska, Elisabeth
Author: Brozowska, Elisabeth
790        1962                **$10**

**Animals' Playground, The**
Illustrator: Seiden, Art
Author: Marshall, Virginia Stone
825        1964                **$6**

**Animals' Vacation, The**
Illustrator: Haber, Shel & Jan
Author: Haber, Shel & Jan
839        1964                **$4**

**Are Dogs Better Than Cats?**
Illustrator: Le Grand
Author: Le Grand
565        1953                **$8**

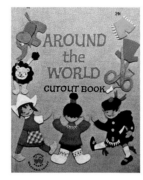

**Around the World Cutout Book**
Illustrator: Galst, Annie
Author: Galst, Annie
826        1964                **$6**

**Astronut and the Flying Bus**
Illustrator: Tallarico, Tony
Author: Lenhart, Ellen
853        1965                **$16**

**Babar and Father Christmas**
Illustrator: Hass, Merle S.
Author: De Brunoff, Jean
592        1940                **$20**

**Babar the King**
Illustrator: De Brunhoff, Jean
Author: De Brunhoff, Jean
602        1953                **$18**

**Baby Animal Friends**
Illustrator: Erickson, Phoebe
Author: Erickson, Phoebe
608        1954                **$7**

**Baby Bunny, The**
Illustrator: Stone, Dick
Author: Evers, Alf
548        1951                **$8**

**Baby Elephant, The**
Illustrator: Burchard, Peter
Author: Brewster, Benamine
541        1950                **$10**

**Baby Huey**
Illustrator: Harvey Cartoon Studios
Author: Harvey Cartoon Studios
787        1961                **$20**

**Baby Raccoon**
Illustrator: Baudoin, Simonne
Author: Berg, Jean Horton
797        1963        **$6**

**Baby Susan's Chicken**
Illustrator: Cummings, Alison
Author: Berg, Jean Horton
546        1951        **$8**

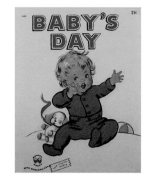

**Baby's Day**
Illustrator: Pointer, Priscilla
Author: Edwards, Annette
663        1953        **$7**

**Baby's First Book**
Illustrator: Schad, Helen
Author: Edwards, Annette
606        1953        **$7**

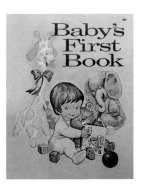

**Baby's First Book**
Illustrator: Schad, Helen
Author: Edwards, Annette
606        1953        **$7**

**Baby's First Christmas**
Illustrator: Dart, Eleanor
738        1959        **$8**

**Baby's First Christmas**
Illustrator: Dart, Eleanor
876        1959        **$6**

**Bambi's Children**
Illustrator: Bartlett, William
Author: Salten, Felix
544        1951        **$10**

**Barbie—The Baby Sitter**
Illustrator: Nankivel, Claudine
Author: Bethell, Jean
849        1964        **$15**

**Bedtime Stories**
Illustrator: Masha
Author: Graham, Eleanor
507        1946        **$15**

**Bedtime Stories**
Illustrator: Masha
Author: Graham, Eleanor
507        1946        **$10**

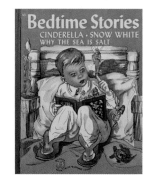

**Bedtime Stories**
Illustrator: Masha
Author: Graham, Eleanor
507        1946        **$6**

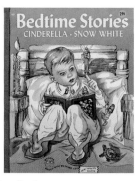

**Bedtime Stories**
Illustrator: Masha
Author: Graham, Eleanor
507          1946          **$4**

**Bible Treasures**
Illustrator: Raw, J. G.
Author: Ryder, Lillian
643          1961          **$7**

**Big Joke, The**
Illustrator: Newell, Crosby
Author: Bonsall, George
628          1955          **$7**

**Big-Little Dinosaur, The**
Illustrator: Jones, Bob
Author: Geis, Darlene
731          1959          **$6**

**Big-Little Dinosaur, The**
Illustrator: Jones, Bob
Author: Geis, Darlene
731          1959          **$3**

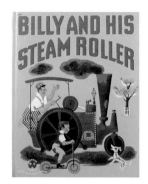

**Billy and His Steam Roller**
Illustrator: Myers, Bernice
Author: Bertail, Inez
557          1951          **$8**

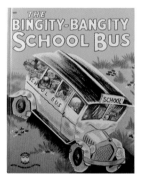

**Bingity-Bangity School Bus, The**
Illustrator: Wood, Ruth
Author: Conkling, Fleur
550          1950          **$25**

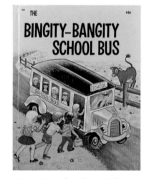

**Bingity-Bangity School Bus, The**
Illustrator: Wood, Ruth
Author: Conkling, Fleur
550          1950          **$5**

**Black Beauty**
Illustrator: Santos, George
Author: Martin, Marcia
595          1952          **$8**

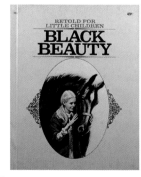

**Black Beauty**
Illustrator: Santos, George
Author: Martin, Marcia
595          1952          **$3**

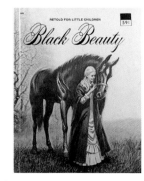

**Black Beauty**
Illustrator: Santos, George
Author: Martin, Marcia
595          1952          **$3**

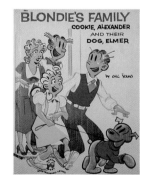

**Blondie's Family—Cookie, Alexander and Their Dog, Elmer**
Illustrator: Young, Chic
Author: Young, Chic
666          1954          **$18**

**Blow, Wind, Blow**
Illustrator: D'amato, Janet & Alex
Author: D'amato, Janet & Alex
740          1960                    **$6**

**Blowaway Hat, The**
Illustrator: Cunningham, Dellwyn
Author: Adelson, Leone
554          1946                    **$8**

**Bootsy**
Illustrator: Lear, Mirian
Author: Erville, Lucienne
741          1959                    **$6**

**Boy Who Wanted to Be a Fish, The**
Illustrator: Le Grand
Author: Le Grand
553          1951                    **$8**

**Boy Who Wouldn't Eat His Breakfast, The**
Illustrator: Brozowska, Elizabeth
Author: Brozowska, Elizabeth
815          1963                    **$6**

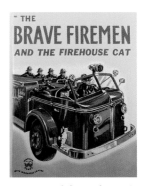

**Brave Firemen and the Firehouse Cat, The**
Illustrator: Medvey, Steven
Author: Bradbury, Bianca
563          1951                    **$8**

**Brave Little Duck, The**
Illustrator: Gayer, Marguerite
Author: Conkling, Fluer
777          1953                    **$6**

**Brave Little Steam Shovel, The**
Illustrator: Myers, Bernice
Author: Bertail, Inez
555          1951                    **$8**

**Brave Little Steam Shovel, The**
Illustrator: Myers, Bernice
Author: Bertail, Inez
555          1951                    **$4**

**Brave Little Tailor, The**
Illustrator: Myers, Bernice
Author: Weigle, Oscar
707          1958                    **$6**

**Bunny Hopwell's First Spring**
Illustrator: Dixon, Rachel
Author: Fritz, Jean
614          1954                    **$7**

**Bunny Hopwell's First Spring**
Illustrator: Dixon, Rachel
Author: Fritz, Jean
614          1954                    **$7**

**Bunny Sitter, The**
Illustrator: Meyerhoff, Nancy
Author: Grilley, Virginia
774          1963                    $6

**Busy Baby Lion, The**
Illustrator: Rik, Jottier
Author: Lucienne, Erville
737          1959                    $7

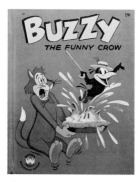

**Buzzy the Funny Crow**
Illustrator: Harvey Cartoon Studios
Author: Harvey Cartoon Studios
821          1963                    $7

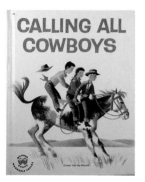

**Calling All Cowboys**
Illustrator: Hawes, Baldwin
Author: Hawes, Baldwin
#536         1950                    $6

**Camping Trip With the Range Rider, A**
Illustrator: Nielsen, Jon
Author: Sutton, Felix
681          1957                    $6

**Can You Guess?**
Formerly: Guess What
Illustrator: Wood, Ruth
Author: Klein, Leonore
701          1953                    $6

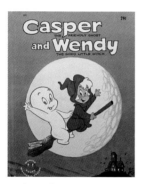

**Casper and Wendy**
Illustrator: Harvey Cartoon Studios
Author: Harvey Cartoon Studios
805          1963                    $8

**Casper and Wendy Adventures**
Illustrator: Harvey Cartoon Studios
Author: Harvey Cartoon Studios
855          1969                    $12

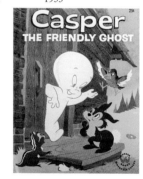

**Casper the Friendly Ghost**
Illustrator: Harvey Cartoon Studios
Author: Harvey Cartoon Studios
761          1960                    $15

**Casper the Friendly Ghost in Ghostland**
Illustrator: Harvey Cartoon Studios
Author: Harvey Cartoon Studios
850          1965                    $8

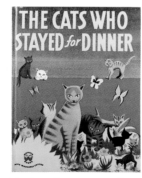

**Cats Who Stayed For Dinner, The**
Illustrator: Burchard, Peter
Author: Rowand, Phyllis
556          1951                    $12

**Child's Garden of Versus, A**
Illustrator: Wood, Ruth
Author: Stevenson, Robert Louis
704          1958                    $6

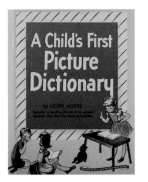

**Child's First Picture Dictionary, A**
Illustrator: Weber, Nettie; Clement, Charles
Author: Moore, Lilian
517          1948          **$10**

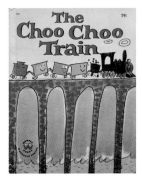

**Choo Choo Train, The**
Illustrator: Kessler, Leonard
Author: Pennington, Lillian Boyer
718          1958          **$6**

**Christmas Favorites**
Formerly: The Wonder Christmas Book
Illustrator: Myers, Lou
869          1951          **$5**

**Christmas Favorites**
Formerly: The Wonder Christmas Book
Illustrator: Myers, Lou
869          1951          **$5**

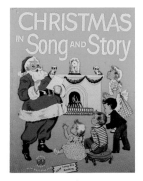

**Christmas in Song and Story**
Illustrator: Scholz, Catherine
Author: Berg, Jean Horton
586          1953          **$6**

**Christmas is Coming**
Illustrator: Cummings, Alison
Author: Martin, Marcia
593          1952          **$10**

**Christmas Puppy, The**
Illustrator: Wilde, Irma
Author: Wilde, Irma
585          1953          **$15**

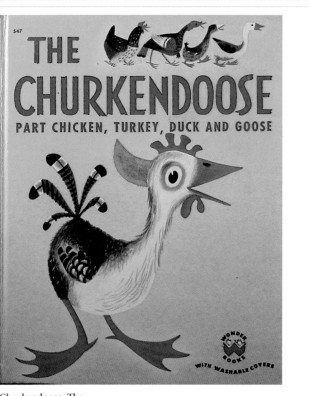

**Churkendoose, The**
Illustrator: Cunningham, Dellwyn
Author: Berenberg, Ben Ross
547          1946          **$25**

**Christmas Songs and Stories**
Illustrator: Scholz, Catherine
Author: Berg, Jean Horton
586          1953          **$12**

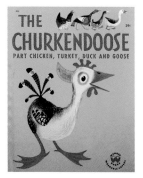

**Churkendoose, The**
Illustrator: Cunningham, Dellwyn
Author: Berenberg, Ben Ross
832        1946        $8

**Churkendoose, The**
Illustrator: Cunningham, Dellwyn
Author: Berenberg, Ben Ross
832        1946        $8

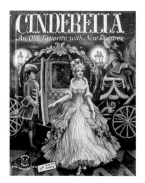

**Cinderella**
Illustrator: Ives, Ruth
Author: Andreas, Evelyn
660        1954        $7

**Cinderella**
Illustrator: Ives, Ruth
Author: Andreas, Evelyn
660        1954        $4

**City Boy, Country Boy**
Illustrator: Weigel, Susi
Author: Lobe, Mira
810        1963        $6

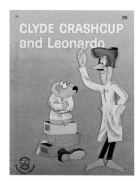

**Clyde Crashcup and Leonardo**
Illustrator: Kurtz, Bob
Author: Kurtz, Bob
837        1965        $18

**Come and See the Rainbow**
Illustrator: Scholz, Catherine
Author: Walters, Marguerite
743        1960        $6

**Come Visit My Ranch**
Illustrator: Hawes, Baldwin
Author: Hawes, Baldwin
536        1950        $10

**Copycat Colt, The**
Illustrator: Steiner, Charlotte
Author: Steiner, Charlotte; Hoff, Virginia
545        1951        $8

**Count the Baby Animals**
Illustrator: Plummer, Virginia
Author: Walters, Marguerite
702        1958        $6

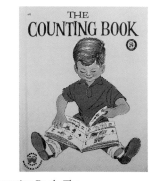

**Counting Book, The**
Illustrator: Riley, Bob
Author: Peter, John
692        1957        $6

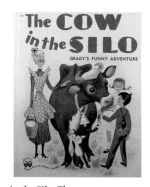

**Cow in the Silo, The**
Illustrator: Cunningham, Dellwyn
Author: Goodell, Patricia
534        1950        $20

**Cowardly Lion, The**
Illustrator: Wood, Ruth
Author: Baum, Frank L.
642      1956          **$22**

**Cozy Little Farm, The**
Illustrator: Angela
Author: Bonino, Louise
502      1946          **$15**

**Cozy Little Farm, The**
Illustrator: Angela
Author: Bonino, Louise
749      1946          **$5**

**Cozy Little Farm, The**
Illustrator: Angela
Author: Bonino, Louise
749      1946          **$3**

**Costume Party, The**
Illustrator: D'amato, Janet & Alex
Author: Morel, Eve
800      1962          **$6**

**Crusader Rabbit**
Illustrator: Krusz, Arthur
Author: Weigle, Oscar
698      1958          **$20**

**December is For Christmas**
Illustrator: Kendrick, Alcy
Author: Scott, Ann
776      1961          **$6**

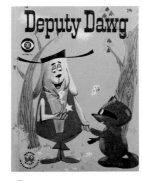

**Deputy Dawg**
Illustrator: Bezada, Herb; Trombetta, Mario
Author: Newell, Crosby
760      1960          **$20**

**Deputy Dawg and the Space Man**
Illustrator: Bezada, Herb; Crapanzano, Joseph
Author: Sand, Helen
773      1961          **$18**

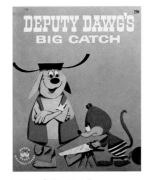

**Deputy Dawg's Big Catch**
Illustrator: Bezada, Herb; Crapanzano, Joseph
Author: Newell, Crosby
770      1961          **$20**

**Dick Whittington and His Cat**
Illustrator: Cunningham, Dellwyn
Author: Weigle, Oscar
705      1958          **$6**

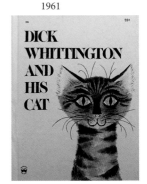

**Dick Whittington and His Cat**
Illustrator: Cunningham, Dellwyn
Author: Weigle, Oscar
705      1958          **$3**

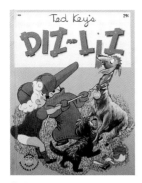

**Diz and Liz**
Illustrator: Allen, Colin
Author: Key, Ted
835      1965      **$13**

**Doll Family, The**
Illustrator: Harris, Martin
Author: Wilson, Dorothy
802      1962      **$8**

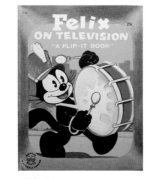

**Dondi**
Illustrator: Deson, Gus; Hasen, Erwin
Author: Deson, Gus; Hasen, Erwin
783      1961      **$15**

**Donkey Who Wanted to Be Wise, The**
Illustrator: Marsia, Robert
Author: Delahaye, Gilbert
771      1961      **$6**

**Dress-Up Parade, The**
Illustrator: Wilde, George
Author: Wilde, Irma
688      1953      **$7**

**Famous Fairy Tales**
Illustrator: Jules, Mervin
Author: Graham, Eleanor
505      1946      **$15**

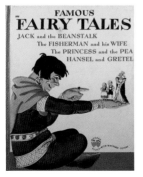

**Famous Fairy Tales**
Illustrator: Jules, Mervin
Author: Graham, Eleanor
505      1946      **$10**

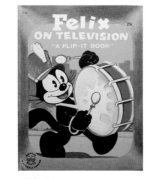

**Felix on Telivision**
Illustrator: Oriolo, Joe
Author: Shapiro, Irwin
716      1956      **$14**

**Felix the Cat**
Illustrator: Sullivan, Pat
Author: Sullivan, Pat
665      1953      **$18**

**Felix the Cat**
Illustrator: Sullivan, Pat
Author: Sullivan, Pat
665          1953          $10

**Felix on Television**
Illustrator: Sullivan, Pat
Author: Sullivan, Pat
665          1953          $10

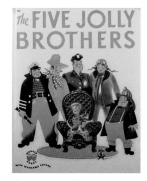

**Five Jolly Brothers, The**
Illustrator: Sinnickson, Tom
Author: Chaffee, Tish
552          1951          $8

**Five Little Finger Playmates**
Illustrator: Steiner, Charlotte
522          1949          $10

**Fixit Man, The**
Illustrator: Wilde, George
Author: Wilde, Irma
756          1952          $6

**Flash Gordon and the Baby Animals**
Illustrator: Berger, Alex
Author: King Features Syndicate
684          1956          $15

**Fluffy Little Lamb**
Illustrator: Baudoin, Simonne
Author: Delahaye, Gilbert
780          1962          $6

**Four Puppies Who Wanted a Home, The**
Illustrator: Frankel, Simon
Author: Bryan, Dorothy & Marguerite
530          1950          $10

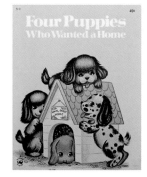

**Four Puppies Who Wanted a Home, The**
Illustrator: Frankel, Simon
Author: Bryan, Dorothy & Marguerite
530          1950          $8

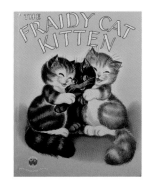

**Fraidy Cat Kitten, The**
Illustrator: Wilde, Irma
Author: Wilde, Irma
542          1950          $10

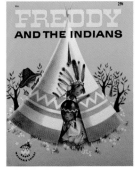

**Freddy and the Indians**
Illustrator: Binst, Claire
Author: Delahaye, Gilbert
816          1963          $6

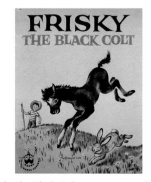

**Frisky the Black Colt**
Illustrator: Steiner, Charlotte
Author: Steiner, Charlotte; Hoff, Virginia
699          1951          $6

**Funny Mixed-Up Story, The**
Illustrator: Wilson, Dagmar
Author: Mcnulty, Faith
734          1959                    **$6**

**Gandy Goose**
Illustrator: Ruhman, Ruth
Author: Jason, Leon
695          1957                    **$18**

**Giraffe Who Went to School, The**
Illustrator: Wilde, Irma
Author: Wilde, Irma
551          1951                    **$8**

**Giraffe Who Went to School, The**
Illustrator: Wilde, Irma
Author: Wilde, Irma
551          1951                    **$8**

**Good Morning, Good Night**
Illustrator: Derwinski, Beatrice
Author: Luther, Frank
583          1953             **$8**

**Funny Mixed-Up Story, The**
Illustrator: Wilson, Dagmar
Author: Mcnulty, Faith
734          1959                    **$6**

**Good Night Fairy Tales**
Illustrator: Weber, Adele; Heins, Doris
Author: Weigle, Oscar
726          1959                    **$6**

**Goose Who Played the Piano, The**
Illustrator: Cunningham, Dellwyn
Author: Evers, Alf
567          1951                    **$10**

**Guess What?**
Illustrator: Wood, Ruth
Author: Klein, Leonore
605          1953                    **$7**

**Hans Christian Andersen's Fairy Tales**
Illustrator: Caraway, James
Author: Andersen, Hans Christian
599          1952                    **$8**

**Happy Birthday Present, The**
Illustrator: Scott, Marguerite
Author: Bates, Barbara S.
564          1951                    **$8**

**Happy Surprise, The**
Illustrator: Wood, Ruth
Author: Klein, Leonore
582          1952          **$8**

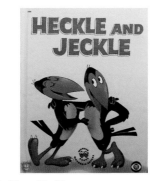

**Heckle and Jeckle**
Illustrator: Jason, Leon
Author: Jason, Leon
694          1957          **$14**

**Heckle and Jeckle Visit the Farm**
Illustrator: Gershen, Irv
Author: Waring, Barbara
712          1958          **$16**

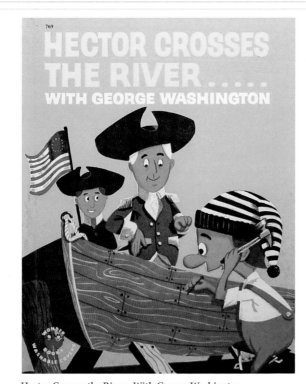

**Hector Crosses the River...With George Washington**
Illustrator: Crapanzano, Joe; Bezada Jr.,Herbert
Author: Newell, Crosby
769          1961          **$18**

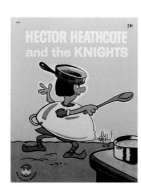

**Hector Heathcoat and the Knights**
Illustrator: Zaffo, George
Author: Bethell, Jean
840          1965          **$18**

**Heidi: Child of the Mountains**
Illustrator: Lerch, Steffie
Author: Spyri, Johanna
532          1950          **$8**

**Heidi: Child of the Mountains**
Illustrator: Lerch, Steffie
Author: Spyri, Johanna
532          1950          **$3**

**Helpful Friends, The**
Illustrator: Bonsall, George; Newell, Crosby
Author: Bonsall, George; Newell, Crosby
631          1955          **$7**

**Henny-Penny**
Illustrator: Ponter, James
685          1954          **$6**

**Henry Goes to a Party**
Illustrator: Anderson, Carl
Author: Anderson, Carl
778        1955              **$15**

**Henry in Lollipop Land**
Illustrator: Anderson, Carl
Author: Anderson, Carl
664        1953              **$16**

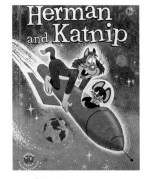

**Herman and Katnip**
Illustrator: Harvey Cartoon Studios
Author: Harvey Cartoon Studios
788        1961              **$17**

**Hide-And-Seek Duck, The**
Illustrator: Wilde, Irma
Author: Wilde, Irma
568        1952              **$8**

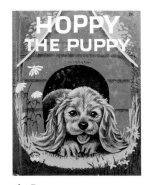

**Hoppy the Puppy**
Formerly: The Roly-Poly Puppy
Illustrator: Berthold
Author: Bates, Barbara S.
751        1950              **$6**

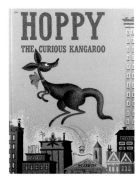

**Hoppy the Curious Kangaroo**
Illustrator: Fraydas, Stan
Author: Fraydas, Stan
579        1952              **$8**

**Hoppy the Curious Kangaroo**
Illustrator: Fraydas, Stan
Author: Fraydas, Stan
579        1952              **$4**

**Horse For Johnny, A**
Illustrator: Moyers, William
Author: Bookman, Charlotte
754        1952              **$6**

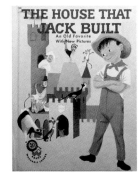

**House That Jack Built, The**
Illustrator: Wilson, Dagmar
724        1959              **$6**

**House That Popeye Built, The**
Illustrator: Sagendorf, Bud
Author: Newell, Crosby
750        1960              **$7**

**How Peter Cottontail Got His Name**
Illustrator: Jackson, Pauline
Author: Burgess, Thornton W.
668        1957              **$7**

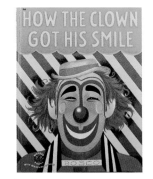

**How the Clown Got His Smile**
Illustrator: Hull, John
Author: Martin, Marcia
566        1951              **$8**

**How the Rabbit Found Christmas**
Illustrator: Kendrick, Alcy
Author: Scott, Ann
#866        1961                    $6

**Hungry Baby Bunny, The**
Illustrator: Seiden, Bea Rabin
Author: Evers, Alf
847        1951                    $3

**Hungry Baby Bunny, The**
Illustrator: Seiden, Bea Rabin
Author: Evers, Alf
847        1951                    $5

**Hungry Little Bunny, The**
Illustrator: Wilde, Irma
Author: Wilde, Irma
531        1950                    $8

**I Can Do Anything...Almost**
Illustrator: Murtagh, Betty
Author: Hartman, Virginia
822        1963                    $5

**I Can Do Anything...Almost**
Illustrator: Murtagh, Betty
Author: Hartman, Virginia
822        1963                    $5

**I Can I Can I Can**
Illustrator: Schad, Helen G.
Author: Schad, Helen G.
676        1958                    $6

**I Love You**
Illustrator: Bonsall, George; Newell, Crosby
Author: Bonsall, George; Newell, Crosby
657        1956                    $7

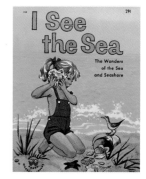

**I See the Sea**
Illustrator: Wood, Ruth
Author: Mcgovern, Ann
768        1961                    $6

**I See the Sky**
Illustrator: Cook, Sunny B.
Author: Peters, Ann
746        1960                    $6

**Insects We Know**
Illustrator: Koehler, Cynthia Iliff
Author: Rood, Ronald N.
747        1960                    $6

**It's a Lovely Day**
Illustrator: Smith, Flora
Author: Walters, Marguerite
632        1956                    $7

**It's a Secret**
Illustrator: Myers, Bernice
Author: Brewster, Benjamin
540          1950          **$10**

It's a Secret
Illustrator: Myers, Bernice
Author: Brewster, Benjamin
540          1950          $4

**Jingle Dingle Book, The**
Illustrator: Ruhman, Ruth
Author: Jason, Leon
675          1957          **$8**

**Johnny Grows Up**
Illustrator: Cummings, Alison
Author: Martin, Marcia
618          1954          **$7**

**Joke on Farmer Al Falfa, A**
Illustrator: Gershen, Irv
Author: Newell, Crosby
736          1959          **$18**

**Jolly Jumping Man, The**
Illustrator: Frankel, Simon
Author: Berg, Jean Horton
537          1950          **$10**

**Just Like Me**
Illustrator: Weisgard, Leonard
Author: Weisgard, Leonard
672          1954          **$6**

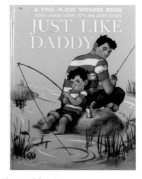

**Just Like Mommy, Just Like Daddy**
Illustrator: Cummings, Alison
Author: Simon, Patty
589          1952          **$8**

**Kewtee Bear's Christmas**
Illustrator: Dixon, Rachel Taft
Author: Reed, Alan & Stout, Bert & Quigley,
Truman
867          1965          **$10**

**Kewtee Bear—Santa's Helper**
Illustrator: Dixon, Rachel Taft
Author: Reed, Alan & Stout, Bert & Quigley,
Truman
652          1956          **$15**

**Kitten's Secret, The**
Illustrator: Barton, Mary
Author: Gossett, Margaret
527          1950          **$12**

**Kitten's Secret, The**
Illustrator: Barton, Mary
Author: Gossett, Margaret
527     1950     $5

**Kittens Who Hid From Their Mother, The**
Illustrator: Werber, Adele; Laslo, Doris
Author: Woodcock, Louise
529     1950     **$10**

**Lassie Come Home**
Illustrator: Drutzu, Anne Marie
Author: Knight, Eric
639     1956     $8

**Lassie's Long Trip**
Illustrator: Hoecker, Hazel
Author: Knight, Jere
674     1957     $8

**Let's Give a Party**
Illustrator: Nigro, Joanne
Author: Newell, Crosby
752     1960     $5

**Let's Give a Party**
Illustrator: Nigro, Joanne
Author: Newell, Crosby
752     1960     $3

**Let's Go Fishing**
Illustrator: Newell, Crosby
Author: Bonsall, George
764     1955     $6

**Let's Go Shopping**
Illustrator: Meyerhoff, Nancy
Author: Brooke, Guyon
693     1958     $6

**Let's Go to School**
Illustrator: Hoecker, Hazel
Author: Edwards, Annette
691     1954     $6

**Let's Go to School**
Illustrator: Hoecker, Hazel
Author: Edwards, Annette
691     1954     $3

**Let's Play Indian**
Illustrator: Chastain, Madye Lee
Author: Chastain, Madye Lee
538     1950     **$10**

**Let's Pretend**
Illustrator: Clarke, Joan
Author: Clarke, Frances
680     1959     $6

**Let's Take a Ride**
Illustrator: Dillon, Corrine
Author: Hope, Laura Lee
673          1954          $6

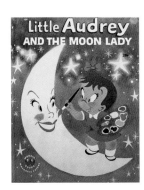

**Little Audrey and the Moon Lady**
Illustrator: Harvey Cartoon Studios
Author: Harvey Cartoon Studios
759          1960          $18

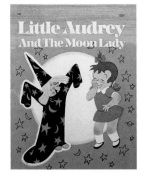

**Little Audrey and the Moon Lady**
Illustrator: Harvey Cartoon Studios
Author: Harvey Cartoon Studios
759          1960          $10

**Little Car That Wanted a Garage, The**
Illustrator: Meshekoff, Edward
Author: Woolley, Catherine
573          1952          $10

**Little Car That Wanted a Garage, The**
Illustrator: Meshekoff, Edward
Author: Woolley, Catherine
573          1952          $6

**Little Cowboy's Christmas, A**
Illustrator: Dart, Eleanor
Author: Martin, Marcia
570          1951          $19

**Little Cowboy's Christmas, A**
Illustrator: Dart, Eleanor
Author: Martin, Marcia
570          1951          $10

**Little Duck Said Quack, Quack, Quack, The**
Illustrator: Kendrick, Alcy
Author: Barnett, Grace & Olive
636          1955          $7

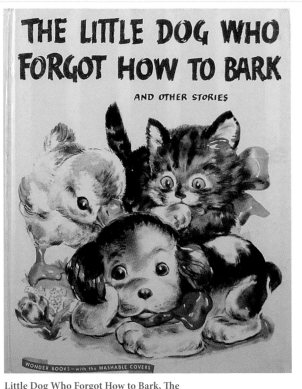

**Little Dog Who Forgot How to Bark, The**
Illustrator: Hopkins, Hildegard
Author: Bailey, Carolyn S.
504          1946          $15

**Little Engine That Laughed, The**
Illustrator: Seiden, Art
Author: Evers, Alf
729          1950                    $6

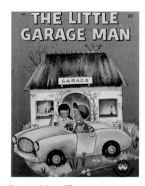

**Little Garage Man, The**
Illustrator: Binst, Claire
Author: Delahaye, Gilgert; Smith, George
744          1960                    $6

**Little John Little**
Illustrator: Steiner, Charlotte
Author: Steiner, Charlotte
558          1951                    $8

**Little Lost Puppy, The**
Illustrator: Spicer, Jesse
Author: Otto, Margaret G.
528          1950                    $10

**Little Peter Cottontail**
Illustrator: Erickson, Phoebe
Author: Burgess, Thornton W.
641          1956                    $7

**Little Peter Cottontail**
Illustrator: Erickson, Phoebe
Author: Burgess, Thornton W.
641          1956                    $4

**Little Peter Cottontail**
Illustrator: Erickson, Phoebe
Author: Burgess, Thornton W.
641          1956                    $3

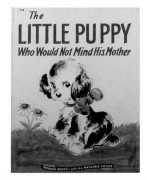

**Little Puppy Who Would Not Mind His
Mother, The**
Illustrator: Hopkins, Hildegarde
Author: Misc.
515          1949                    $12

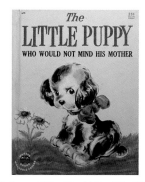

**Little Puppy Who Would Not Mind His
Mother, The**
Illustrator: Hopkins, Hildegarde
Author: Fyleman, Rose
679          1949                    $4

**Little Red Caboose That Ran Away, The**
Illustrator: Burchard, Peter
Author: Curren, Polly
715          1952                    $6

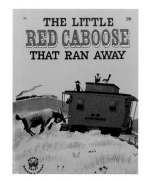

**Little Schoolhouse**
Illustrator: Elgin, Kathleen
Author: Newell, Crosby
710          1958                    $6

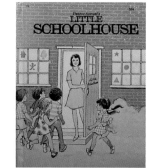

**Little Schoolhouse**
Illustrator: Elgin, Kathleen
Author: Newell, Crosby
710          1958                    $3

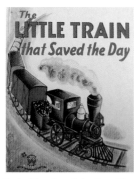

**Little Train That Saved the Day, The**
Illustrator: Steiner, Charlotte
Author: Steiner, Charlotte
571          1952                    $8

**Little Train That Saved the Day, The**
Illustrator: Steiner, Charlotte
Author: Steiner, Charlotte
571          1952                    $6

**Little Train That Won a Medal, The**
Illustrator: Loeb, Anton
Author: Geis, Darlene
512          1947                    $15

**Littlest Angel, The**
Illustrator: Evans, Katherine
Author: Tazewell, Charles
755          1960                    $10

**Littlest Angel, The**
Illustrator: Evans, Katherine
Author: Tazewell, Charles
755          1960                    $5

**Littlest Christmas Tree, The**
Illustrator: Hauge, Carl & Mary
Author: Burgess, Thornton W.
625          1954                    $15

**Littlest Christmas Tree, The**
Illustrator: Hauge, Carl & Mary
Author: Burgess, Thornton W.
625          1954                    $5

**Littlest Snowman, The**
Illustrator: De Santis, George
Author: Tazewell, Charles
720          1958                    $12

**Littlest Snowman, The**
Illustrator: De Santis, George
Author: Tazewell, Charles
720          1958                    $4

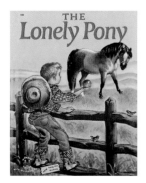

**Lonely Pony, The**
Illustrator: Oogjen, Barbara & Thomas
Author: Christopher, John
645          1956                    $7

**Look Who's Here!**
Illustrator: Gaulke, Gloria
Author: Walters, Marguerite
834          1964                    $5

**Look Who's Here!**
Illustrator: Gaulke, Gloria
Author: Walters, Marguerite
834          1964                    $5

**Lord's Prayer, The**
Catholic Version
Illustrator: Brulé, Al
647C          1956          $7

**Lord's Prayer, The**
Protestant Version
Illustrator: Brulé, Al
647P          1956          $7

**Luno the Soaring Stallion**
Illustrator: Kirkel, Stephen; Bezada, Herb
Author: Bethell, Jean
831          1964          $14

**Magic Bus, The**
Illustrator: Gergely, Tibor
Author: Dolbier, Maurice
516          1948          $25

**Magic Word, The**
Illustrator: Dart, Eleanor
Author: Zolotow, Charlotte
578          1952          $8

**Magilla Gorilla and the Super Kite**
Illustrator: Hanna-Barbera Productions, Inc.
Author: Elias, Horace J.
707          1976          $10

**Make-Believe Book, The**
Illustrator: Newell, Crosby
Author: Newell, Crosby
634          1959          $7

**Make-Believe Parade, The**
Illustrator: Wilkin, Eloise
Author: Margo, Jan
520          1949          $20

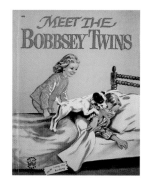

**Meet the Bobbsey Twins**
Illustrator: Dillon, Corinne
Author: Hope, Laura Lee
623          1954          $10

**Merry Christmas Book, The**
Illustrator: Scholz, Catherine
Author: Berg, Jean Horton
820          1953          $6

**Merry Christmas Mr. Snowman!**
Illustrator: Wilde, Irma
Author: Wilde, Irma
818          1951          $8

**Merry Christmas Mr. Snowman**
Illustrator: Wilde, Irma
Author: Wilde, Irma
818          1951          $6

**Mighty Mouse and the Scarecrow**
Illustrator: Chad
Author: Sutton, Felix
678          1954                    $16

**Mighty Mouse to the Rescue**
Illustrator: Gershen, Irv
Author: Waring, Barbara
717          1958                    $17

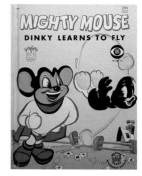

**Mighty Mouse—Dinky Learns to Fly**
Illustrator: Chad
Author: Sutton, Felix
677          1953                    $16

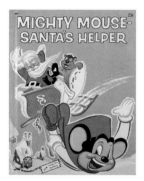

**Mighty Mouse—Santa's Helper**
Illustrator: Chad
Author: Sutton, Felix
662          1955                    $20

**Minute-and-a-Half-Man**
Illustrator: Kirkel, Stephen
Author: Newell, Crosby
758          1960                    $18

**Mister Magoo**
Illustrator: Nofziger, Ed
Author: Newell, Crosby
708          1958                    $16

**Monkey See Monkey Do**
Illustrator: Moyers, William
Author: Tooze, Ruth
521          1949                    $12

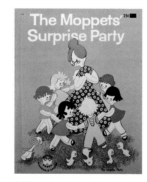

**Moppets' Surprise Party, The**
Illustrator: Newell, Crosby
Author: Newell, Crosby
794          1955                    $6

**Morning Noises**
Illustrator: Gree, Alain
Author: Gree, Alain
795          1962                    $6

**Most Beautiful Tree in the World, The**
Illustrator: Weisgard, Leonard
Author: Weisgard, Leonard
653          1956                    $10

**Mother Goose**
Illustrator: Hirsch, Joseph
501          1946                    $15

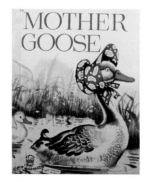

**Mother Goose**
Illustrator: Hirsch, Joseph
501          1946                    $15

**Mr. Bear Squash-You-All-Flat**
Illustrator: Angela
Author: Gipson, Morrell
523          1950          **$100**

**Mr. Wishing Went Fishing**
Illustrator: Wilde, George
Author: Wilde, Irma
584          1952          **$10**

**Mrs. Goose's Green Trailer**
Illustrator: Weisgard, Leonard
Author: Potter, Miriam Clark
633          1956          **$7**

**Muskie and His Friends**
Illustrator: Kirkel, Stephen; Bezada, Herb
Author: Bethell, Jean
828          1963          **$18**

**My A B C Book**
Illustrator: Seiden, Art
610          1953          **$7**

**My A B C Book**
Illustrator: Seiden, Art
610          1953          **$3**

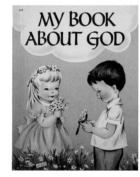

**My Book About God**
Illustrator: Varga, Judith
644          1956          **$7**

**My First Book of Jokes**
Illustrator: D'amato, Janet & Alex
Author: D'amato, Janet & Alex
799          1962          **$6**

**My First Book of Prayers**
Illustrator: Ives, Ruth
Author: Juergens, Mary
661          1953          **$7**

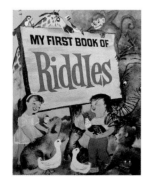

**My First Book of Riddles**
Illustrator: D'amato, Janet & Alex
Author: D'amato, Janet & Alex
745          1960          **$6**

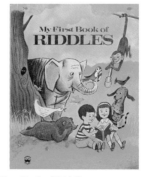

**My First Book of Riddles**
Illustrator: D'amato, Janet & Alex
Author: D'amato, Janet & Alex
745          1960          **$2**

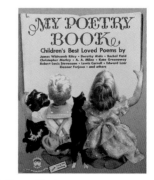

**My Poetry Book**
Illustrator: Smith, Flora
Author: Pierce, June
621          1954          **$7**

**My Wonder Book of Dolls**
Illustrator: Wohlberg, Meg
Author: Hamilton, Antoinette
721     1959        **$10**

**Night Before Christmas, The**
Illustrator: Leone, Sergio
Author: Moore, Clement C.
858     1965        **$6**

**Night Before Christmas, The**
Illustrator: Leone, Sergio
Author: Moore, Clement C.
858     1965        **$6**

**Nine Friendly Dogs, The**
Illustrator: Goldsborough, June
Author: Sutton, Felix
622     1954        **$7**

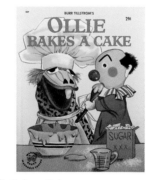

**Nine Rabbits and Another**
Illustrator: Dixon, Rachel Taft
Author: Potter, Miriam Clark
845     1957        **$5**

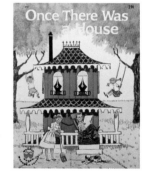

**Noisy Clock Shop, The**
Illustrator: Seiden, Art
Author: Berg, Jean Horton
539     1950        **$10**

**Nonsense Alphabet, The**
Illustrator: Seiden, Art
Author: Lear, Edward
725     1959        **$6**

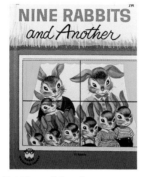

**Ollie Bakes a Cake**
Illustrator: Meyerhoff, Nancy
Author: Bethell, Jean
829     1964        **$20**

**Once There Was a House**
Illustrator: Wood, Ruth
Author: Wynnw, Milton
842     1965        **$5**

**Once Upon a Time**
Formerly: The Cow in the Silo
Illustrator: Cunningham, Dellwyn
Author: Goudell, Patricia
700     1950        **$8**

**Over in the Meadow**
Illustrator: Wood, Ruth
Author: Wadsworth, Olive A.
796     1962        **$6**

**Pecos Bill**
Illustrator: Canizares, Stephenie
Author: Walsh, Henry
767     1961        **$10**

**Pelle's New Suit**
Illustrator: Wilde, George
Author: Beskow, Elsa
803      1962      **$6**

**Peter Cottontail and Reddy Fox**
Illustrator: Hauge, Carl & Mary
Author: Burgess, Thornton W.
843      1954      **$5**

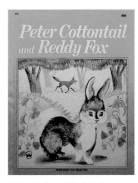

**Peter Cottontail and Reddy Fox**
Illustrator: Hauge, Carl & Mary
Author: Burgess, Thornton W.
843      1954      **$4**

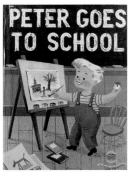

**Peter Goes to School**
Illustrator: Doremus, Hal W.
Author: House, Wanda Rogers
600      1953      **$7**

**Peter Goes to School**
Illustrator: Doremus, Hal W.
Author: House, Wanda Rogers
600      1953      **$3**

**Peter Hatches an Egg**
Illustrator: Marlier, Marcel
Author: Bienvenu-Brialmont, Louise
772      1962      **$6**

**Peter Hatches an Egg**
Illustrator: Marlier, Marcel
Author: Bienvenu-Brialmont, Louise
772      1962      **$3**

**Peter Pan**
Illustrator: Derwinski, Beatrice
Author: Martin, Marcia
597      1952      **$8**

**Peter Rabbit**
Illustrator: Phoebe, Erickson
Author: Potter, Beatrix
812      1947      **$6**

**Peter Rabbit**
Illustrator: Erickson, Phoebe
Author: Potter, Beatrix
513      1947      **$15**

**Peter Rabbit and Reddy Fox**
Illustrator: Hauge, Carl & Mary
Author: Burgess, Thorton W.
611      1954      **$8**

**Peter Rabbit and Reddy Fox**
Illustrator: Hauge, Carl & Mary
Author: Burgess, Thornton W.
611      1954      **$6**

**Petey Parakeet**
Illustrator: Cook, Sunny B.
Author: Bonsall, George; Newell, Crosby
798          1963                    $6

**Picinic at the Zoo, The**
Illustrator: Myers, Bernice & Lou
Author: Libbey, Ruth Everding
613          1954                    $7

**Pinocchio**
Illustrator: Seiden, Art
Author: Andreas, Evelyn
615          1954                    $7

**Pinocchio**
Illustrator: Seiden, Art
Author: Andreas, Evelyn
615          1954                    $3

**Playful Little Dog, The**
Illustrator: Robertson, Maurice
Author: Berg, Jean Horton
562          1951                    $8

**Playtime For Nancy**
Illustrator: Stolgerg, Doris
Author: Hyde, Margaret O.
560          1951                    $10

**Polly's Christmas Present**
Illustrator: Wilde, Irma
Author: Wilde, Irma
819          1953                    $6

**Polly's Christmas Present**
Illustrator: Wilde, Irma
Author: Wilde, Irma
819          1953                    $3

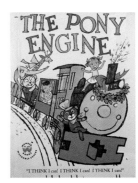

**Pony Engine, The**
Illustrator: Prestopino, Grgorio
Author: Garn, Doris
626          1957                    $7

**Popeye**
Illustrator: Sagendorf, Bud
Author: Sagendorf, Bud
667          1955                    $16

**Popeye Goes on a Picnic**
Illustrator: Sagendorf, Bud
Author: Newell, Crosby
697          1958                    $6

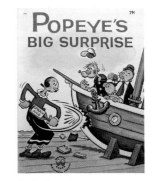

**Popeye's Big Surprise**
Illustrator: Sagendorf, Bud
Author: Waring, Barbara
791          1962                    $8

**Puff the Magic Dragon**
Illustrator: Tallarico, Tony
Author: Newman, Paul
851        1965                $7

**Puppy on Parade, The**
Illustrator: Hoecker, Hazel
Author: Grilley, Virginia
617        1956                $7

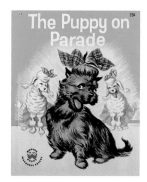

**Puppy on Parade, The**
Illustrator: Hoecker, Hazel
Author: Grilley, Virginia
617        1956                $3

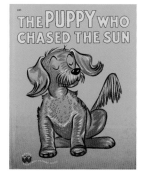

**Puppy Who Chased the Sun, The**
Illustrator: Le Grand
Author: Le Grand
535        1950                $10

**Puppy Who Found a Boy, The**
Illustrator: Wilde, George & Irma
Author: Wilde, George & Irma
561        1951                $8

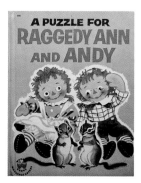

**Puzzle For Raggedy Ann and Andy, A**
Illustrator: Dixon, Rachel Taft
Author: Gruelle, Johnny
683        1957                $16

**Quiet Book, The**
Illustrator: Kendrick, Alcy
Author: Flynn, Helen M.
654        1958                $7

**Quiet Little Indian, The**
Illustrator: Wood, Ruth
Author: Geis, Darlene
709        1958                $6

**Rabbits Give a Party, The**
Illustrator: Baudoin, Simonne
Author: Dermine, Lucie
811        1963                $5

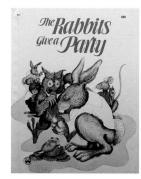

**Rabbits Give a Party, The**
Illustrator: Baudoin, Simonne
Author: Dermine, Lucie
811        1963                $3

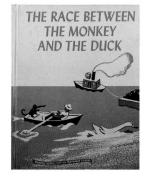

**Race Between the Monkey and the Duck, The**
Illustrator: Hurd, Clement
Author: Hurd, Clement
510        1940                $20

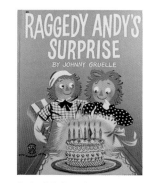

**Raggedy Andy's Surprise**
Illustrator: Sinnickson, Tom
Author: Gruelle, Johnny
604        1953                $18

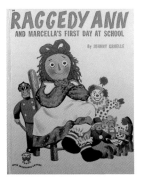

**Raggedy Ann and Marcella's First Day at School**
Illustrator: Sinnickson, Tom
Author: Gruelle, Johnny
588          1952          **$22**

**Raggedy Ann's Christmas Surprise**
Illustrator: Sinnickson, Tom
Author: Gruelle, Johnny
868          1952          **$16**

**Raggedy Ann's Merriest Christmas**
Illustrator: Sinnickson, Tom
Author: Gruelle, Johnny
594          1952          **$22**

**Raggedy Ann's Merriest Christmas**
Illustrator: Sinnickson, Tom
Author: Gruelle, Johnny
594          1952          **$22**

**Raggedy Ann's Secret**
Illustrator: Wood, Ruth
Author: Gruelle, Johnny
727          1959          **$15**

**Raggedy Ann's Tea Party**
Illustrator: Wilde, George & Irma
Author: Gruelle, Johnny
624          1954          **$18**

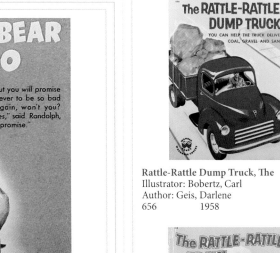

**Randolph, the Bear Who Said No**
Illustrator: Walker, Nedda
Author: Nelson, Faith
509          1946          **$35**

**Rattle-Rattle Dump Truck, The**
Illustrator: Bobertz, Carl
Author: Geis, Darlene
656          1958          **$7**

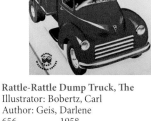

**Rattle-Rattle Train, The**
Illustrator: Bobertz, Carl
Author: Geis, Darlene
655          1957          **$7**

**Really Truly Treasure Hunt, The**
Illustrator: Newell, Crosby
Author: Bonsall, George
793          1954                    $6

**Rolling Wheels**
Illustrator: Dauber, Elizabeth
Author: Elting, Mary
762          1950                    $6

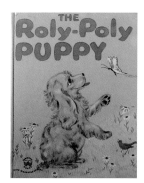

**Roly-Poly Puppy, The**
Illustrator: Berthold
Author: Bates, Barbara S.
549          1950                    $8

**Romper Room Book, A—Can Your Guess?**
Illustrator: Wood, Ruth
Author: Klein, Leonore
701          1953                    $6

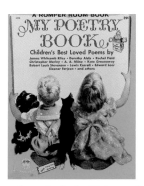

**Romper Room Book, A—My Poetry Book**
Illustrator: Smith, Flora
Author: Pierce, June
621          1954                    $7

**Romper Room Book of Happy Animals, The**
Illustrator: Jones, Robert
Author: Weigle, Oscar
687          1957                    $6

**Romper Room Book of Nursery Songs, The**
Illustrator: Schlesinger, Alice
Author: Cummins, Dorothy Berliner
619          1954                    $7

**Romper Room Book, A—What Time Is It?**
Illustrator: Zabinski, Joseph
Author: Peter, John
689          1954                    $6

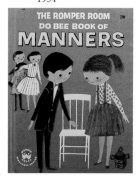

**Romper Room Do Bee Book of Manners, The**
Illustrator: Seiden, Art
Author: Claster, Nancy
763          1960                    $6

**Romper Room Laughing Book, The**
Illustrator: Nankivel, Claudine
Author: Claster, Nancy
808          1963                    $6

**Romper Room Safety Book, The**
Illustrator: Seiden, Art
Author: Claster, Nancy
854          1965                    $6

**Runaway Baby Bird, The**
Illustrator: Mazza, Adriana
Author: Walters, Marguerite
748          1960                    **$6**

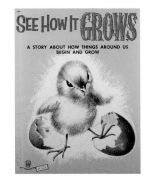

**See How It Grows**
Illustrator: Smith, Flora
Author: Walters, Marguerite
630          1954                    **$7**

**Sheri Lewis Wonder Book, The**
Illustrator: Wood, Ruth
Author: Newell, Crosby
781          1961                    **$13**

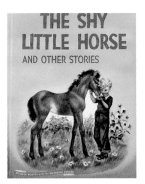

**Shy Little Horse, The**
Illustrator: Robinson
Author: Scott, Therese
511          1947                    **$15**

**Silly Sidney**
Illustrator: Cummings, Art
Author: Bethell, Jean
841          1965                    **$18**

**Silver Chief**
Illustrator: Hauge, Carl & Mary
Author: Weigle, Oscar
650          1956                    **$18**

**Sleeping Beauty**
Illustrator: Ives, Ruth
Author: Andreas, Evelyn
635          1956                    **$7**

**Sleeping Beauty**
Illustrator: Ives, Ruth
Author: Andreas, Evelyn
635          1956                    **$2**

**Sleepy-Time For Everyone**
Illustrator: Castagnoli, Martha
Author: Castagnoli, Martha
612          1954                    **$7**

**Snow White and the Seven Dwarfs**
Illustrator: Seiden, Art
659          1955                    **$7**

**Snow White and the Seven Dwarfs**
Illustrator: Seiden, Art
659          1955                    **$3**

**Snowman's Christmas Present, The**
Illustrator: Wilde, Irma
Author: Wilde, Irma
572          1951                    **$13**

**Snowman's Christmas Present, The**
Illustrator: Wilde, Irma
Author: Wilde, Irma
572          1951                    **$13**

**Snowman's Christmas Present, The**
Illustrator: Wilde, Irma
Author: Wilde, Irma
572          1951                    **$10**

**So This is Spring!**
Illustrator: Dixon, Rachel
Author: Fritz, Jean
844          1954                    **$5**

**So This is Spring!**
Illustrator: Dixon, Rachel
Author: Fritz, Jean
844          1954                    **$4**

**Songs to Sing and Play**
Illustrator: Wood, Ruth
Author: Weigle, Oscar
753          1960                    **$6**

**Sonny the Bunny**
Illustrator: Seiden, Art
Author: Martin, Marcia
591          1952                    **$8**

**Sonny the Lucky Bunny**
Illustrator: Seiden, Art
Author: Martin, Marcia
848          1952                    **$5**

**Sonny the Lucky Bunny**
Illustrator: Seiden, Art
Author: Martin, Marcia
848          1952                    **$4**

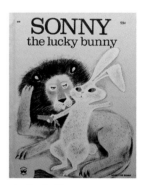

**Sonny the Lucky Bunny**
Illustrator: Seiden, Art
Author: Martin, Marcia
848          1952                    **$2**

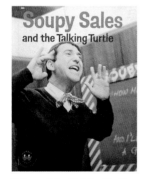

**Soupy Sales and the Talking Turtle**
Illustrator: Tallarico, Tony
Author: Bethell, Jean
860          1965                    **$8**

**Stacks of Caps**
Formerly: Monkey See, Monkey Do
Illustrator: Moyers, William
Author: Tooze, Ruth
722          1949                    **$6**

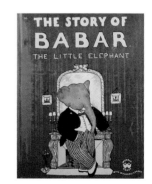

**Story of Babar, The**
Illustrator: De Brunhoff, Jean
Author: De Brunhoff, Jean
590          1952                    **$18**

**Story of the Christ Child, The**
Illustrator: Lap, Pranas
Author: Edwards, Annette
587      1953      **$8**

**Storytime Favorites**
Illustrator: Leob, Anton
Author: Scott, Theresa Ann
514      1947      **$15**

**Storytime Favorites**
Illustrator: Leob, Anton
Author: Scott, Theresa Ann
514      1947      **$10**

**Storytime Favorites**
Illustrator: Leob, Anton
Author: Scott, Theresa Ann
514      1947      **$5**

**Summer Friends**
Illustrator: Wood, Ruth
Author: Krinsky, Jeanette
739      1960      **$6**

**Surprise Doll, The**
Illustrator: Lerch, Steffie
Author: Gipson, Morrell
519      1949      **$40**

**Surprise Doll, The**
Illustrator: Lerch, Steffie
Author: Gipson, Morrell
519      1949      **$40**

**Surprise For Felix, A**
Illustrator: Oriolo, Joe
Author: Sullivan, Pat
728      1959      **$10**

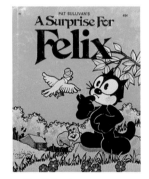

**Surprise For Felix, A**
Illustrator: Oriolo, Joe
Author: Sullivan, Pat
728      1959      **$5**

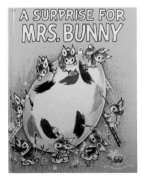

**Surprise For Mrs. Bunny, A**
Illustrator: Steiner, Charlotte
Author: Steiner, Charlotte
601      1953      **$8**

**Surprise For Mrs. Bunny, A**
Illustrator: Steiner, Charlotte
Author: Steiner, Charlotte
601      1953      **$5**

**Surprise Party, The**
Illustrator: Newell, Crosby
Author: Newell, Crosby
620      1955      **$7**

**Ten Little Fingers**
Illustrator: Pointer, Priscilla
Author: Pointer, Priscilla
714        1954                    **$6**

**Ten Little Fingers**
Illustrator: Pointer, Priscilla
Author: Pointer, Priscilla
714        1954                    **$2**

**Ten Little Fingers**
Illustrator: Pointer, Priscilla
Author: Pointer, Priscilla
714        1954                    **$2**

**Terrytoon Space Train, The**
Illustrator: Gershen, Irv
Author: Waring, Barbara
711        1958                    **$18**

**There Was Once a Little Boy**
Illustrator: Cook, Sunny B.
Author: Budney, Blossom
719        1959                    **$6**

**This Magic World**
Illustrator: Koehler, Cynthia Iliff
Author: Koehler, Cynthia Iliff
723        1959                    **$6**

**This Magic World**
Illustrator: Koehler, Cynthia Iliff
Author: Koehler, Cynthia Iliff
723        1959                    **$2**

**Three Little Kittens and Other Nursery Tales**
Illustrator: Dixon, Rachel Taft
Author: Graham, Eleanor
503        1946                    **$15**

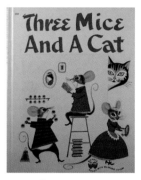

**Three Mice and a Cat**
Illustrator: Seiden, Art
Author: Berg, Jean Horton
533        1950                    **$25**

**Three Little Pigs and Little Red Riding Hood, The**
Illustrator: Peller, Jackie; Tamburine, Jean
609        1954                    **$7**

**To Market, to Market**
Illustrator: Seiden, Art
Author: Potter, Miriam Clark
775        1961                    **$6**

**Tom Corbett's Wonder Book of Space**
Illustrator: Vaughn, Frank
Author: Martin, Marcia
603          1953                    **$20**

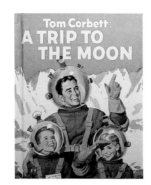

**Tom Corbett: A Trip to the Moon**
Illustrator: Vaughn, Frank
Author: Martin, Marcia
713          1953                    **$18**

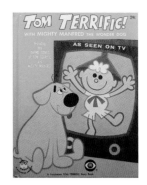

**Tom Terrific With Mighty Manfred the Wonder Dog**
Illustrator: Bartsch, Arthur
Author: Newell, Crosby
703          1958                    **$16**

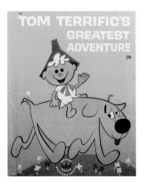

**Tom Terrific's Greatest Adventure**
Illustrator: Newell, Crosby
Author: Newell, Crosby
735          1959                    **$15**

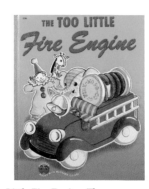

**Too Little Fire Engine, The**
Illustrator: Flory, Jane
Author: Flory, Jane
526          1950                    **$10**

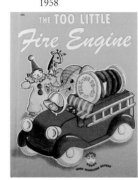

**Too Little Fire Engine, The**
Illustrator: Flory, Jane
Author: Flory, Jane
526          1950                    **$5**

**Traveling Twins, The**
Play money
Illustrator: Smalley, Janet
Author: Berg, Jean Horton
With money
596     1953        **$15**
Without money
596     1953        **$5**

**Trick on Deputy Dawg, A**
Illustrator: Kirkel, Stephen; Bezada, Herb
Author: Bethell, Jean
830          1964                    **$20**

**Tuggy the Tuboat**
Illustrator: Hauge, Carl & Mary
Author: Berg, Jean Horton
696          1958                    **$6**

**Tutu the Little Fawn**
Illustrator: Morel, Eve
Author: Simon, Romain
836          1964                    **$6**

**Twelve Days of Christmas, The**
Illustrator: Mars, W. T.
651          1956                    $8

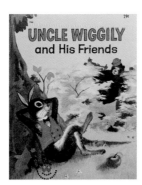

**Uncle Wiggily and His Friends**
Illustrator: Leone, Sergio
Author: Garis, Howard R.
766          1961                   $16

**Uncle Wiggily's Adventures**
Illustrator: Leone, Sergio
Author: Garis, Howard R.
765          1961                    $4

**Visit to the Dentist, A**
Illustrator: Wallace, Lucille
Author: Garn, Dr. Bernard J.
732          1959                    $5

**Visit to the Dentist, A**
Illustrator: Wallace, Lucille
Author: Garn, Dr. Bernard J.
732          1959                    $4

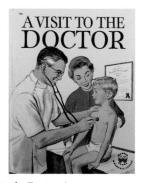

**Visit to the Doctor, A**
Illustrator: Dowd, Vic
Author: Berger, Knute; Tidwell & Haseltine
733          1960                    $6

**Visit to the Hospital, A**
Illustrator: Rossi, Ken
Author: Chase, Francine
690          1958                    $6

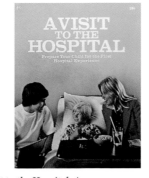

**Visit to the Hospital, A**
Illustrator: Rossi, Ken
Author: Chase, Francine
690          1958                    $3

**Waiting For Santa Claus**
Illustrator: Cummings, Alison
Author: Martin, Marcia
865          1952                    $7

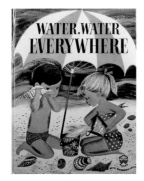

**Water, Water Everywhere**
Illustrator: Seiden, Art
Author: Raphael, Ralph B.
607          1953                    $7

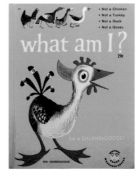

**What Am I?**
Formerly: The Churkendoose
Illustrator: Cunningham, Dellwyn
Author: Berenberg, Ben Ross
832          1946                    $8

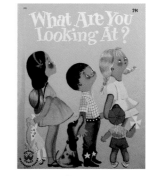

**What Are You Looking At?**
Illustrator: Bonsall, George; Newell, Crosby
Author: Bonsall, George; Newell, Crosby
792          1954                    $6

**What Can We Do With Blocks?**
Illustrator: Herric, Pru
Author: Shaine, Frances
833          1964          **$6**

**What Happened to Piggy?**
Illustrator: Hauge, Carl & Mary
Author: Potter, Miriam Clark
629          1955          **$35**

**What Is That?**
Illustrator: Hampson, Denman
Author: Hampson, Denman
789          1961          **$6**

*Front cover*          *Back cover*

**What Time Is It?**
Illustrator: Zabinski, Joseph
Author: Peter, John
689          1954          **$3**

**What's For Breakfast?**
Illustrator: Wilde, Irma
Author: Wilde, Irma
846          1950          **$5**

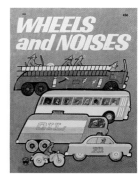

**Wheels and Noises**
Illustrator: Dauber, Elizabeth
Author: Elting, Mary
524          1974          **$5**

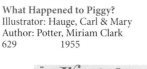

**Wheels and Noises**
Illustrator: Dauber, Elizabeth
Author: Elting, Mary
524          1950          **$8**

**Who Does Baby Look Like?**
Illustrator: Rowand, Phyllis
Author: Rowand, Phyllis
525          1950          **$10**

**Who Goes There?**
Illustrator: D'amato, Janet & Alex
Author: D'amato, Janet & Alex
779          1961          **$6**

**Who Has My Shoes?**
Illustrator: Kessler, Leonard
Author: Kessler, Leonard
801          1963          **$125**

**Who Is My Friend?**
Illustrator: Mc Laughlin, Birdice
Author: Corum, Louise
646          1959          **$7**

**Who Likes Dinner?**
Illustrator: Cunningham, Dellwyn
Author: Beyer, Evelyn
598          1953          **$8**

**Who Lives Here?**
Illustrator: Varga, Judith
Author: Varga, Judith
669          1958          $7

**Who Lives on the Farm?**
Illustrator: Jackson, Pauline
Author: Elting, Mary
518          1949          $10

**Who Will Play With Me?**
Illustrator: Dillon, Corinne
Author: Sutton, Margaret
559          1951          $8

**Whose Hat Is That?**
Illustrator: Kessler, Leonard
Author: Kessler, Leonard
742          1960          $10

**Why the Bear Has a Short Tail**
Illustrator: Sari
Author: Williams, Louise B.
508          1946          $25

**Whose Hat Is That?**
Illustrator: Kessler, Leonard
Author: Kessler, Leonard
742          1960          $6

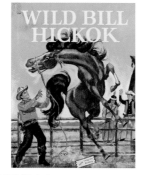

**Wild Bill Hickok**
Illustrator: Nielsen, Jon
Author: Sutton, Felix
649          1956          $20

**Wizard of Oz, The**
Illustrator: Sinnickson, Tom
Author: Baum, Frank L.
543          1951          $12

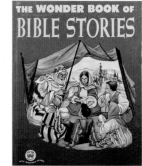

**Wonder Book of Bible Stories, The**
Illustrator: Frost, Bruno
Author: Juergens, Mary
577          1951          $8

**Wonder Book of Birds, The**
Illustrator: Koehler, Alvin
Author: Koehler, Cynthia Iliff
757      1961      **$6**

**Wonder Book of Birds, The**
Illustrator: Koehler, Alvin
Author: Koehler, Cynthia Iliff
757      1961      **$2**

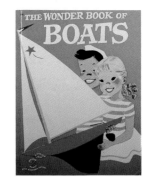

**Wonder Book of Boats, The**
Illustrator: Hurst, Earl Oliver
Author: Hurst, Earl Oliver
580      1953      **$8**

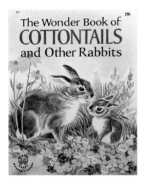

**Wonder Book of Christmas, The**
Illustrator: Myers, Lou
575      1951      **$10**

**Wonder Book of Christmas, The**
Illustrator: Myers, Lou
575      1951      **$6**

**Wonder Book of Clowns, The**
Illustrator: Schucker, James
Author: Weigle, Oscar
638      1955      **$8**

**Wonder Book of Cottontails and Other Rabbits, The**
Illustrator: Koehler, Alvin
Author: Koehler, Cynthia Iliff
852      1965      **$4**

**Wonder Book of Counting Rhymes, The**
Illustrator: Parsons, Virginia
Author: Pierce, June
682      1957      **$6**

**Wonder Book of Counting Rhymes, The**
Illustrator: Parsons, Virginia
Author: Pierce, June
682      1957      **$2**

**Wonder Book of Cowboys, The**
Illustrator: Vaughn, Frank
Author: Peters, Lisa
640      1956      **$7**

**Wonder Book of Favorite Nursery Tales, The**
Illustrator: Peller, Jackie; Tamburine, Jean
730      1953      **$6**

**Wonder Book of Finger Plays and Action Rhymes, The**
Illustrator: Wood, Ruth
Author: Pierce, June
627      1955      **$7**

Wonder Book of Firemen and Fire
Engines, The
Illustrator: Weisner, William
Author: Peters, Lisa
637          1956          **$10**

Wonder Book of Firemen and Fire
Engines, The
Illustrator: Weisner, William
Author: Peters, Lisa
637          1956          **$5**

Wonder Book of Fish, The
Illustrator: Koehler, Cynthia Iliff & Alvin
Author: Koehler, Cynthia Iliff & Alvin
782          1961          **$6**

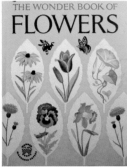

Wonder Book of Flowers, The
Illustrator: Koehler, Cynthia Iliff
Author: Koehler, Cynthia Iliff
784          1961          **$5**

Wonder Book of Fun, The
Illustrator: Cunningham, Dellwyn
Author: Orleans, Ilo
576          1951          **$8**

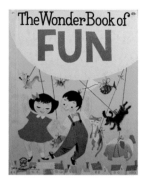

Wonder Book of Fun, The
Illustrator: Cunningham, Dellwyn
Author: Orleans, Ilo
576          1951          **$4**

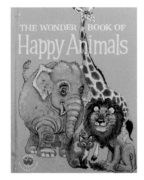

Wonder Book of Happy Animals, The
Illustrator: Jones, Robert
Author: Weigle, Oscar
687          1957          **$6**

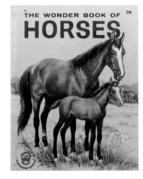

Wonder Book of Horses, The
Illustrator: Koehler, Alvin
Author: Koehler, Cynthia Iliff
857          1965          **$4**

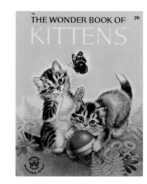

Wonder Book of Kittens, The
Illustrator: Koehler, Cynthia Iliff
Author: Waring, Barbara
786          1963          **$6**

Wonder Book of Nursery Songs, The
Illustrator: Schlesinger, Alice
Author: Cummins, Dorothy Berliner
619          1954          **$7**

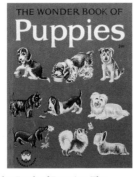

Wonder Book of Puppies, The
Illustrator: Koehler, Cynthia Iliff & Alvin
Author: Koehler, Cynthia Iliff & Alvin
804          1963          **$6**

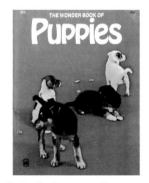

Wonder Book of Puppies, The
Illustrator: Koehler, Cynthia Iliff & Alvin
Author: Koehler, Cynthia Iliff & Alvin
804          1963          **$3**

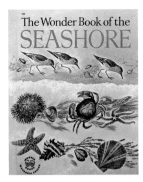

**Wonder Book of the Seashore, The**
Illustrator: Koehler, Alvin
Author: Koehler, Cynthia Iliff
785        1962        **$5**

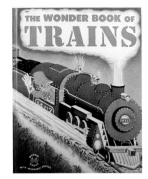

**Wonder Book of Trains, The**
Illustrator: Sinnickson, Tom
Author: Peters, Lisa
569        1952        **$10**

**Wonder Book of Trees, The**
Illustrator: Koehler, Alvin
Author: Koehler, Cynthia Iliff
827        1964        **$6**

**Wonder Book of Trees, The**
Illustrator: Koehler, Alvin
Author: Koehler, Cynthia Iliff
827        1964        **$3**

**Wonder Book of Trucks, The**
Illustrator: Schusker, James
Author: Peters, Lisa
616        1954        **$7**

**Wonder Book of Trucks, The**
Illustrator: Schusker, James
Author: Peters, Lisa
616        1954        **$3**

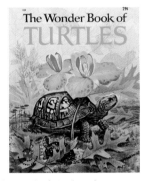

**Wonder Book of Turtles, The**
Illustrator: Koehlerm Cynthia & Alvin
Author: Morel, Eve
838        1964        **$4**

**Wonderful Tar-Baby, The**
Illustrator: Cunningham, Dellwyn
Author: Harris, Joel Chandler
581        1952        **$18**

**Everyone's Egg**
The Flintstones
Illustrator: Hanna-Barbera Productions, Inc.
Author: Elias, Horace J.
927        1976                    **$8**

**Fix-It Man, The**
The Flintstones
Illustrator: Hanna-Barbera Productions, Inc.
Author: Elias, Horace J.
917        1976                    **$8**

**Fred Flintstone's Suprising Corn**
The Flintstones
Illustrator: Hanna-Barbera Productions, Inc.
Author: Elias, Horace J.
918        1976                    **$8**

**Fred's Big Cleaning Day**
The Flintstones
Illustrator: Hanna-Barbera Productions, Inc.
Author: Elias, Horace J.
None       1976                    **$8**

**Pebbles and Bamm-Bamm Find Things to Do**
The Flintstones
Illustrator: Hanna-Barbera Productions, Inc.
Author: Elias, Horace J.
919        1976                    **$8**

**Wilma's Busy Day**
The Flintstones
Illustrator: Hanna-Barbera Productions, Inc.
Author: Elias, Horace J.
939        1976                    **$8**

**Big Blooming Rosebush, The**
Huckleberry Hound
Illustrator: Hanna-Barbera Productions, Inc.
Author: Elias, Horace J.
944        1976                    **$8**

**Great Pizza Hunt, The**
The Jetsons
Illustrator: Hanna-Barbera Productions, Inc.
Author: Elias, Horace J.
790        1976                    **$8**

**Mosquito Flying Day**
Yogi Bear
Illustrator: Hanna-Barbera Productions, Inc
Author: Elias, Horace J.
924        1976                    **$8**

**Playtime in Jellystone Park**
Yogi Bear
Illustrator: Hanna-Barbera
Productions, Inc.
Author: Elias, Horace J.
926        1976            **$8**

**Yogi Bear and the Baby Skunk**
Yogi Bear
Illustrator: Hanna-Barbera
Productions, Inc.
Author: Elias, Horace J.
921        1976                    **$8**

# Section 5: *Treasure Books*

Treasure Books, Inc. of New York printed Treasure Books from 1952 to 1956. Around 1957 some Treasure Book titles were published as Wonder Books.

The books measured 6-5/8 x 7-7/8 inches and contained 28 full-color pages. Treasure Books were produced similar to Little Golden® Books where the front and back covers were stapled together and covered with a paper spine. The spines changed four times over the books' short life: light tan (1952), very pale red (1953), very dark red (late 1953), and yellow with thin colored stripes (around 1954).

Treasure Books were tested and approved by Oak Lane Country Day School of Temple University, Philadelphia, Pennsylvania.

**How to determine Treasure Book editions:**
There are no markings to distinguish a first edition from a reprint, but you can use the book number of the last title listed on the back of the book to approximate dates. If the copyright of the last number listed on the back covers matches the copyright of your book, you probably have a first edition.
The back covers ended in the following numbers:
853 [1952]
857, 861, 863, 865, 869 [1953]
873, 878, 882, 887, 893 [1954]
899, 902, 903 [1955]
906 [1956]

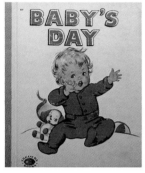

**Baby's Day**
Illustrator: Pointer, Priscella
Author: Edwards, Annette
859          1953          **$12**

**Big & Little**
Illustrator: Hull, John
Author: Hull, John
883          1954          **$10**

**Big & Little**
Glittered cover
Illustrator: Hull, John
Author: Hull, John
883          1954          **$10**

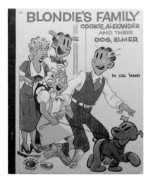

**Blondie's Family**
Illustrator: Young, Chic
Author: Young, Chic
887          1954          **$16**

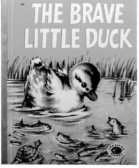

**Brave Little Duck, The**
Illustrator: Gayer, Marguerite
Author: Conkling, Fleur
854          1953          **$12**

**Cinderella**
Illustrator: Ives, Ruth
Author: Andreas, Evelyn
879          1954          **$10**

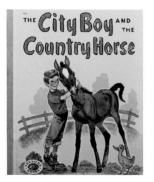

**City Boy and the Country Horse, The**
Illustrator: Woyers, William
Author: Bookman, Charlotte
850          1952          **$12**

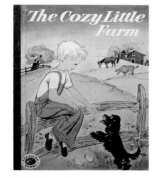

**Cozy Little Farm, The**
Illustrator: Angela
Author: Bonino, Louise
878          1946          **$10**

**Dress-Up Parade, The**
Illustrator: Wilde, George
Author: Wilde, Irma
861          1953          **$18**

**Felix On Television**
Illustrator: Oriolo, Joe
Author: Shapiro, Irwin
904          1956          **$18**

**Felix the Cat**
Illustrator: Sullivan, Pat
Author: Sullivan, Pat
872          1953          **$18**

**Fixit Man, The**
Illustrator: Wilde, George
Author: Wilde, Irma
851          1952          **$12**

**Flash Gordon**
Illustrator: Berger, Alex
905          1956          **$18**

**Flash Gordon**
Glittered cover
Illustrator: Berger, Alex
905          1956          **$18**

**Help Mr. Willy Nilly**
Illustrator: Tamburine, Jean
Author: Fritz, Jean
886          1954          **$13**

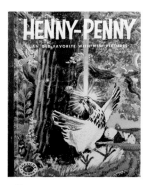

**Henny-Penny**
Illustrator: Ponter, James
882          1954          **$10**

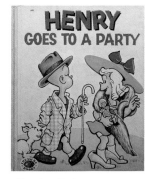

**Henry Goes to a Party**
Illustrator: Anderson, Carl
Author: Anderson, Carl
897          1955          **$18**

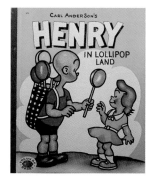

**Henry in Lollipop Land**
Illustrator: Anderson, Carl
Author: Anderson, Carl
871          1953          **$18**

**It's Fun to Peek**
Illustrator: Wilson, Dagmar
Author: Berg, Jean Horton
899          1955          **$10**

**Just Like Me**
Illustrator: Weisgard, Leonard
Author: Weisgard, Leonard
881          1954          **$12**

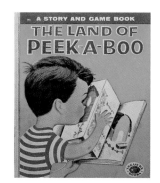

**Land of Peek-A-Boo, The**
Illustrator: Newell, Crosby
Author: Bonsall, George
901          1955          **$15**

**Let's Go to School**
Illustrator: Hoecker, Hazel
Author: Edwards, Annette
893          1954          **$16**

**Let's Play Train**
Illustrator: Weisgard, Leonard
Author: Weisgard, Leonard
870          1953          **$25**

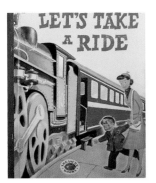

**Let's Play Nurse and Doctor**
Illustrator: Stang, Judy
Author: Stang, Judy
863          1953          **$12**

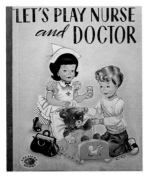

**Let's Take a Ride**
Illustrator: Wilder, George
Author: Martin, Marcia
862          1953          **$12**

**Let's Take a Trip in Our Car**
Plastic car in cover
Illustrator: Schucker, James
Author: Sutton, Felix
890          1954          **$25**

**Little Engine That Laughed, The**
Illustrator: Seiden, Art
Author: Evers, Alf
857          1950          **$12**

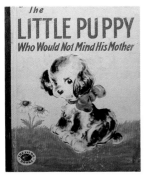

**Little Puppy Who Would Not Mind His Mother, The**
Illustrator: Hopkins, Hidegarde
877          1949          **$12**

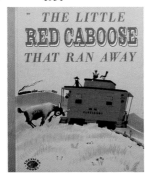

**Little Red Caboose That Ran Away**
Illustrator: Burchard, Peter
Author: Curren, Polly
852          1952          **$12**

**Magic Clown, The**
Illustrator: Schucker, James
Author: Sutton, Felix
876          1954          **$16**

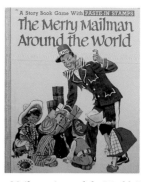

**Merry Mailman Around the World, The**
Illustrator: Wood, Ruth
Author: Martin, Marcia
892             1955                    **$20**

**Merry Mailman, The**
Illustrator: Wood, Ruth
Author: Martin, Marcia
865         1953              **$12**

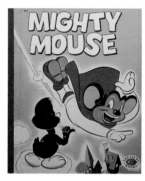

**Mighty Mouse**
Illustrator: Chad
Author: Sutton, Felix
860         1953              **$18**

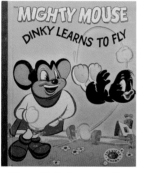

**Mighty Mouse Dinky Learns to Fly**
Illustrator: Chad
Author: Sutton, Felix
866         1953              **$18**

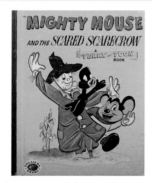

**Mighty Mouse and the Scared Scarecrow**
Illustrator: Chad
Author: Sutton, Felix
884         1954              **$18**

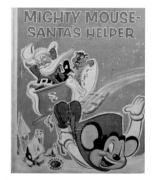

**Mighty Mouse—Santa's Helper**
Illustrator: Chad
Author: Sutton, Felix
896         1955              **$18**

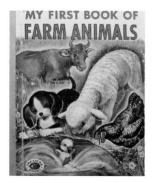

**My First Book of Farm Animals**
Illustrator: Wilde, Irma
Author: Edward, Annette
858         1953              **$12**

**My First Book of Prayers**
Illustrator: Ives, Ruth
Author: Juergens, Mary
868         1953              **$10**

**My Own Book of Fun and Play**
Illustrator: Riley, Bob
Author: Peter, John
885         1954              **$10**

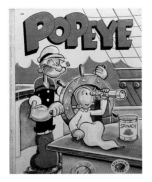

**Popeye**
Illustrator: Sagendorf, Bud
888            1955            **$16**

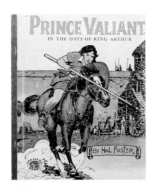

**Prince Valiant**
Illustrator: Foster, Hal
Author: Foster, Hal
874            1954            **$20**

**Really Truly Treasure Hunt, The**
Illustrator: Newell, Crosby
Author: Bonsall, George
891            1954            **$13**

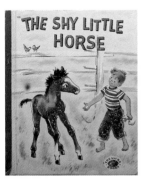

**Shy Little Horse, The**
Illustrator: Robinson
Author: Scott, Therese
880            1947            **$10**

**Snow White and the Seven Dwarfs**
Illustrator: Seiden, Art
898            1955            **$12**

**Sparkie—No School Today**
Illustrator: Jason, Leon
Author: Jason, Leon
902            1955            **$16**

**Ten Little Fingers**
Illustrator: Pointer, Pricella
Author: Pointer, Pricella
875            1954            **$10**

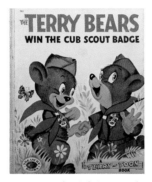

**Terry Bears Win the Cub Scout Badge, The**
Illustrator: Moore, Robert J
Author: Sutton, Felix
903            1955            **$18**

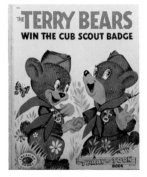

**Terry Bears Win the Cub Scout Badge, The**
Glittered Cover
Illustrator: Moore, Robert J.
Author: Sutton, Felix
903            1955            **$18**

**Things to Make and Do For Christmas**
Cut-uut activities
Illustrator: Shelly, Duke
Author: Shelly, Duke
867            1953            **$20**

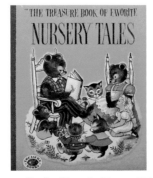

**Treasure Book of Favorite Nursery Tales, The**
Illustrator: Peller, Jackie; Tamburine, Jean
856            1953            **$12**

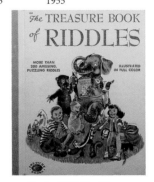

**Treasure Book of Riddles, The**
Illustrator: Wood, Ruth
Author: North, Robert
855            1950            **$12**

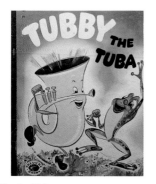

Tubby the Tuba
Illustrator: Chad
Author: Tripp, Paul
873          1954          **$18**

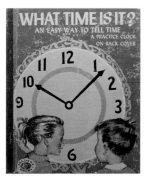

What Time is It?
Illustrator: Zabinski, Joseph
Author: Peter, John
889          1954          **$10**

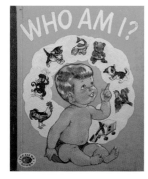

Who Am I?
Illustrator: Schad, Helen G.
Author: Schad, Helen G.
864          1953          **$12**

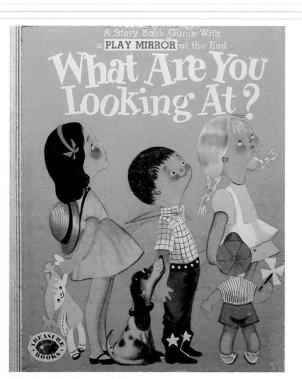

What Are You Looking At?
Mirror in book.
Illustrator: Bonsall. George; Newell, Crosby
Author: Bonsall, George; Newell, Crosby
895          1954          **$16**

Who is That?
Mirror in book.
Illustrator: Schad, Helen G.
Author: Schad, Helen G.
906          1956          **$16**

Wonderful Animal Band, The
Illustrator: Burchard, Peter
Author: Luther, Frank
869          1953          **$10**

Wonderful Treasure Hunt, The
Illustrator: Wilde, George
Author: Wilde, Irma
853          1952          **$12**

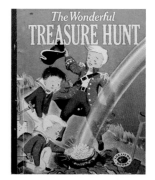

Wonderful Treasure Hunt, The
Illustrator: Wilde, George
Author: Wilde, Irma
853          1952          **$12**

# Section 6: *Jolly Books*

## By Avon Publishing
## Designed and Produced by Book Creators, Inc., New York, New York

Jolly Books measured 6-1/2 x 8-1/4 inches. The covers were wrapped around from front to back, similar to Wonder Books. The pages were stitched together with the first and last pages pasted to the inside covers.

Book numbers 201 through 208 were produced under the art direction of Charles Payzant (1898-1980) and contained 32 pages. In the 1940s Payzant had been an art director for Walt Disney on *Dumbo, Peter and the Wolf* from *Make Mine Music* and *A Night on Bald Mountain/Ave Maria* from *Fantasia*. Some of his background painting also appeared in *Pinocchio, Snow White and the Seven Dwarfs, Bambi* and *The Three Caballeros*. He left Disney in the late

1940s to illustrate children's books. After Payzant left Jolly Books in 1952, the page count was reduced to 28 pages.

The following publisher's description of their books was printed on the back cover:

Jolly Books are the newest and finest books for children to be offered to the public. Prepared with the most careful attention under the guidance of child psychologists, each story is designed to entertain and stimulate the mind of the young child. Some of the world's finest artists have combined their talents to produce beautiful, full color pictures on every page. Sturdily bound, with handsome washable covers, they will give hours of enjoyment over and over again.

**Bible Stories For Children**
Illustrator: Nielsen, Jon
Author: Sprague, Dorothy
220          1953                    $8

**Boo, the Little Indian**
Illustrator: O'Connor, Kendal; Bushman, Bruce
Author: Abbott, Peter
206          1952                    $10

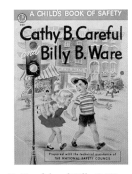

**Cathy B. Careful and Billy B. Ware**
Safety book
Illustrator: Dart, Eleanor
Author: Summit, Mildred
222          1953                    $12

**Coyboy Jack the Sheriff**
Illustrator: Battaglia, Aureluis
Author: Tabor, Tommie
223          1953                    $10

**Fun in the Firehouse**
Illustrator: Sari
Author: O'Hearn, Nila
221          1953                    $10

**Jolly A B C Book of Toys**
Illustrator: Corcos, Lucille
218          1953                    $8

**Jolly Book of Mother Goose, The**
Illustrator: Jervis, Margaret
Author: Jervis, Margaret
216          1953                    $16

**Jolly Bunny Book, The**
Illustrator: Holland, Sylvia
Author: Sellew, Chatherine F.
209          1953                    $12

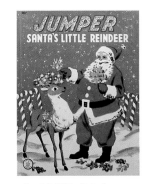

**Jumper, Santa's Little Reindeer**
Illustrator: Payzant, Charles
Author: Shannon, Terry
207          1952                    $16

**Little Engine Out West**
Illustrator: Payzant, Charles; Knight, John J.
Author: O'Hearn, Nila
212     1953     **$8**

**Little Peter What's-My-Name**
Illustrator: Marks, Mickey Klar
Author: Bracker, Charles
224     1953     **$12**

**Magic Key, The**
Illustrator: Holland, Sylvia
Author: Francis, Mary
203     1952     **$60**

**Moko, the Circus Monkey**
Illustrator: Parmelee, Ted
Author: Payzant, Charles
202     1952     **$35**

**Old MacDonald Had a Farm...**
Illustrator: Jervis, Margaret
210     1953     **$8**

**Owl and the Pussycat, The**
Illustrator: Lear, Edward
Author: Jervis, Margaret
217     1953     **$25**

**Please Come to My Party**
Illustrator: Eliot, Duval
Author: Otto, Susan
205     1952     **$8**

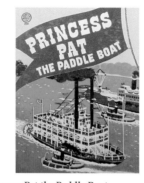

**Princess Pat the Paddle Boat**
Illustrator: Payzant, Charles; Knight, John J.
Author: Johnstone, Muriel
214     1953     **$12**

**Rumpus the Remarkable Kitten**
Illustrator: Bracker, Charles E.
Author: Bracker, Charles E.
211     1953     **$25**

**Spoodles the Puppy Who Learned**
Illustrator: Totten, Bob
Author: Black, Irma Simonton
201     1952     **$12**

**Tippy Runs Away**
Illustrator: Holland, Sylvia; Knight, John J.
Author: Bertail, Inez
204     1952     **$15**

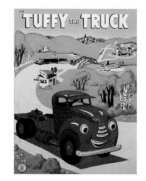

**Tuffy the Truck**
Illustrator: Davidovich, Basil
Author: Wyler, Rose
208     1952     **$8**

**Up Goes the House**
Illustrator: Dormus, Robert
Author: Gustavson, Harry
219        1953        **$8**

**When Grandma Was a Girl**
Illustrator: Sari
Author: Summit, Mildred
215        1953        **$8**

**Whose Little Boy Are You?**
Illustrator: Brackers, Charles
Author: Witsen, Betty Van
213        1953        **$10**

# Section 7: *Little Owl Books*

## Published by Cross Publications

Little Owl Books measured the exact same size as Little Golden® Books. They also had the side staple binding with gold foil spine covering. This was a very short-lived series with only four titles published in 1954. Each book contained 28 pages with full-color pictures. Any book found will be a first edition.

The following was printed on the copyright page of each book:

To the Parents:
New Little Owl Books are designed especially for your child "to-grow-up-with." All children want to grow wiser like the symbolic wise little owl, and one of the first and best loved ways for them to discover what is happening in the world about them is from happy discussions of clearly illustrated picture books. Little Owl Books train while they entertain. From them children gain knowledge and understanding of the ways of people and things, while they develop a most valuable sense of security and pride in "just knowing ahead of actual experiencing." You will note Little Owl Books contain stories with up-to-the-minute interests. We suggest your child start his own library of Little Owl Books with this issue. And that you and he be watchful for new titles that will frequently appear on the counters. It is our sincere hope that each new book will be a joy to own.
*The Publisher*

**Candles for the Queen**
Illustrator: Sawyer, Juen
Author: Jewel, Janice
102        1954        **$12**

**Johnny's Space Trip**
Illustrator: Stone, Charles
Author: Sell, Mike
103        1954        **$15**

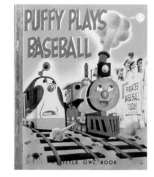

**Puffy Plays Baseball**
Illustrator: De Bevere, Maurice
Author: Taylor, Mary
104        1954        **$15**

**TV Pals**
Illustrator: Ottenheimer, Fred
Author: May, Eileen
101        1954        **$12**

# Section 8: *Pied Piper Books*

## Designed and Produced by Domesday Press, Inc.
## Binding by F. M. Charlton Co., Inc.

Pied Piper Books measured 6-1/4 x 7-5/8 inches. The books had stiff cardboard front and back covers with a fabric hinge and were covered with dust jackets. The pages were attached to the cover by three staples down the center of the book. Each book contained 32 pages with full-color pictures. Each title's number was only printed at the upper left corner of the dust jacket. If your book is missing its dust jacket, you will not find a number on the book.

There are no markings on the books to designate the edition. Most of the books had solid yellow back covers with the Pied Piper logo at the bottom left. The dust jacket back cover is the only place to find the other available titles listed. The jackets listed the following: Books 1-4 listed four titles, 5-8 listed eight titles, 9-12 listed 12 titles, and 13-16 listed 16 titles. If you own a jacketed book that lists your book's number and was not in the groupings I mentioned above, it's probably not a first edition.

Example: You own book number 4, and the last title number listed on its dust jacket is number 12. Your book is a reprint edition.

I have also come across some books that have the front cover artwork continuing to the back of the book, instead of the solid yellow back cover.

The Samuel Lowe Company, which produced Bonnie Books, later published some of the Pied Piper titles.

In 1935 George Arthur Hornby (1912-1990) started Domesday Press in his Connecticut home. By 1936 the company had outgrown the home and moved to Providence, Connecticut. The *New York Times* published news of his death on Oct. 3, 1990. In the article his daughter, Ann Guilfoyle, states that her father helped design the first 12 Little Golden Books.

**The following was printed on the dust jackets back flyleaf:**

Pied Piper Books bring to children in a beautiful and durable format the very best of the old stories and the most promising of the new. Every title is illustrated in full color by a leading artist. These books are designed and produced by The Domesday Press.

**Animal Stories**
Illustrator: Gregori
10          1946                    $12
With dust jacket                    $25

**Bobby Snoozes**
Illustrator: Flory, Arthur
Author: Flory, Arthur
04          1945                    $12
With dust jacket                    $25

**Boniface the Bunny**
Illustrator: Werth, Kurt
Author: Laskey, Muriel
01          1945                    $12
With dust jacket                    $25

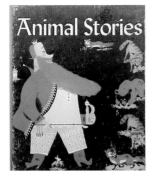

**Cyril the Squirrel**
Illustrator: Werth, Kurt
Author: Laskey, Muriel
13          1946                    $12
With dust jacket                    $25

**Dancing Goat, The**
Illustrator: Keyser, Evelyn
Author: Lynn, Anne
06          1945                    $12
With dust jacket                    $25

**Elves and the Shoemaker, The**
Illustrator: Dorcas
Author: Patric, Mary
09          1946                    $12
With dust jacket                    $25

**Famous Fairy Tales**
Illustrator: Barnes, Catherine
02          1945                    **$15**
With dust jacket                    **$25**

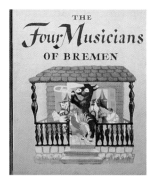

**Four Musicians of Bremen**
Illustrator: Keyser, Evelyn
Author: Keyser, Evelyn
14          1946                    **$12**
With dust jacket                    **$25**

**Mrs. Duck and the Milkman**
Illustrator: Randall, Ken
Author: Weenolsen, Hebe
16          1946                    **$15**
With dust jacket                    **$25**

**Pandora**
Illustrator: Weihs, Erika
Author: Patric, Mary
08          1945                    **$18**
With dust jacket                    **$30**

**Sing Song**
Illustrator: Kohs, Marion R.
Author: Rossetti, Christina
03          1945                    **$12**
With dust jacket                    **$25**

**Some Day**
Illustrator: Sari
Author: Cunninghan, Virginia
07          1945                    **$12**
With dust jacket                    **$25**

**Storyland**
Illustrator: Paflin, Roberta
Author: Patric, Mary
12          1946                    **$12**
With dust jacket                    **$25**

**Ugly Duckling, The**
Illustrator: Yeakey, Carol
Author: Patric, Mary
15          1946                    **$12**
With dust jacket                    **$25**

**What Am I?**
Illustrator: Flory, Jane
Author: Flory, Jane
05          1945                    **$12**
With dust jacket                    **$25**

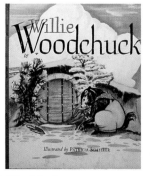

**Willie Woodchuck**
Illustrator: Scheirer, Patricia
Author: Holt, Marion E.
11          1946                    **$12**
With dust jacket                    **$25**

**Child's Book of Birds, A**
Illustrator: Henderson, Luis M.
20          1946                    **$12**
With dust jacket                    **$25**

# Section 9: *A Star-Bright Book*
## By Childrens Press, Inc.

A Star Bright Book measured 6-1/2 x 7-6/8 inches. The book's cover was produced in the same fashion as a Little Golden® Book, using the side stapled hinge design. The spine's textured paper covering was dark red. Each book contained 38 pages of black and white and full-color pictures. The book's number is located toward the bottom of the title page on the left. Finding a first edition is very easy, since none of the titles had more then one printing.

Books numbered S-300 through S-304 were prepared under the direction of Laura Oftedal of the University of Chicago Laboratory School. Numbers S-305 through S-307 were the Story-Book Science series edited by Illa Podendorf, also of the University of Chicago Laboratory School.

**Bad Mousie**
Illustrator: Trientje
Author: Dudley, Martha
303          1947          **$10**

**Captain Joe**
Illustrator: Trientje
Author: Friskey, Julilly
306          1947          **$8**

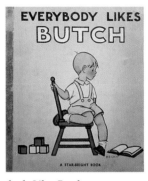

**Everybody Likes Butch**
Illustrator: Becky
Author: Bryant, Bernice
301          1947          **$8**

**Farmer Collins**
Illustrator: Trientje
Author: Kohler, Julillu
305          1947          **$8**

**Football Trees**
Illustrator: Adams, Pauline
Author: Kohler, Julilly
307          1947          **$8**

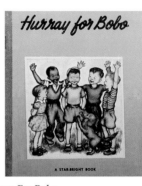

**Hurray For Bobo**
Illustrator: Schwartz, Berta
Author: Savage, Joan
304          1947          **$6**

**Peter Rabbit**
Illustrator: Erickson, Phoebe
300          1947          **$10**

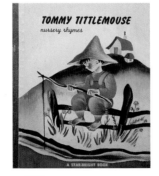

**Tommy Tittlemouse**
Illustrator: Evans, Katherine
302          1947          **$10**